LEARNING TO LEAD

LEARNING TO LEAD

YOUTH ORGANIZING
IN IMMIGRANT COMMUNITIES

Veronica Terriquez

A Volume in the American Sociological Association's
Rose Series in Sociology

Russell Sage Foundation • New York

DOI: https://doi.org/10.7758/gert1126

Library of Congress Cataloging in Publication Control Number: 2025039906
ISBN 9780871548528 (paperback) / ISBN 9781610448994 (ebook)

Cover art: *Seeds of Change* by Lizet Valencia, Digital illustration/Graphic design.
©2025 Lizet Valencia. Reprinted with permission.

The paper used in this publication meets the minimum requirements of
American National Standard for Information Sciences — Permanence of Paper
for Printed Library Materials. ANSI Z39.48-1992.

Text design by Suzanne Nichols. Front matter DOI: https://doi.org/10.7758
/gert1126.2907

RUSSELL SAGE FOUNDATION
112 East 64th Street, New York, New York 10065
10 9 8 7 6 5 4 3 2 1

The Russell Sage Foundation

The Russell Sage Foundation, one of the oldest of America's general purpose foundations, was established in 1907 by Mrs. Margaret Olivia Sage for "the improvement of social and living conditions in the United States." The foundation seeks to fulfill this mandate by fostering the development and dissemination of knowledge about the country's political, social, and economic problems. While the foundation endeavors to assure the accuracy and objectivity of each book it publishes, the conclusions and interpretations in Russell Sage Foundation publications are those of the authors and not of the foundation, its trustees, or its staff. Publication by Russell Sage, therefore, does not imply foundation endorsement.

Previous Volumes
in the Series

Forthcoming Titles

The Rose Series in Sociology

The American Sociological Association's Rose Series in Sociology publishes books that integrate knowledge and address controversies from a sociological perspective. Books in the Rose Series are at the forefront of sociological knowledge. They are lively and often involve timely and fundamental issues on significant social concerns. The series is intended for broad dissemination throughout sociology, across social science and other professional communities, and to policy audiences. The series was established in 1967 by a bequest to ASA from Arnold and Caroline Rose to support innovations in scholarly publishing.

JOANNA DREBY
AARON MAJOR
STEVEN F. MESSNER
KATHERINE TRENT

EDITORS

To the next generation of changemakers: May your efforts to fight for the well-being of your communities and the natural environment be guided by the hard-earned lessons of those who came before you.

Contents

═ Illustrations ═

Figures

Tables

= About the Author =

Veronica Terriquez directs the UCLA Chicano Studies Research Center and is a professor of Chicana/o and Central American Studies and Urban Planning.

═ Acknowledgments ═

THIS BOOK reflects a long-standing commitment to understanding how young people from immigrant communities cultivate the capacity to collectively effect change. The passion, commitment, and creativity of students I met at Skyline High School in Oakland, California, at the turn of the millennium inspired me to launch this line of research. Although the project would take years to fully take shape, it ultimately came to life through data collected in the 2010s—made possible by the insight, generosity, and collaboration of countless individuals.

Foremost, I am deeply grateful to the young people, their mentors, and community members who shared their experiences, completed surveys, and offered thoughtful reflections. I also owe a profound debt of gratitude to the many student and youth researchers who joined me in the field—an energetic team whose contributions were essential to every stage of this work.

The rigorous scholarship of those who have long advanced our understanding of immigrants, youth of color, and working-class communities shaped my analysis. I am especially grateful for the intellectual and infrastructural support provided by multiple research centers and the generous backing of private philanthropy and academic funders who enabled me to collect extensive and rich data.

I am particularly thankful to Manuel Pastor and his team at the University of Southern California Equity Research Institute for their unwavering partnership. I also extend heartfelt thanks to John Rogers, the late Jeannie Oakes, Ruth Milkman, Pedro Noguera, Paul Ong, and Irene Bloemraad—each of whom played a foundational role in shaping how I approached the questions at the heart of this book. Meanwhile, the Stanford Center for Advanced Study in the Behavioral Sciences offered a rare gift of time while I worked on drafts of the manuscript.

My sincere appreciation also goes to the Rose Series at the Russell Sage Foundation's staff, anonymous reviewers, workshop participants, editors, and all others whose thoughtful feedback greatly strengthened the manuscript.

This research has been a collective endeavor, and I acknowledge many of the people who have been a part of this work over the years by name in an online appendix. Here, I must extend my deepest thanks to Monica Iannessa and my family for their patience and support as I dedicated myself to this project. Their love and understanding sustained me as I conducted the research and writing that brought this book to life.

Chapter 4 reprints material from Terriquez, Veronica. 2017. "Legal Status, Civic Organizations, and Political Participation Among Latino Young Adults." *The Sociological Quarterly* 58(2): 315–36. https://doi.org/10.1080/00380253.2017.1296756. Copyright © 2017 Midwest Sociological Society, reprinted by permission of Informa UK Limited, trading as Taylor & Francis Ltd, https://www.tandfonline.com on behalf of Midwest Sociological Society.

═ Chapter 1 ═

Ain't No Power Like
the Power of the Youth

O N THE evening of June 10, 2014, hundreds of high school students crowded into a meeting of the Los Angeles Unified School
District (LAUSD), the nation's second-largest school district, as
members voted 5–1 to redirect more than $138 million of its budget to
schools serving the highest-need students.[1] They were witnessing the
outcome of the Equity is Justice campaign, which sought to address
resource disparities in schools serving primarily Latinx immigrant and
African American communities.[2]

Carolyn Hernandez, then sixteen years old, led chants for the over-
flow crowd who could not enter the packed boardroom. "Say what?"
she would call out over the mic, to which her peers responded in
unison: "Ain't no power, like the power of youth, 'cause the power of
youth don't stop!" The U.S.-born daughter of Guatemalan immigrants,
Carolyn was among the adolescent leaders from youth organizing
groups who had spearheaded an intergenerational effort to advance
this funding policy change. She was a member of South Central Youth
Empowered thru Action (SCYEA), an organizing group run out of the
Community Coalition and based in South Central Los Angeles. Serving
a community experiencing widespread disinvestment, the Community
Coalition established SCYEA in 1991 to address interracial violence
between Latinx and African American youth. Involving youth leaders
across five South Central high schools, the group brought together
largely second-generation immigrant and African American youth to
address shared concerns around under-resourced, poor-performing
schools and neighborhood health and safety, as well as to train its
members in nonpartisan voter registration and education.

Carolyn was one of the more than four thousand children of immigrants whom I surveyed, interviewed, or observed over the 2010s. All
were involved in grassroots campaigns to change policies, get out the
vote, and educate broader publics about issues affecting their communities. Supported by nonpartisan 501(c)3 organizations, these youths

1

https://doi.org/10.7758/gert1126.1342

stood alongside their diverse peers, including African American adolescents, in taking sustained collective actions to address systemic inequalities. As they tackled issues related to education, health, environmental justice, immigrant rights, housing, municipal funding, voting rights, and other areas, they secured policy wins and increased voter turnout in progressive regions like Los Angeles, as well as in less-welcoming regions for immigrants in which support for President Donald Trump's Make America Great Again (MAGA) agenda was strong.

Like most of the adolescent organizing groups across the United States, SCYEA focuses on youth like Carolyn, who grew up navigating a stressful local environment characterized by poverty, a significant gang presence, regular gun violence, and heavy-handed policing.[3] Making things more challenging, her neighborhood included a high concentration of mixed-status families, with one or more members undocumented and at risk of deportation.[4] Carolyn herself lived with five relatives in a small apartment and attended severely under-resourced schools, including Fremont High School, which enrolled a high concentration of low-income students and English-language learners and had one of the lowest college-going rates in the district.

SCYEA's programming had a profound effect on Carolyn. To contextualize the inequality that its members experienced, SCYEA organizers took them on field trips to visit schools in more affluent parts of the district to see their superior facilities and learn about their better-resourced programs. These trips to other parts of the city strengthened the youths' resolve to fight to secure more resources for their own schools. In the year leading up to the LAUSD funding vote, Carolyn and her peers learned about the complexities of district budgeting processes, strategized with youth leaders from other parts of the school district, attended school board meetings, and conducted extensive community outreach. "Even during summer school, we were making presentations, protesting, doing our signs, making art, doing everything we could for the campaign," she recalled.

Through this work, Carolyn and her peers formed relationships with school administrators and teachers who might support their cause, while also learning to communicate with people who might not share their viewpoints or enthusiasm. Though Carolyn knew she would graduate before she could directly benefit from the Equity is Justice campaign, she nonetheless felt that she was "doing this for the younger people coming along—like my younger sister, my neighbors, my friends' younger brothers and sisters. We're doing this for our future generations so that they can have resources and a safe space, so that they are able to thrive and really achieve their fullest potential."

Carolyn and engaged youth like her are at the heart of this book. I examine how low-income, second-generation immigrant adolescents acquire the capacities to lead inclusive and equity-minded grassroots campaigns. I use the term *second-generation* as a shorthand to encompass both 1.5-generation adolescents—those born abroad but raised in the United States—and U.S.-born adolescents who were raised by at least one immigrant parent. These young people often navigate government institutions on behalf of parents who might not have the time or language proficiency to do so.[5] A segment of this young population, particularly girls, also works alongside peers and adult allies to alter the policies and practices of these institutions so that they better serve their communities.

In examining the political activism of second-generation adolescents, I focus on members of SCYEA and other youth organizing groups. Drawing on extensive observations, I elaborate on the concept of political socialization, the ongoing or interactive process through which individuals acquire knowledge about, attitudes toward, and a sense of agency in the public arena.[6] I argue that adolescents can experience a transformative political socialization that enables them to insert their voices in political processes and address injustices facing their communities. Regardless of whether adolescents reside in regions relatively welcoming of immigrants, this socialization typically entails

- support for the developmental needs of adolescents whose families experience poverty and immigration-related challenges, as well as systemic and interpersonal racism, sexism, and/or homophobia;

- exposure to a critical civics education outside of the classroom that deepens their understanding of diversity, social inequality, and policy debates; and

- guidance in civic action that facilitates collective influence over democratic decision-making.

Through a range of activities, adolescents overcome multiple barriers, assuming active roles in policy change and voter education campaigns. In taking part in and contributing to intensive programming that is responsive to local regional dynamics, these young people come to embrace intersectional politics, tackling an array of issues that resonate with their communities.

My argument is based on survey, interview, and other data gathered throughout the 2010s, primarily from California but also from a national survey of youth organizing groups. I demonstrate how organizational activities support the healthy development of young people facing multiple adversities, facilitate the informed analysis of social issues and power, and involve adolescents in government decision-making processes. In the United States, a country in which rights and freedoms are unequally distributed, this transformative socialization process has profound implications for the political incorporation of second-generation immigrants and their abilities to play a role in defining the future of their communities, broader regions, and the nation as a whole.

The Identities and Politics of the Young Second Generation

Nationally, the proportion of young people with immigrant parents remains quite large. In 2020, about 28 percent of U.S. residents younger than thirty were immigrants by birth or the children of immigrants. Among this second generation, 85 percent were people of color, meaning they identify as Latinx, Asian American and Pacific Islander (AAPI), black, or some other race that is not white.[7]

Coming of age during a time of political unrest and exacerbated social inequalities, these racially diverse young people face compounded challenges, especially if their parents come from modest backgrounds.[8] Decades of deindustrialization and government disinvestment have shredded the public safety net, leaving such families to navigate the rising costs for higher education, decent housing, quality health care, and nutritious food. At the same time, living-wage jobs have become increasingly scarce. Adding to these burdens, many of these young people came of age during the worst pandemic in the United States in a century. For those in mixed-status families, the lack of legal protections intensifies economic hardships and stress.[9] Sadly, intensified anti-immigrant hostility has further signaled to these families that they are unwelcome.[10]

Aside from economic and immigration-related challenges, young Latinx, AAPI, and black children of immigrants face high rates of criminalization, especially if those children are boys.[11] They are also vulnerable to attacks on women's and LGBTQ rights, and while global climate change threatens the future of their entire generation, adolescents from low-income backgrounds disproportionately face toxic local environmental conditions that pose more immediate risks to their health. Within these trying political, economic, and environmental conditions, young people must survive and determine how to carve out a better future for themselves and their communities.

Figure 1.1   California's Population Younger than Thirty, by Race or Ethnicity and Immigrant Background

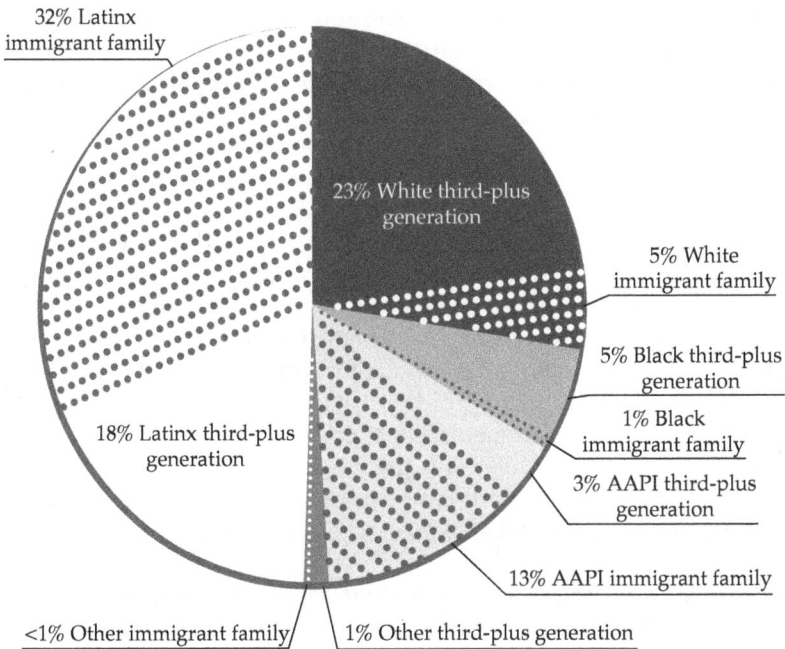

32% Latinx immigrant family

23% White third-plus generation

5% White immigrant family

5% Black third-plus generation

1% Black immigrant family

3% AAPI third-plus generation

18% Latinx third-plus generation

13% AAPI immigrant family

<1% Other immigrant family

1% Other third-plus generation

Source: Author's calculations based on the 2020 Current Population Survey.
Note: Percentages add up to more than 100 percent due to rounding error.

The Intersectional Identities and Activism of California's Second-Generation Majority

In a nation where immigrants form a large portion of the population, understanding how the young second-generation acquires the capacities to participate in its democratic processes is critical. The country's most populous state, California, is a prime laboratory for observing the political engagement of the children of immigrants; in 2020, they composed about 50 percent of California's population younger than age thirty, and 70 percent of individuals in this age group were people of color (see figure 1.1).[12] Those of Latinx origin—primarily of Mexican and Central American descent—made up about half of this age cohort, with most having at least one immigrant parent. Meanwhile, Asian American youth of wide-ranging ethnic backgrounds (including those with one white parent) composed 15 to 16 percent of the population. Although most white and black youth tended to be raised by U.S.-born parents (such children are referred to as the third-plus generation), a minority were growing up in immigrant and refugee families.

These ethnically and racially diverse young people are less likely than their elders to identify with binary gender categories (male or female) or as heterosexual.[13] Youth organizing groups have embraced LGBTQ+ youth, supporting cultural and political changes around the treatment of sexual minorities and people who do not identify with their gender assigned at birth.

In terms of social status, while some children of immigrants are faring quite well and successfully incorporating into the United States' economic and social institutions, others encounter barriers.[14] Overall, youth whose parents possess high levels of education, entrepreneurial skills, or economic capital tend to have better educational and economic prospects than those whose parents arrive with limited education and economic resources.[15] Some children of immigrants also encounter blocked pathways to citizenship for themselves or family members, which can significantly constrain their upward mobility, cause significant anxiety, and expose them to the risks of family separation.[16] Relatedly, persisting racism also poses challenges, especially for those with darker skin.[17]

One might expect these challenges to dampen civic engagement, but interestingly, the political incorporation of the second generation does not always align with socioeconomic outcomes. For example, the children of Asian and Latinx immigrants differ significantly in their average socioeconomic status, yet they exhibit similar levels of political participation.[18] And though a parent's or child's undocumented or precarious legal status may limit economic mobility, it can also, in certain contexts, spur political mobilization.[19]

The concept of intersectionality can help guide activism. Rooted in the intellectual production and activism of women of color in the 1960s and 1970s, intersectionality is an analytic framework and set of social practices for understanding the convergences of various identities and power.[20] Emphasizing the interconnectedness among categories of difference, the concept tends to resonate with the low-income children of immigrants, as it spurs them to reflect on how multiple systems of oppression have shaped their marginalization or privilege. And, as evidenced by early-twenty-first-century millennial-led movements (such as the Occupy, Black Lives Matter, Dreamer, and climate movements), intersectional frameworks can propel young people to form coalitions and alliances as they propose inclusive solutions to shared problems.[21]

To be clear, second-generation youth exhibit unequal political trajectories, and only a minority become deeply invested in civic affairs.[22]

Some remain politically disengaged, exhibiting apathy or skepticism toward U.S. politics.[23] Others will develop political behaviors and dispositions reflective of their non-immigrant peers, including those that distance themselves from undocumented compatriots.[24] Meanwhile, a small but tenacious group become civic leaders who advocate on behalf of immigrant and other marginalized communities, drawing on lessons learned from their mentors and elders, while also developing their own novel ways to respond to present circumstances. This book focuses on the last group: an influential minority who take informed and strategic actions to demand more accountable and representative government institutions.

The Political Socialization of Second-Generation Adolescents

Though examples abound of highly visible teenage activism at home and abroad, adolescents are rarely regarded as serious political actors in contemporary U.S. society.[25] This perception stems from the visibility of young adults as frontline participants in social movements and the dominance of middle-aged and older individuals in formal positions of power.[26] Yet adolescents can also become influential change agents who drive policy changes and boost voter turnout, utilizing strategies that engage their contemporaries in collective efforts.

As demonstrated by extensive research, adolescents have the potential to experience intensified learning and overcome environmental challenges from childhood.[27] The teenage years represent a stage of human development marked by heightened brain plasticity and rapid neurobiological, psychosocial, and cognitive changes that foster resilience and support self-direction. As adolescents progress through the teenage years, they begin to reflect more deeply on their values, beliefs, and aspirations; they also attempt to make sense of their identities, find a purpose, and chart out their future.[28]

Adolescence, then, constitutes a critical period for developing deep political interests, commitments, and capacities.[29] While youth are undoubtedly protagonists in their own political development, their political socialization also depends on exposure to civic action and on their social environment.[30] Interactions with agents of political socialization— parents, schools, media (especially social media for today's generation), and civic organizations—can inform whether and how adolescents decide to get involved in politics.[31]

The ways in which these socializing agents foster adolescent political engagement vary widely. White, middle-class nonimmigrant youth— particularly cisgender males (*cisgender* refers to people whose gender self-identification conforms to normative gender roles)—disproportionately enjoy access to socializing agents that prepare them to exercise political power.[32] By contrast, low-income, second-generation immigrant youth often remain do not get such access, hampering their abilities to exercise political influence.

Researchers have long argued that parents serve as key agents of children's political socialization.[33] However, because immigrant parents disproportionately encounter legal, informational, linguistic, class-related, and other challenges to direct engagement in formal political processes, they are rarely equipped to model political participation for their children.[34] Carolyn was rare among the second-generation youth I encountered in that her immigrant mother was also a politically active member of the Community Coalition (SCYEA's host organization) who reinforced what her daughter was learning in her youth organizing group. More representative was Lucia Ortega, a fellow SCYEA member raised by parents who worked multiple jobs. "Putting food on the table was a priority, and politics was not something they were involved in," she told me. "I've had to explain [political] things to my parents."[35]

Schools are another important agent of political socialization in the lives of young people, but institutions serving low-income youth can be constrained by various factors. Teachers may have scant classroom time to guide students in taking civic action on social issues, as accountability testing has narrowed social studies curricula.[36] They may also be inexperienced in such curricula or afraid of raising politically contentious issues, and indeed, educators have come under attack for discussing issues of race, diversity, and inclusion.[37] As such, quality action-oriented civics curricula that attend to the community concerns of diverse youth remains rare and even controversial.[38] Like most other members of youth organizing groups, Carolyn was disappointed with her high school's failure to connect local current events to coursework material. The lessons she received were "about the three branches of government, and when it comes to all those decisions that were made, it was all historical," she lamented. Most of her school's teachers lacked personal ties to South Central Los Angeles and did not discuss local issues in the classroom. In failing to make local connections, schools miss opportunities to deepen students' understandings of their everyday concerns and how they might make a difference.

Social media represents another agent of political socialization, but how it affects young people's political engagement can vary widely. At times, social media can expand political views and encourage youth to take action.[39] It can also spread disinformation or simply reinforce preexisting offline behaviors.[40] Carolyn's experience reflected the latter. She explained that SCYEA alumni often posted on "events that are going on in the community, or on situations that happen when it comes to black and brown folks," whereas other, less politically active Fremont students "may just repost a meme or share a family picture without thinking about it too much."

Certain types of civic associations can cultivate adolescents' abilities to engage in politics. Second-generation youth primarily access civic groups through their high schools, but some also join through community and religious institutions. Notably, student government, community service groups, and debate and drama clubs that are publicly oriented—meaning that they involve members in collective activities requiring public service or interactions with public audiences—can pave the way to political participation.[41] In fact, when adolescents join associations in which they are expected to speak in public forums, perform community service, or plan group events, they exhibit greater political participation as young adults compared with similarly situated peers.[42]

This holds true whether the association is political or apolitical, though the priorities of each differ qualitatively. Student government serves as an example of an apolitical association, with students typically working together on school-oriented activities like rallies, school assemblies, dances, and community service activities. Often, members of student government must campaign for positions and speak in public, but they rarely advocate for government policy changes or work to get out the vote in government elections. Apolitical, publicly oriented associations like student government or community service groups thus offer youth limited preparation for future political participation and do not necessarily encourage members to critique social structures and invest in political solutions to social problems or racial inequality.[43] In fact, they may even train young people to maintain the status quo, a status quo that in many cases is failing them.

Take, for example, a well-meaning high school civic group in a low-income community that engages adolescent members in local park clean-ups. Youths may be providing an important service and learning valuable coordination skills, but they will not be prompted to question why the park is strewn with litter in the first place: Does the local government have funds for park maintenance and cleanup? Are equitable resources devoted to park maintenance in affluent white neighborhoods and not to those in areas with immigrant and non-white residents? By contrast, socializing agents can prime young people to analyze power and social inequalities, as well as insert their own voice in government decision-making and electoral processes. This book focuses on such socializing agents—SCYEA and other youth organizing groups that enhance adolescents' abilities to collectively respond to systemic injustices through political processes.

Youth Organizing Groups and Transformative Political Socialization

Like many alumni of youth organizing groups, Carolyn remained highly engaged in politics after high school. As a student at San Francisco State University, she provided strategic support for its black Student Union (aligned with the Black Lives Matter movement), serving as a bridge between Latinx and black students. She also worked with Goodwill, which partnered with the city of San Francisco in a campaign to reduce wasteful water use. Her earlier youth organizing experience gave her confidence to continue to be politically engaged in college, even though she was, as a freshman, one of the youngest activists in her school. "I felt like I was in my element back doing community work," she recalled of joining campaigns in college.

Carolyn's college political participation was facilitated by the transformative political socialization she experienced as an adolescent member of SCYEA. Because of the aforementioned constraints on parents, schools, and other agents of political socialization, youth organizing groups play a powerful role in orienting the adolescent children of immigrants to the U.S. political system. They create a space for such adolescents to work alongside diverse peers to make sense of social injustices, advance policy changes, or get out the vote. The transformative political process goes beyond enabling young people to access the prerequisite knowledge and civic skills necessary for participation; it also equips members with the tools to understand structural inequalities and overcome hardships deriving from their social statuses. In doing so, youth organizing groups afford members the freedom to collectively reimagine how institutions might better serve their communities, while providing them invaluable formative experience in working toward systemic change.[44]

Youth organizing groups offer important insights into the types of programming that foster a transformative socialization. Owing to their dense networks, dissemination of best practices, and extensive collaboration, these groups represent an identifiable "organizational field" subject to what Paul DiMaggio and Walter Powell call "isomorphic processes"—that is, the constraints and opportunities that lead organizations with shared goals to resemble one another.[45] Because of these pressures, as youth organizing groups have expanded across the United States, they have developed shared approaches for supporting young people's leadership.[46] Most groups adopt a similar operating structure. They typically convene a core group of leaders on a regular basis, often once or twice a week after school or during lunchtime. While the issue areas they tackle can vary (for example education, housing, immigration, or voting rights), these core leaders spearhead campaigns by becoming well-versed on their issues, conducting public outreach, and securing support for their campaign goals from adult allies and decision-makers.

My extensive observations of these groups have led me to identify three main shared components of youth organizing that advance a trans-formative political socialization. As further described in the following pages, these groups attend to their members' developmental needs, offer members a critical civics education, and provide them guidance in civic action. To be clear, groups incorporate this programming with varying levels of fidelity and success. Yet overall, when second-generation immi-grant youth take part in and contribute to groups' comprehensive pro-gramming, they increase their capacities to exercise political power.

Attending to Developmental Needs

Positive interventions can make a difference for adolescents who struggle with multiple hardships. As research by neuroscientists and psychologists has demonstrated, supportive environments can stimulate positive neurological adaptations that allow youth to recover from setbacks and thrive in the present.[47] Youth organizing groups, whose members have often experienced poverty, immigration-related chal-lenges, and other struggles, devote resources to members' academic, professional, economic, and personal success. SCYEA, for example, often sets aside one hour of its three-hour after-school meetings for homework or college preparation. SCYEA helped Carolyn with the college application process and gave advice on what to expect once admitted. The group also takes high school juniors on college tours facilitated by SCYEA alumni who share their experiences of adapting to college life.

This academic support and college preparation appears to pay off. John Rogers, Miguel Carvente, and I found that SCYEA members were more likely to attend four-year universities than youth from similar socioeconomic backgrounds who did not belong to a youth organizing group.[48] In addition, many SCYEA members appreciate such help, and once in college they were not embarrassed to seek additional academic support, understanding that their lack of academic preparation was a systemic rather than personal failure.

In addition to academic support, groups increasingly incorporated healing and self-care activities to help members cope with stress through-out the 2010s. Distinct from community organizing groups targeting adults, grassroots youth organizing groups offer these age-appropriate services to help them recover from adversity.[49] Groups like SCYEA recog-nize that members can experience significant stress stemming from immi-gration, poverty, or neighborhood violence, in addition to school- and campaign-related pressures. Like many SCYEA members, Carolyn appreciated the attention paid to her emotional well-being:

> My favorite part of our meetings is the circle at the end, where we are being vulnerable. Everyone has the chance to share how they are feeling — like who had a bad day, or like who's feeling sad, who wants to share. Everyone just steps into the middle and then [we hold] our hands showing unity and supporting one another.

In this circle practice Carolyn described, SCYEA members learned about the African principle of *umoja*, or the understanding that the circle is only as strong as its weakest link. Reflecting members' own ethnic cultures or those of their peers, these strategies help youth pro- cess adversities and expand their emotional capacities for collective action.[50]

A Critical Civics Education

Having laid the emotional groundwork for collective action, youth organizing groups offer members a rigorous and targeted civics education. "I always left CoCo [Community Coalition] learning something new that I'm not being taught at school," Carolyn recalled of SCYEA's biweekly meetings, in which she and her peers discussed how local governments shape local policies, learned about school district budgeting processes, and conducted peer surveys to gauge their concerns. Building on their members' growing confidence and academic skills, youth organizing groups help members analyze the structural causes of community problems, social policies, power dynamics, and the various systems of oppression affecting their communities. This civics education (sometimes referred to as political education) frequently entails interactive workshops and can include elements of youth-led participatory action research, in which students conduct their own campaign-related research.

Like civil rights organizations before them, SCYEA and other youth organizing groups aim to cultivate politicized collective identities.[51] Curricula often align with Cathy Cohen and colleagues' lived civics approach, which raises awareness of adolescents' own identities and teaches them to think about power, privilege, and inclusive approaches to social change through an intersectional lens. To this end, SCYEA and most other groups regularly incorporate ethnic studies and other topics that center local histories, ethnic communities, and members' multiple identities. For example, young staff members contextualized SCYEA's equity and justice and other campaigns within the history of earlier black and Latino youth movements and local grassroots organizing and introduced young leaders to movement elders. As a Guatemalan American growing up in a city with a very large Mexican population, Carolyn met older Central American immigrant community leaders. She also learned about the histories and experiences of her fellow community members, including those of her black and LGBTQ+ peers. In sum, the curricula expose members to root causes and solutions to community problems, while developing members' pride in their own identities and promoting solidarity.

Guidance in Civic Action

Youth organizing campaigns' efforts may operate on a small scale (for example, promoting healthy and ethnic food options in school cafeterias), or they may require broad-based coalitions and years of work (such as fighting for access to government subsidized health care for undocumented youth). Regardless of the scale of the campaign, groups provide members vital guidance in civic action. Youth develop basic civic skills such as public speaking, running meetings, and planning events. Additionally, in collaborating with adult allies, adolescents receive extensive guidance in executing collective action strategies aimed at advancing campaign goals.

As described by Ben Kirshner, youth organizing groups function as apprenticeships: Young staff and experienced members model effective action, coach members in taking action themselves, and then fade into the background once members have sufficiently developed their skills.[52] Members have the opportunity to rehearse talking points and speeches among peers and increase their confidence. "We always practice what we have to say before we talk to others and say it in public," Carolyn said. Members also learn to strategically leverage their skills to influence policy and voter turnout. As Carolyn noted, when youth testify at public hearings or meet with decision-makers, "the organizers are very particular about preparing people to represent others when they speak." Additionally, members plan events small and large, from teach-ins at their school to larger community gatherings aimed at broader audiences. "[Staff] would help us make sure we get people's attention, that we are clear [about] why we're rallying, and that our presentations stick in people's minds," Carolyn explained.

Many groups train adolescent leaders in how to properly collect signatures or register voters. "We would have role-plays for phone banking, door knocking, voter registration," recounted Carolyn. Often guided by a more experienced youth leader, SCYEA youth practice scenarios in which they approach potential voters or stakeholders, including those who might be uninformed or opposed to their causes.

Together, these three elements—attention to developmental needs, a critical civics education, and guidance in civic action—constitute a transformative political socialization process that augments adolescents' capacities to effectively participate in grassroots policy change and electoral campaigns. By incorporating such comprehensive programming, youth organizing groups develop their members' voice and agency, engendering a bottom-up political consciousness grounded in local community concerns.

Civic Infrastructure and Localized Political Contexts

Youth organizing groups tend to be embedded within larger ecosystems of civil society organizations, including those focused on labor, civil, and immigrant rights. They often join more established and larger organizations to help fill a void left by political parties, which have largely failed to adequately engage with and mobilize recent waves of non-European immigrants and refugees.[53]

These immigrant-serving civic infrastructures tend to differ across geographic contexts.[54] Immigration scholars have long noted that the context of reception—the social, economic, and political conditions that immigrants encounter in their host society—can shape immigrants' integration outcomes, including their political engagement.[55] At a regional or municipal level, civic associations and their affiliated movements respond to "localized political contexts" that differ in their degree of accommodation or hostility toward newcomers.[56]

This holds true for youth organizing groups that operate in a range of political environments. While similarities exist across the field, my research shows that youth organizing groups also make local adaptations to their curricula, political strategies, and programming as they prepare youth to exercise their voice in political debates. For example, Community Coalition serves a historically black and now majority Latinx South Central Los Angeles. The organization has become an integral component of a larger civil and immigrant rights social movement infrastructure that influences school district, city, and county policies. Youth in this organization prioritize and celebrate black and brown alliances as they pursue ambitious campaigns alongside established civil rights, immigrant rights, and labor organizations with significant access to political elites. The social and political dynamics of the South Central Los Angeles context, however, differ in many ways from those in other regions that lack a well-networked and allied civil society ecosystem. Groups adapt their programs to different local contexts—for example, operating differently in Los Angeles than they do in hostile areas where the majority of voters embrace an antiimmigrant agenda.

Yet regardless of the local context, youth organizing groups enhance members' abilities to engage in political debates around a wide range of concerns. Unlike a dominant political party, these civic associations are not invested in reproducing the status quo and can thus alter long-term local political dynamics as they expand the political power and networks of second-generation youth. As, such, a transformative political socialization can accelerate the political incorporation of immigrant communities.

Data and Methods

This book draws on multiple waves of surveys and interviews systematically collected from 2011 to 2021. However, my first exposure to these groups occurred when I was a college student in 1996 and briefly volunteered for Californians for Justice (CFJ) in Oakland; its door-to-door campaign at the time aimed to educate voters about Proposition 209, which sought to end affirmative action in California. The organization was in its founding year and had not yet developed the robust youth programming that it would later finetune and expand. Nonetheless, CFJ trained me on how to relay a nonpartisan message to voters and track the results of those efforts. CFJ showed me, a college student who was concerned about the political attacks on immigrants and young people of color across California in the 1990s, how I could address these concerns by engaging in political action beyond protesting.

Since then, I have remained connected to youth organizing groups in a range of capacities. In my research, I observed the alumni of high school organizing groups become young adults. Some took on roles in the immigrant youth movement fighting for the Dream Act and other progressive political efforts, while others went on to work in the public sector. A smaller number worked for or became elected officials. My casual observations led me to believe that these nonpartisan youth organizing groups might be impactful training grounds for low-income second-generation immigrants who might not otherwise receive significant exposure to politics as adolescents. However, as a researcher committed to scientific inquiry, I wanted to assess whether my observations reflected a broader pattern. I therefore leveraged the networks and trusting relationships I had developed over the years to embark on an expansive study of these groups.

In 2011, I had the opportunity to examine broader civic engagement patterns as part of the California Young Adult Study (CYAS), a mixed-methods investigation examining youth transitions to adulthood. It surveyed 3,020 young adults, including a representative sample as well as purposive samples of undocumented youth activists and alumni of youth organizing groups. My research team and I conducted more than three hundred in-depth interviews with survey participants. This data offers ample evidence that adolescent youth organizing groups develop members' capacities to engage in politics.

This 2011–2012 study prompted me to look more deeply into these organizations. Through additional surveys and staff interviews conducted throughout the decade that followed, I refined survey measures and my conceptualization of politicization processes. Consequently, this book also draws on national and statewide survey data collected from youth organizing staff, a membership census of a subset of youth organizing groups, 278 interviews of youth and staff, and other data collected between 2013 and 2021. Over the years, I witnessed the field of youth organizing groups expand and become more interconnected, thanks to the movement of staff across organizations as well as the emergence of intermediary groups that provided these organizations with training and technical assistance. In the online methodological appendix to this book, I further detail my connection to the field, my approach to data collection, and the various sources of data.[57]

Leveraging observations, interviews, and data collected over a decade, I completed an in-depth and rigorous analysis of the organizational practices that engender a transformative political socialization. To be sure, youth organizing groups are not monolithic. My findings indicate that organizational practices vary, as do the effectiveness of the training and developmental supports young people receive across organizations or even within the same organization. Yet the general pattern remains consistent: Adolescents who participate in and contribute to this comprehensive programming increase their capacity to exercise civic leadership in and beyond their communities. At a time when reactionary forces are scapegoating immigrants and democratic institutions are under attack, this empirical research offers a blueprint for facilitating the leadership of second-generation youth in standing up for their communities, developing coalitions, and advancing solutions to pressing public concerns.

Organization of the Book

This book highlights how young people, mainly the children of immigrants and refugees, come to collectively advocate for their communities. I divide my findings into two sections.

Part I (chapters 2 through 4) demonstrates how youth organizing in California fits into broader legacies of civil rights and related social movement activism, offering an overview of youth organizing groups and the outcomes associated with second-generation adolescents' involvement. Chapter 2 describes the historical context in which youth organizing groups grew in number, drawing on a 2019 national survey about their membership, campaign issue areas, and networks in California and across the country. Influenced by late twentieth-century movements, nonprofit 501(c)3 youth organizing groups multiplied as an alternative approach to preventing violence and gang activity.

In chapter 3, I demonstrate how political incorporation pathways differ between members of adolescent youth organizing groups and their counterparts from similar backgrounds. I summarize some of the self-selection mechanisms into these groups and members' self-reported gains in developmental outcomes, critical civic knowledge, and the capacity to take political action, which arguably enable participants to more effectively lead in adolescence and into adulthood.

Chapter 4 takes an in-depth look at the political socialization of some of California's most vulnerable immigrant youth—those who lack legal documentation. In 2011, undocumented young adult leaders successfully advocated for the California Dream Act—an initiative that provided in-state tuition for undocumented immigrants. How did immigrant youth leaders learn to exercise political power so effectively? Survey and interview data demonstrate that a disproportionate number of these young adult immigrants began learning to take political action as adolescents while participating in youth organizing groups. As they reached adulthood, they developed coordinated networks to promote a shared immigrant rights agenda. And finally, thanks to the LGBTQ+ leaders within their ranks, these young immigrants adopted intersectional frameworks that facilitated coalition-building and left an imprint on subsequent youth organizing efforts.

In part II of the book (chapters 5 through 8), I describe the components of the transformative socialization process in greater depth while attending to localized contexts of reception. Although California as a whole remains more receptive to immigrants than many other states in the country, it includes regions with moderate to modest support for immigrant rights. In addressing regional differences, I extend the applicability of my study to geographic areas outside of the state, noting how demographics and political dynamics help define local adaptations to organizational programming.

Chapter 5 focuses on one aspect of youth development that sustains young people as they engage in politics: healing and self-care. As an illustrative example, I feature Resilience Orange County (ROC), a Santa Ana group founded by participants of the Dream movement. Specifically, I show how this group incorporated healing and self-care activities that helped young people process and recover from emotional hardships.

Offering lessons for groups working with young people who must endure multiple stressors, ROC adapted its program to respond to a localized context that had a history of criminalizing youth and immigrants.

Chapter 6 spotlights two organizations in Oakland, Asian Youth Promoting Advocacy and Leadership (AYPAL) and Youth Together (YT), to explore the critical civics education that their youth organizing members receive. Similar to other groups, these organizations implemented curricula attending to members' multiple identities. In orienting members toward intersectional and coalitional politics, these groups adapted their curricula to highlight local ethnic histories and multiracial social movements.

The next two chapters detail how young people benefit from guidance in civic action in two very different localized political contexts. Chapter 7 demonstrates how members of InnerCity Struggle (ICS) in Los Angeles's Eastside neighborhood acquired civic skills and applied them in collective action. In a localized context that was welcoming of immigrant rights, youth leveraged Eastside and citywide civic infrastructures to wage bold grassroots campaigns. In contrast, chapter 8 demonstrates how members of 99Rootz and other groups learned to effectively take action in the hostile context of California's Central Valley, where older white conservative voters held significant political power. While political opposition in this area often inhibited youth organizing groups from launching ambitious policy change campaigns, members of Latinx, Southeast Asian, Filipinx, and Punjabi descent, as well as other backgrounds, successfully increased voter turnout.

Briefly featuring Future Leaders of America based in California's Central Coast, chapter 9 concludes the book by summarizing my findings. I also discuss the implications of this research for initiatives seeking to support new cohorts of young people in engaging in collective struggles for the well-being and self-determination of their communities.

Over the course of a decade, I have had the opportunity to observe the trajectories of former members of youth organizing groups as they entered adulthood. Many remained active in and beyond their community, regardless of their college and career paths. Among them is Carolyn, who developed a passion for environmental justice and found employment at an environmental mitigation firm soon after graduating from college. During her free time, she contributed to her community by volunteering at SCYEA, promoting a variety of political causes over social media, and regularly participating in voter mobilization efforts. Carolyn also drew on her organizing experience and bilingual language skills during the COVID-19 pandemic, knocking on doors to assist her Latinx and black neighbors in signing up online for vaccine appointments. "I feel like canvassing [door to door] comes so naturally now," she asserted, "because we've done it constantly throughout the youth program."

Like so many alumni of youth organizing groups who underwent a transformative political socialization, Carolyn learned to lead in ways that centered immigrant and other low-income community members' needs. While some youth I observed went on to make headlines in local, state, or even national campaigns, many were like Carolyn: engaged behind the scenes. As regular voters (when eligible), these young people remained steadfast in protecting their communities during difficult times and committed to efforts that expand opportunity.

Experienced in engaging others to support a range of causes, young people like Carolyn play an important role in defining the future of their communities. *Learning to Lead* thus offers a roadmap for supporting upcoming generations in collective struggles for justice.

PART I

INHERITING STRUGGLES AND FORGING NEW PATHS

HISTORICAL CIVIL rights and social movements inform contemporary youth organizing, which in turn shapes future political landscapes. Youth organizing thus carries forward the legacies of the past while projecting new possibilities for the future. Offering a statewide analysis of youth organizing in California, part I of this book illustrates this continuity while recognizing that newer generations play a role in furthering their political incorporation and responding to contemporary concerns. In chapter 2, I outline how California's youth organizing field connects to the political activism of prior generations and how these organizations share characteristics with those across the United States. Chapter 3 draws on statewide data to make the case that these settings bolster second-generation immigrant youths' civic capacities, facilitating their ongoing contributions to the political debates affecting their communities. Subsequently, in chapter 4, I show how adolescent experience enabled a cohort of young immigrants to help shape a national immigrant rights movement. Taken together, these chapters offer statewide evidence that comprehensive programming engenders a transformative political socialization, propelling young participants to take their place among community leaders who came before them.

= Chapter 2 =

Rooted in Resistance:
The Origins and State
of the Nonprofit Youth
Organizing Field

L IAN CHEUN was barely three weeks old when she and her parents
  escaped from the Khmer Rouge labor camp in Northern Cambodia
  where they had been imprisoned. "The journey was wild," Lian
said. Her family crossed four borders and spent several years in a Thai
refugee camp before resettling in Oakland, California, in 1984, right
before her fifth birthday. Even after reaching safety, the Cambodian
civil war and genocide remained with them—she remembered her
father's night terrors, his screams, and "the fear in his voice" throughout
her childhood years. Lian encountered yet more violence in the various
low-income multiracial neighborhoods where she lived while her parents struggled to find safe and stable housing. She attended Roosevelt
Middle School, where her seventh-grade friends "were starting to get
pregnant, dropping out, joining gangs, forming cliques," she said.
"There were fights pretty much every day."

Lian was fourteen and finishing ninth grade when, on a whim, she
joined a campaign run by Youth of Oakland United, a project of People
United for a Better Oakland. She helped collect survey data to docu-
ment youth opposition to a city council plan to impose a curfew on
minors and mobilized young people to attend a city council hearing in
which she spoke for the group. The curfew was subsequently tabled.
"That was when I first learned about power," Lian said, grasping that
she and her peers could collectively influence local policies. "It was my
first campaign."

Since that success, Lian has spent two decades as an organizer—
initially as a young participant, then as a staff member, and now as executive director of Khmer Girls in Action (KGA) in Long Beach. Her history
and accomplishments reflect the experiences of many young people of

23

https://doi.org/10.7758/gert1126.5319

color who are the children of immigrants and who join youth organizing groups, as well as their continuing commitment as adults to address political concerns affecting their communities. In many ways, Lian's career as an organizer ran parallel to the evolution of California youth organizing groups. Relying on a national survey, in-depth interviews, participant observations, and secondary research further detailed briefly in the appendix and more thoroughly in the online appendix, this chapter follows Lian's story and summarizes the history of nonprofit groups that grew in number between the mid-1990s and 2020. Importantly, this chapter also shows how groups in California compared with those in the rest of the United States. While youth organizing groups were more common in California than in other states, the data suggests that they played a role in advancing immigrant political incorporation across the country.

The Late Twentieth-Century Lineage of Contemporary Youth Organizing

Scholars have long noted that social movements do not occur in isolation but rather build off geographically proximate and contemporary movements. David Meyer and Nancy Whittier coined the concept *social movement spillover* to describe how earlier actions influence the ideologies, strategies, tactics, and structures of subsequent movements.[1] In California, this spillover results from intergenerational mentorship and a somewhat romanticized collective memory of local organizing efforts during the civil rights era. Accordingly, nonprofit youth organizing groups initially looked to the social movements of the mid-to-late twentieth century for guidance and inspiration. In doing so, organizers leveraged these earlier movements to demonstrate to young leaders the possibilities of advancing change, rather than drawing on lessons from the conflicts within and limitations of earlier struggles.

The Black Panther Party

As the young civil rights and labor leaders of the mid-to-late twentieth century aged, they often remained active in local politics and progressive efforts for decades.[2] Some counseled the founders, young adult staff, and members of youth organizing groups established in the 1990s and 2000s. In Oakland, for example, youth organizers have drawn on the legacy of the Black Panther Party for Self-Defense. Founded in 1966 in Oakland, the Black Panther Party quickly developed chapters across the nation that radicalized and inspired political action among black youth and their allies. After the original party disbanded, some leaders continued their activism in Oakland and elsewhere, working in local government and advising Lian and many other adolescents as they addressed the concerns of young people of color.[3]

One of these former Panthers is Millie Cleveland, who for much of the 1990s directed the Violence Prevention Project at the West Oakland Mental Health Center. A Detroit native who led high school walkouts as a teenager, she had witnessed firsthand how young people with few positive outlets for developing their talents and skills got caught up in violence and the criminal justice system. Millie is a mother of two young men and a talented organizer with long-standing ties to local labor unions that have sometimes supported youth organizing efforts. Notably, in the 1990s, she helped develop youth organizing efforts and campaign strategies. She also leveraged her conflict mediation skills to bring together racially diverse youth and to broker relationships with decision-makers. Millie was a key adult ally for Lian in the Oakland Kids First Initiative and a co-founder of Youth Together (YT), a group discussed in this chapter.

Another important figure is David Hilliard, who hosted tours of key Black Panther sites in Oakland. In the 1990s and early 2000s, the Black Panther tour was a staple field trip of youth organizing groups, contributing to their members' political education and featuring Hilliard's "I was there" account of the party's origins, purpose, and accomplishments. During these tours, Hilliard described how the Black Panthers not only promoted a political agenda that centered black communities but also made inroads in building cross-racial coalitions.[4] As an observer on three separate occasions, I saw how tour guides shared their perspectives on the rationale behind and key accomplishments of the party without delving deeply into the internal tensions within and demise of the party. The Black Panthers' 1966 Ten-Point Program—which listed demands involving food, education, housing, criminal justice, and the military—prompted young people to analyze present-day injustices and inequalities and to understand how their efforts might connect to previous activism. And thus, in the summer of 2020, I witnessed youth leaders reference the historic 1966 program as they announced their own California platform at a statewide network videoconference coordinated by the intermediary, YO! Cali.

Another important mentor to young organizers was Anthony Thigpenn, a former Black Panther and a well-known political strategist in Los Angeles progressive politics. Thigpenn helped develop a multiracial approach for addressing the systemic inequalities laid bare during the 1992 LA uprising. Thigpenn became a guiding force in the systematic youth voter education and mobilization efforts that emerged in the 2010s and described in chapter 8 of this book.

Asian American Civil Rights Activists

Contemporary youth organizing groups also draw from the experiences of Asian Americans who were involved in the civil rights movement. Among these were Yuri Kochiyama, a tireless Asian American civil rights leader and native Angeleno who has settled in Oakland and established fruitful and long-lasting connections with young Asian Americans and other leaders of color. Known for her pioneering work with Malcolm X in building Asian-black solidarity, she also helped to win reparations for Japanese Americans interned during World War II and continued to fight for political prisoners and support other causes until late in life. Other examples include Pam Tau Lee, a Chinese American, and Lillian Galedo, a Filipina American activist, both of whom participated in the historic fight against the eviction of elderly Asian American residents from San Francisco's International Hotel. As founders of the Chinese Progressive Association and Filipinos Advancing Justice, both women deeply invested in mentoring Asian American youth organizers.

Beginning in the mid-to-late 1970s, David Kakishiba, a community activist and the son of a Japanese internee, helped establish successful youth programs for ethnically diverse Asian American youth. Another important leader was Warrick Liang, who as a youth was involved in the anti-war movement and debates over Asian American studies at the University of California, Berkeley. Later, he worked with Cambodian and Lao youth in an overseas Thai refugee camp. Returning to the United States, Liang ran the Richmond Youth Project, which jump-started youth organizing among Southeast Asian and other racially diverse youth in Richmond, Virginia.

Chicano and Latinx Movements

The United Farm Workers (UFW) and the related Chicano movement, as well as subsequent immigration and labor movements in the 1980s and early 1990s, paved the way for youth organizing in Latinx communities. Based in the agricultural and politically conservative region of California's Central Valley, the UFW built strong connections with the Chicano movement of the late 1960s and early 1970s. Led by charismatic leaders Cesar Chavez and Dolores Huerta, the UFW recruited university students and other young California volunteers. Chavez was the founder; Huerta, his valued right hand, became the group's prominent legislative advocate. She has supported youth-led campaigns since the 1990s, and in the 2010s, her Bakersfield-based foundation sponsored a youth organizing group.

Activists who participated in the UFW and Chicano movement as youth became valued mentors in ongoing campaigns for civil rights, immigrant rights, environmental justice, women's rights, and labor organizing, opening doors for younger leaders to participate in interconnected activist efforts. In Merced, Cecilia Mendoza, who joined the UFW in 1966, offered her home as a meeting space for 99Rootz, an organization featured in chapter 8. María Elena Durazo, a former UFW volunteer, became the first Chicana president of the largely Latinx immigrant union, UNITE HERE. When she later served as executive secretary-treasurer of the Los Angeles County Federation of Labor, she secured monetary and political support for undocumented youth activists. Chicana activist Betita Martínez hosted events for young Bay Area youth and mentored organizers in the 1990s and early 2000s. Finally, Antonia Hernández, former Chicana youth activist and first woman director of the Mexican American Legal Defense Fund (MALDEF), later provided key funding to Los Angeles youth organizing groups as the president of the California Community Foundation.

Some Chicano civil rights and UFW activists urged labor unions such as the Service Employees International Union (SEIU) to become more racially inclusive, put immigrant rights on its agenda, and address broader economic and educational inequalities facing people of color.[5] During the 1990s, Gabriel Hernandez, an activist in the Central American sanctuary movement and SEIU organizer, was a driving force in building a network of Bay Area Chicano and Central American youth trained in grassroots organizing. Meanwhile, beginning in the 2000s in Los Angeles, SEIU janitors and classified school employees' unions also offered their political muscle to support youth organizing campaigns.

Labor and Immigrant Rights Groups

Campaigns on behalf of immigrant and refugee rights, efforts linked to labor rights struggles, also shaped youth organizing efforts in California in the early 1990s. In San Francisco and Los Angeles, community leaders established organizations and social networks to help refugees fleeing U.S.-supported wars in El Salvador and Guatemala.[6] These organizers highlighted the fact that Central Americans were largely political refugees with experiences distinct from those of Mexicans, who primarily migrated for economic reasons.[7]

As for Mexican immigrants, the Coalition for Humane Immigrant Rights of Los Angeles and Hermandad Mexicana Nacional were both founded in response to the 1986 Immigrant Reform and Control Act to help mostly undocumented Mexican immigrants gain access to amnesty.

The law gave legal status to U.S. immigrants who arrived before 1982, but it also barred employing—and criminalized—those who did not qualify, including Central Americans escaping U.S.-supported wars.[8] Thus, many of the Mexican and Central American migrants who had arrived after the 1982 cutoff date remained undocumented.

Consequently, immigrant rights issues became increasingly salient in the 1990s, as opposition to the growing Mexican and Central American populations from the Republican Party and other groups mounted.[9] In response, MALDEF, Centro Legal de la Raza, and the Spanish Speaking Unity Council shifted resources from civil rights to immigrant rights advocacy, and some Asian American civil rights groups also developed programs on immigrant and refugee rights. Meanwhile, the labor movement recruited new immigrants into its ranks, providing the immigrant rights movement with political muscle.[10]

Thus, California developed a civic infrastructure and public leadership linking civil rights, labor rights, immigrant rights, and refugee rights, connections sometimes facilitated by UFW activists. In some communities, Native American elders also played a role, introducing the preservation of Indigenous cultural traditions and attention to the natural environment as important priorities. And while some elder movement activists contended with racial tensions, many others successfully modeled multiracial and cross-sector alliances, providing younger generations concrete examples of how collective action can make a difference.[11] Therefore, by the time youth organizing groups began growing in number in the 1990s, an influential segment of veteran leaders were already attentive to issues affecting racially diverse people of color, including more recently arrived immigrants and refugees from low-income and working-class backgrounds.

The Growth of Youth Organizing in California

Adolescents have long played a role in social movements, particularly in policy debates and voter outreach; their ties to nonpartisan, nonprofit 501(c)3 organizations as vehicles for engagement are relatively new. In the late 1980s and 1990s, social movement leaders and youth advocates responded to growing concerns about street gangs, rising interracial violence, and the crack epidemic.[12] These challenges unfolded against a backdrop of deindustrialization and the disappearance of living-wage jobs. During this period, government agencies increasingly divested from education and social programs aimed at low-income youth, instead reallocating resources to militarize police forces, expand the prison industrial complex, and enforce zero-tolerance school discipline policies.[13] Consequently, black youth, along with the children of immigrants and refugees—including Mexicans, Central Americans, and Southeast Asians—faced heightened criminalization.[14] To further complicate the lives of low-income diverse youth, immigrant rights and civil rights came under attack in California.[15] Within this context, social movement leaders and youth advocates developed programs that combined the strategies of grassroots community organizing groups with those of apolitical youth service programs that attend to young people's developmental needs.[16] In California, some of the earliest nonprofit youth organizing groups emerged in the San Francisco Bay Area and Los Angeles, where they encountered somewhat more favorable localized political contexts for organizing the children of immigrants and refugees.

The Early Days

Local ballot measures in San Francisco and Oakland secured funding for groups that supported youth organizing. Youth Making a Change was among the first groups to achieve longevity. Established in 1991 as a program of San Francisco's Coleman Advocates, it was led by Margaret Brodkin, a well-known local activist with roots in New York's settlement houses.[17] The program emerged from a successful community-driven campaign among high school–age youth that led voters to approve Measure J, also called the Children's Amendment. This initiative set aside 2.5 percent of the assessed value of local property taxes for children's services and established the San Francisco Department of Children, Youth, and Families to disperse the funds to local organizations. This landmark victory paved the way for other similar campaigns, demonstrating adolescents' potential to work alongside adult allies in shaping policy priorities and establishing an ongoing source of funding for youth programs.

For example, across the bay in Oakland, Lian was part of a coalition of youth-serving organizations (including People United for a Better Oakland, East Bay Asian Youth Center, West Oakland Mental Health Center, and Centro de Juventud) and other advocates whose efforts secured voter approval of Measure K, also known as the Kids First Measure, in November 1996. Similar to San Francisco's Measure J, Measure K set aside 2.5 percent of the city's unrestricted general fund to create the Oakland Fund for Children and Youth. As a high school student, Lian worked with peers to pass Measure K, making a video contrasting the resources allocated for youth in the Oakland Hills, a well-off area, with those for youth in the lower-income flatlands. Lian remembered "doing so many presentations to get more and more folks to endorse Kids First." In their Kids First campaign, youth organizers like Lian sought to counter the widespread superpredator tropes that depicted young people of color (especially young men) as criminals in 1990s mainstream media. They presented alternative images of youth of color as children who deserved the opportunity to succeed and thrive.[18] Through this successful Measure K lobbying effort, Lian and her peers learned the importance of securing support from a broad coalition of racially diverse stakeholders, including established civil rights organizations, religious groups, parents, educators, and representatives of youth-serving organizations.

Benefiting from eventual support from the Oakland Fund for Children and Youth, various youth organizing groups emerged in the mid-1990s. Among them was Oakland Kids First!, incorporated after the passage of Measure K, as well as CFJ, founded in 1996 and operating youth organizing groups in four communities. Chapter 6 of this book features Youth Together, also founded in 1996 to address the root causes of inter-racial violence, and AYPAL, founded in 1998 to engage diverse Asian American youth in education and racial justice efforts. These groups consistently involved the children of immigrants and refugees, often alongside or in coalition with nonimmigrant black youth. Oakland-based organizations such as the Center for Third World Organizing and the School of Unity and Liberation provided vital training and support for these emerging nonprofits.

In Los Angeles, youth organizing emerged in force after the 1992 civil unrest and 1994 passage of Proposition 187, which sought to deny government services (including K–12 education) to undocumented immigrants. Within this context, Karen Bass (who eventually became a representative in Congress and later mayor of Los Angeles) and Chicana civil rights activist Sylvia Castillo founded the Community Coalition. The group began organizing high school–age youth in 1994 after the civil unrest exposed interracial violence between black and brown youth. Meanwhile, in East Los Angeles, ICS proposed alternative ways to reduce crime and violence, fought Proposition 187, and enlisted Latinx youth in efforts to improve local schools. As described in chapter 7, this group has engaged in ambitious intergenerational campaigns involving youth and parents.

A Growing Influence

While some of the earliest youth organizing groups primarily concentrated on addressing education, violence, and criminalization concerns, others tackled different issues through their campaign efforts. For example, Youth United for Community Action, established in 1994 in

East Palo Alto, and Youth for Environmental Justice, established in 1997 by Communities for a Better Environment and serving small cities in southeastern Los Angeles County, organized around environmental justice. Another group was KGA, founded in 1997 to promote reproductive justice for Cambodian girls in Long Beach. Its mission later expanded to include boys and address other issues important to youth. And in 2001, the Coalition for Humane Immigrant Rights of Los Angeles (CHIRLA) established Wise Up!, which was among the first U.S. youth organizing groups to focus on undocumented youth.

In the 2000s and 2010s, the staff and alumni of established groups supported the expansion of youth organizing efforts across the state. They developed new organizations, offered technical assistance and training, and served as bridges to a growing number of philanthropic and government supporters. Drawing on their experience as more seasoned organizers, some staff spearheaded training on power analysis (a process now commonly used by youth and other organizers to develop campaigns) and integrated voter engagement (an approach to voter outreach that incorporates grassroots organizing), enabling groups to develop more sophisticated and ambitious campaigns. Moreover, alumni and staff ties to the immigrant youth and Black Lives Matter movements deepened intersectional approaches to groups' programming and campaign strategies.

By the late 2010s, grassroots organizing groups engaged adolescents across the state, including in more conservative and moderate regions that lacked the civic infrastructures of Los Angeles and the Bay Area. Thanks, in part, to funding from private foundations, as well as the technical assistance from intermediary organizations that provided staff training, policy analysis, and campaign coordination, among other services, youth organizing groups became increasingly connected, sharing best practices for supporting youths' leadership and campaign strategies. Because of this, their programming similarly promoted their members' transformative political socialization. Still, groups varied in terms of organizational structures and programmatic strengths. Their training curricula and campaign tactics also responded to their localized political context.

California's Youth Organizing Groups in National Context

Since the 1990s, the number of nonprofit youth organizing groups across the United States has grown.[19] Back then, only about a dozen or so organizations in California prioritized supporting the leadership of adolescents in grassroots campaigns, KGA among them.[20] Another

39 began organizing adolescent youth in the first decade of the 2000s, some by expanding or shifting existing programs and others by creating new community-based organizations. By the 2010s, roughly 44 groups had begun to focus on youth organizing. Another 15 more established groups also involved youth, but it was unclear from website or survey data at what point in time they began devoting resources to engaging high school–aged youth in policy change or electoral campaigns. By 2019, just prior to the COVID-19 pandemic, 110 California-based non-profit youth organizing groups involved low-income adolescents in grassroots campaigns.

Although these 501(c)3 groups have different campaign foci and organizing strategies, I contend that they can be considered what DiMaggio and Powell call an organizational field, subject to isomorphic pressures that foster similarities among them.[21] Thanks in part to the intermediaries that convened them, youth organizing groups were often well networked; their members attended some of the same staff training sessions, went to the same statewide or regional conferences, and often worked in coalition. Regarding personnel, alumni from existing groups who were recruited to join the staff or in some cases lead sister organizations—Lian Cheun among them—contributed to cohesion among these organizations. In the pages that follow, I draw on a 2019 national field scan survey of youth organizing groups to describe their members, campaigns, and programming. I contextualize California-based groups by comparing them with those operating outside of the state. Sponsored by the Funders Collaborative on Youth Organizing, the survey excludes groups that primarily target middle- or upper-class youth or were tied to religious or conservative movements. More information about the survey sample and methodology can be found in the appendix.

The Core Members of Youth Organizing Groups

The 2019 national survey asked staff to describe their organizations' core leaders, broadly defined as regular participants in group activities. The analysis presented here focuses on 110 groups that involved high school–aged adolescents. However, it is important to note that in approximately 3 out of 4 of these groups, young adults age eighteen to twenty-five also made up the core leaders. Young adult members often help mentor adolescents and can play a significant role in leading campaigns. Middle school youth were involved in 38 percent of programs, though they tended to play minimal roles in campaigns; however, these early adolescent members began receiving age-appropriate developmental supports and gained exposure to a politicizing critical civics education.

Nationally, youth organizing groups largely target young people of color in low-income communities. And in California, these young people were disproportionately the children of immigrants. Young women, individuals who identify as nonbinary, and LGBTQ+ youth also tended to be highly represented. Given their diversity and the multiple layers of adversity many members faced, groups adopted an intersectional approach to tackling issues that resonated with these youth.

Immigrant and Racial-Ethnic Representation

Youth organizing groups intentionally bolster the capacities of racially diverse members to inject their voices into political debates and electoral campaigns. The children of immigrants dominated many youth organizing groups in California and other immigrant destinations.[22] These groups function as engines of immigrant incorporation as the children of immigrants practice solidarity with peers of nonimmigrant parentage.

The 2019 national survey asked staff to identify the demographic groups "significantly" represented among core leaders (see figure 2.1).[23] California groups tended to include comparatively high representation of 1.5-generation immigrants—those who had arrived in the United States as small children, had attended U.S. schools for some years, and typically spoke English.[24] Specifically, staff respondents in 64 percent of California groups indicated that 1.5-generation immigrants and refugee youth were significantly represented among core leaders, while staff at 55 percent of California groups indicated the same of undocumented youth, including those who were at the time eligible for Deferred Action for Childhood Arrivals (DACA), which provides recipients protection from deportation and work authorization. These figures were 46 percent and 34 percent, respectively, in other states.

The survey questionnaire did not contain a separate question about the representation of U.S.-born children of immigrants, as staff sometimes could not distinguish between second- and later-generation immigrant and refugee members. However, it is safe to assume that in most groups, second-generation immigrants greatly outnumbered 1.5-generation youth, reflecting broader demographic trends. For example, in forty-three California groups featured in the subsequent chapter, 19 percent of members were 1.5 generation, and 53 percent were second generation, while only 28 percent were of nonimmigrant parentage.

Young people of color prevail in the memberships of youth organizing groups. Countering the segregation often found across and within

Figure 2.1   Demographic Groups Well-Represented Among Youth Leaders

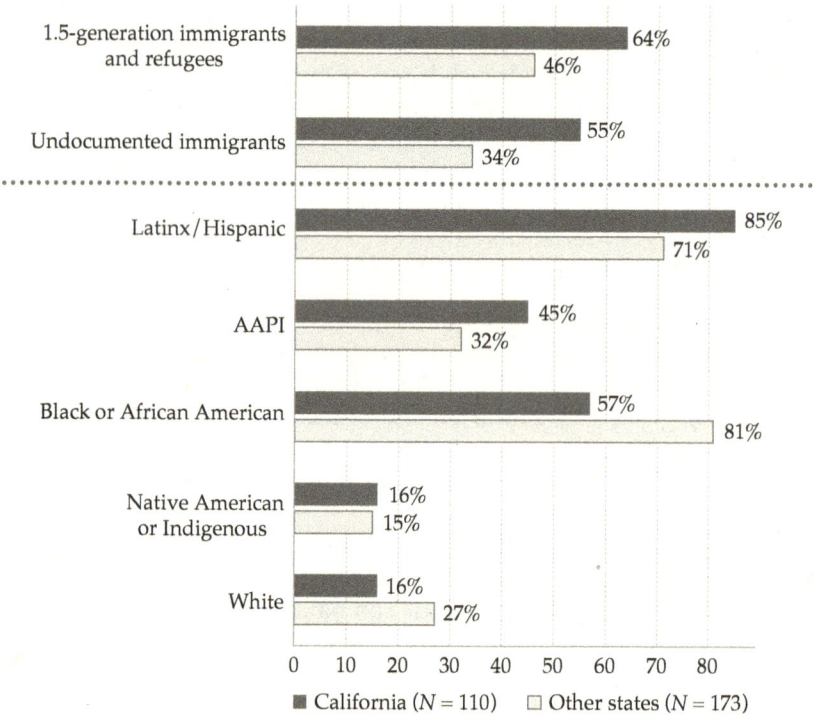

Source: Author's calculations based on FCYO Field Scan 2019.

schools, groups foster cross-racial alliances.[25] Accordingly, youth organizing groups tended to encourage participation in a multiracial democracy characterized by collaboration and alliances across difference.[26]

People of Latinx and AAPI descent were particularly well represented in California organizations, compared with those in other states. For example, 85 percent of California groups reported a significant representation of Latinx youth among their core leaders; many of those leaders were of Mexican origin, but a substantial proportion were of Central American origin as well. Only one group, CARECEN (the Central American Resource Center), explicitly targeted Central American youth.

AAPI youth overall participated in significant numbers in 48 percent of groups. Notably, within this broader category of youth, Southeast Asian youth were well represented in 26 percent of groups (disaggregated results not depicted in figure 2.1). As Lian's story reminds us, Southeast Asian youth of Cambodian, Vietnamese, and Lao origin, including Mien and Hmong ethnicities, disproportionately encountered challenges related to refugee resettlement in high-poverty communities. In addition, 16 percent of youth organizing groups involved Pacific Islander youth, including young Filipinx, who represent the largest AAPI ethnic group in California.

Black and white youth made up a larger share of core leaders outside of California than they did within the state. Still, 57 percent of California groups reported that black youth were significantly represented among their leadership. This did not mean that they formed a large proportion of members, considering that only 6 percent of young people in the state identified as black. Nonetheless, in a few groups, such as the Black Organizing Project and Brotherhood Crusade, which included Belizean and Caribbean youth from immigrant families, most youth leaders identified as black. Meanwhile, the memberships of Oakland's Black Alliance for Just Immigration and San Diego's Partnership for New Americans in San Diego had a significant representation of black youth of Caribbean or sub-Saharan African descent.

Survey results also indicate that Native Americans and other Indigenous youth were well represented in 16 percent of California groups and at similar levels elsewhere in the United States. The California Native Vote Project in Los Angeles County and True North, serving Del Norte County and adjacent tribal lands near the Oregon border, included both U.S. Native and Indigenous members from Mexico and Central America; staff recognized the shared history of genocide, colonization, and displacement among these groups.[27] Meanwhile, in California's Central Coast, the Mixteco Indígena Community Organizing Project (MICOP) Tequio youth program explicitly focuses on Indigenous youth whose families primarily hailed from Oaxaca and other parts of southern Mexico.

Reflecting the racial composition of low-income communities in the state, white youth made up a smaller share of core leaders in California compared with other states. White youth tended to join groups in Northern California and in rural areas, where they lived in greater numbers alongside or near immigrant communities.

Gendered Patterns of Leadership

Girls and young women disproportionately comprised groups' core leadership, especially in California (see figure 2.2). Because immigrant parents tend to enforce stricter rules on daughters than on sons, girls possibly join these adult-supervised groups as a means of getting out of the house after school and on weekends.[28] Moreover, these girls arguably are well equipped to handle these efforts because community activism, to some degree, extends the gendered care work in many immigrant

Figure 2.2   Gender Representation Among Youth Leaders

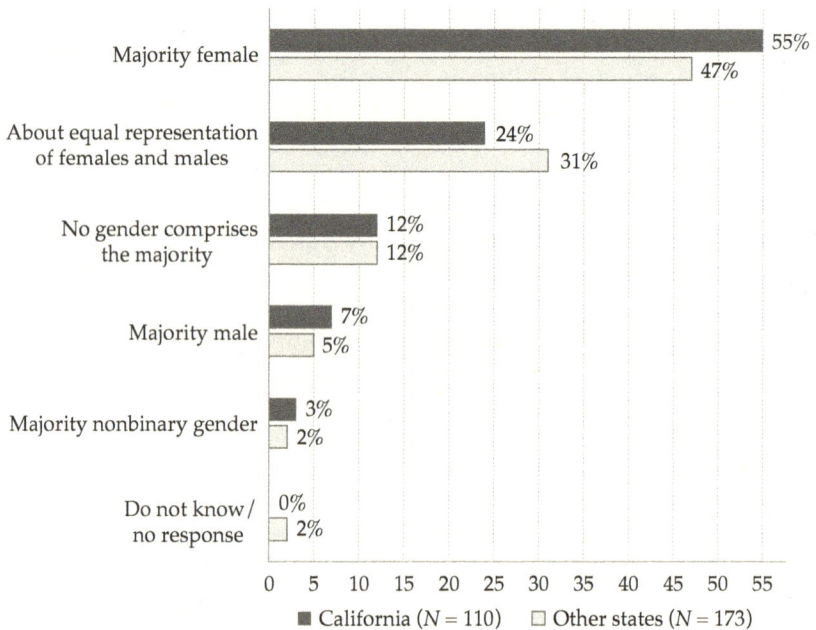

Source: Author's calculations based on FCYO Field Scan 2019.

families.[29] Yet, familial dynamics aside, their involvement extends the oft-overlooked history of women of color taking leadership roles in grass-roots efforts.[30] Indeed, young women were highly visible and effective in the immigrant rights movement and the 2020 uprisings demanding racial justice.[31]

Male-identified youth made up the majority in a relatively small number of groups. The disengagement of boys of color from formal youth organizations may partly stem from their criminalization, pressure to financially support their families, and the greater freedom they experience to spend unstructured time outside the home.[32] Meanwhile, nonbinary leaders were particularly well represented in groups tending to focus on LGBTQ issues.

Many youth organizing groups adopted curriculum and practices that aimed to offer safe spaces for and contribute to the positive identity development of LGBTQ+ youth. Hence, unsurprisingly, LGBTQ+ youth were significantly represented among core leaders in more than half of groups in California, and about half of groups elsewhere, with about

Figure 2.3   Groups with Significant LGBTQ+ Representation Among Youth Leaders

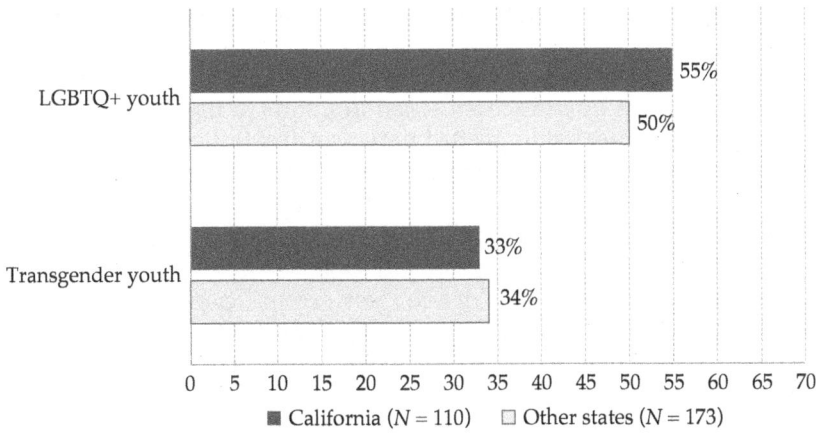

■ California (*N* = 110)   □ Other states (*N* = 173)

Source: Author's calculations based on FCYO Field Scan 2019.
Note: The first set of bars indicates that groups may include transgender youth within the broader LGBTQ+ category.

one-third of groups confirming the involvement of transgender youth among their leadership (see figure 2.3).[33]

Primary Issues in Youth Organizing Campaigns

Youth organizing groups engage adolescents in political processes through low-risk campaigns, addressing various issues of salience to immigrant and other low-income communities. These youth-led campaigns often align with progressive social movements, and some also encourage nonpartisan electoral participation. The link between social movement and electoral participation remains understudied, and youth organizing groups serve as a model of how the two can be intertwined.[34] For example, in 2020, KGA, Lian Cheun's organization, aligned with Black Lives Matter activists in advocating for increased city investments in youth and social service programs rather than policing. At the same time, members conducted nonpartisan voter education on how state and local measures might impact the funding available to support these vital community programs.

Through groups like KGA, second generation adolescents learn to adapt a variety of strategies that bend the course of local institutions and promote their immigrant community's political incorporation.[35] As young leaders execute campaigns, they serve as bridges between their immigrant communities and other political actors, including nonimmigrant peers, social movement leaders, adult allies, registered voters, and elected officials.

To be clear, adolescents' political activism typically focused on local civic action due to school schedules, limited transportation, and the costs and supervision needed for travel. Youths' efforts sometimes advanced modest reforms, such as new crosswalks for children's safety, or small increases in local voter turnout. Occasionally, ambitious youth-led campaigns realized major victories that garnered local or national media attention.

Young leaders tended to define their groups' campaign priorities, although they sometimes inherited campaigns determined by previous cohorts of members. The 2019 staff survey captured issue areas that groups sought to address (see figure 2.4). Results show that the largest proportion of groups in California (59 percent) and in other states (65 percent) engaged in education-related campaigns. Education-related concerns resonate with many second-generation adolescents from poor neighborhoods, given that their schools tend to be under-resourced, evince below-average college-going rates, and have a history of punitive disciplinary practices.[36] Importantly, youth organizing groups were among the proponents of the Local Control Funding Formula, a 2013 policy signed by then Governor Jerry Brown that increased funding for high-needs students and mandated community input into budget priorities. About 40 percent of California groups involved their members in this K–12 budgetary process, sometimes by sending them to board meetings with specific demands. Fresno Barrios Unidos, for example, demanded increased spending on restorative justice—which focuses on repairing the harm arising from unwanted behaviors—as an alternative to punitive school discipline policies such as suspension and expulsion.

Survey results indicate that health issues were the second most common emphasis nationally. Broadly defined, health issues include environmental pollution, unsafe housing conditions, school safety, and any other concern with health implications.[37] Youth organizations and their coalitions claimed notable health campaign victories, including expanding health care for undocumented immigrants as well as strengthening school-based health, mental health, and reproductive health services.[38]

Serving as a bridge between social movements and electoral politics, California groups were especially likely to engage members in voter outreach, with varying levels of frequency and intensity. Some groups

Figure 2.4   Primary Campaign Issue Areas

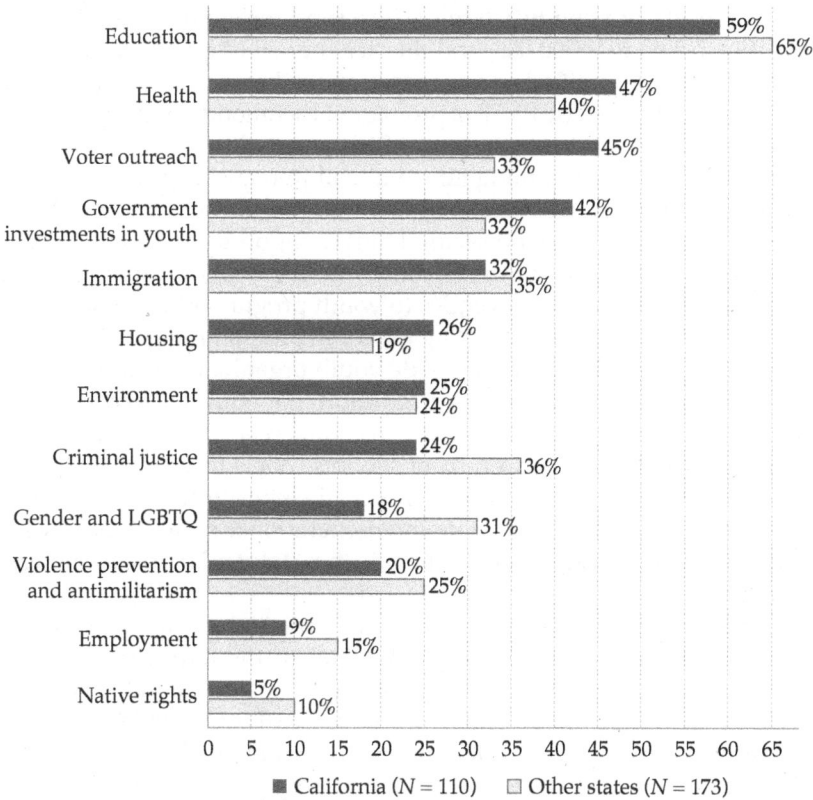

Issue Area	California (N = 110)	Other states (N = 173)
Education	59%	65%
Health	47%	40%
Voter outreach	45%	33%
Government investments in youth	42%	32%
Immigration	32%	35%
Housing	26%	19%
Environment	25%	24%
Criminal justice	24%	36%
Gender and LGBTQ	18%	31%
Violence prevention and antimilitarism	20%	25%
Employment	9%	15%
Native rights	5%	10%

Source: Author's calculations based on FCYO Field Scan 2019.

occasionally staged voter outreach events; a smaller percentage made labor-intensive and systematic phone banking efforts to get out the vote. For example, at the time of the survey, twenty groups were part of the statewide Power California network, which trained members to explain the importance of voting to young voters of color and walk them through the process. In 2018, these collective efforts increased overall turnout among young voters by 2.5 percentage points in targeted communities across the state.[39] As documented by political scientists, nonpartisan community-based organizations can be better equipped than political parties in educating and mobilizing voters in immigrant communities.[40]

About 42 percent of youth organizing groups in California and 32 percent elsewhere sought to increase government spending on youth and other programs. In 2018, Lian, who had earlier participated in the 1995 Oakland Kids First campaign, spearheaded a coalition to persuade the city of Long Beach to create a fund for youth programs. The coalition asked for $500,000, and the city council ultimately committed $200,000.[41] This qualified success came on the heels of another funding victory spearheaded by RYSE, a prominent Richmond youth organizing group. Its campaign led to the city of Richmond's 2018 decision to establish a fund for programming aimed at children and youth. As veteran youth advocates (introduced earlier), Margaret Brodkin advised this effort, and Millie Cleveland secured SEIU support for it. Meanwhile, in Santa Ana, a coalition of groups convinced the city council to devote a portion of marijuana tax revenues to youth programming. Other coalitional efforts to secure city funding for youth programming took place in Sacramento and Stockton. Statewide youth organizing groups, including KGA, affiliated with a broad coalition that educated voters about the possibilities for increasing taxes on commercial property in order to fund schools and other government services. While their 2020 campaign did not yield changes in state tax policy, the effort introduced second-generation youth to a statewide intergenerational network of leaders and offered them insights on how to influence state and municipal budget processes.

Survey results also indicate that about a third of groups also tackled immigration issues. During the latter half of the 2010s, particularly during Trump's first presidency, comprehensive immigration reform seemed out of reach. Some groups sought to save DACA, which provided a reprieve from deportation for eligible undocumented youth who had arrived in the United States as children. Groups also focused on statewide or local immigration issues, including the closing of immigration detention centers, health care access for immigrants, and sanctuary cities.

During the 2010s, affordable housing became a more salient issue, especially in California, as increased demand and skyrocketing costs increasingly displaced low-income residents from central cities. Reflecting the views of many young leaders across the state, one organizer from South Central stated, "We've been working to improve our community and had lots of wins over the years, but then we made it more attractive to affluent folks, who are now buying homes, buying up the shops, and displacing those of us who fought so hard to make it better." As such, fights for affordable housing were driven not just by the economic hardships faced by youth and their families but also by the desire to safeguard community cohesion.

Youth addressing the housing crisis often collaborated with Right to the City and other coalitions. Doing so paved the way for youth to join local and statewide efforts to cancel or delay rent payments during the COVID-19 pandemic for families at-risk of eviction.

About one in four youth organizing groups in and outside of California pursued environmental justice and efforts to address climate change. The California 501(c)3 youth organizing groups in this study were not at the forefront of the youth climate strikes of 2019, although many joined in solidarity, enabling members to engage in this international action. Instead, the groups featured here tended to join longer-term environmental justice campaigns, often in tandem with organizations with technical expertise. For example, in the Central Valley, decades of extensive toxic pesticide spraying across vast tracts of farmland contributed to highly polluted air, land, and water across the region. In response, the Youth Leadership Institute, ACT for Women and Girls, and Loud for Tomorrow participated in larger campaigns to tackle these ongoing environmental issues. Other groups like Communities for a Better Environment in Southeast Los Angeles fought to strengthen regulations around toxic dumping by local industries, while Central Coast Alliance for a Sustainable Economy campaigned against the pollution created by agricultural industries and the Oxnard commercial seaport.

Perhaps because of their comparatively smaller proportions of African American members, groups in California were less likely than those in other states to address criminal justice issues especially affecting black communities. Nevertheless, 24 percent of California groups reported focusing on criminal justice reforms prior to the 2020 uprisings. Often aligned with the Black Lives Matter movement, these campaigns involved issues like police accountability. The Urban Peace Movement in Oakland, for example, demanded the prosecution of two county sheriffs accused in 2018 of illegally recording confidential conversations between juvenile suspects and their attorneys. Meanwhile the Los Angeles–based Youth Justice Coalition supported Senate Bill 395, approved in 2017, which prevents police officers from interrogating youth age fifteen or younger until after they have consulted with legal counsel.

California groups were less likely than those in other states (18 percent compared with 31 percent) to prioritize gender and LGBTQ issues, possibly because they benefited from a more gender- and LGBTQ-inclusive policy environment than did many other states. Still, examples abounded of campaigns addressing these issues in California. Local and statewide campaigns brought attention to the criminalization of boys and young men of color who experience high rates of school suspension and expulsion, as well as incarceration. Addressing women's experiences, the Youth Leadership Institute's #MErcedTOO campaign pointed out sexual misconduct in the Merced Unified High School District; the Young Women's Freedom Center in San Francisco noted gender-based violence in women's prisons; and Visalia-based ACT for Women and Girls participated in Central Valley campaigns focused on reproductive justice.

A handful of California groups tackled transgender and LGBTQ issues. In 2016, for example, youth members of the Gender & Sexualities Alliance Network, formerly the Gay and Straight Alliance, worked in coalition with other LGBTQ rights groups to advocate successfully for Assembly Bill 1732, which requires all single-stall bathrooms in California to be labeled as gender-neutral.

While California groups were less likely to focus on violence prevention, gun reform, or demilitarization than other groups, many were inspired to mobilize against gun violence in 2018 after the Parkland, Florida, school shootings gained national attention. Specifically, members of youth organizing groups across the state joined March for Our Lives walkouts and protests in solidarity with other groups focused on gun reform.[42] Meanwhile, other groups serving young people in the juvenile justice system, like Fathers and Families of San Joaquin County in Stockton and Motivating Intergenerational Leadership for Public Advancement (MILPA) in Salinas, advocated to provide more services for young people who had been exposed to the criminal justice system as a means of preventing future violence. And in 2016, in an example of demilitarization success, the Los Angeles–based Labor Community Strategy Center successfully demanded that the Los Angeles Unified School District withdraw from the U.S. Department of Defense 1033 program, which had provided the district with an armored vehicle, grenade launchers, and automatic weapons.

Groups in California also spearheaded fewer campaigns dedicated to Native and Indigenous rights compared with groups in other states. In this area, the California Native Vote Project worked with other groups to conduct voter outreach, promote education reforms that incorporate Indigenous histories, and eliminate monuments and holidays that celebrate individuals responsible for American genocide. Coincidentally, Native American youth organizing groups in California, including the California Native Vote Project, tended to define Native peoples to include Indigenous youth from Mexico and Guatemala.[43] Meanwhile MICOP's Tequio youth program was more narrowly focused on Mexican Indigenous youth's demands for language, culture, and community recognition.

Working in Coalition

"KGA helped us understand how other groups were facing similar circumstances, and that we were fighting over crumbs," said Jenn Heng, a former adolescent member of the group who eventually joined the staff under Lian's leadership. "They got us to form relationships with people of other racial backgrounds," they explained. These interracial and intergenerational relationships pave the way for trusting coalitions central to the campaigns of KGA and other youth organizing groups.

Figure 2.5   Frequency of Intergenerational Campaign Alliances

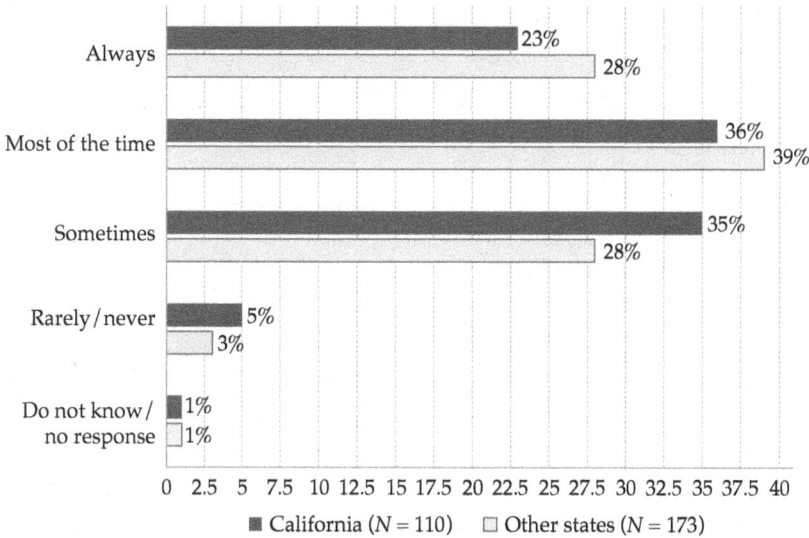

Always — California 23%, Other states 28%
Most of the time — California 36%, Other states 39%
Sometimes — California 35%, Other states 28%
Rarely/never — California 5%, Other states 3%
Do not know/no response — California 1%, Other states 1%

0 2.5 5 7.5 10 12.5 15 17.5 20 22.5 25 27.5 30 32.5 35 37.5 40

■ California (N = 110)   □ Other states (N = 173)

Source: Author's calculations based on FCYO Field Scan 2019.

For example, KGA worked with a broad-based coalition to advocate for an effort known as the People's Budget of Long Beach, seeking to build off the organization's 2018 victory in establishing a city fund for youth programming. The coalition brought together diverse stakeholders — including the Long Beach Gray Panthers, the Language Access Coalition, Black Lives Matter, the Housing Justice Coalition, and the Clergy Laity United for Economic Justice — to demand government investments supporting Long Beach's immigrant, refugee, racially diverse, and low-income residents.[44] These coalitional efforts, Heng explained, required adolescent members to practice "holding their ground" or making their case in ways that would earn the respect and attention of older allies who otherwise might dismiss them because of their age.

Coalitions and networks served multiple purposes beyond achieving instrumental campaign or voter education goals. They exposed youth members to different approaches to affecting change, informed policy change strategies, and enabled groups to obtain technical expertise. Adolescents also gained access to mentors, including seasoned organizers.

Survey results in figure 2.5 demonstrate the frequency of youth organizing participation in intergenerational campaign alliances. In all,

Figure 2.6   Geographic Focus of Networks and Alliances

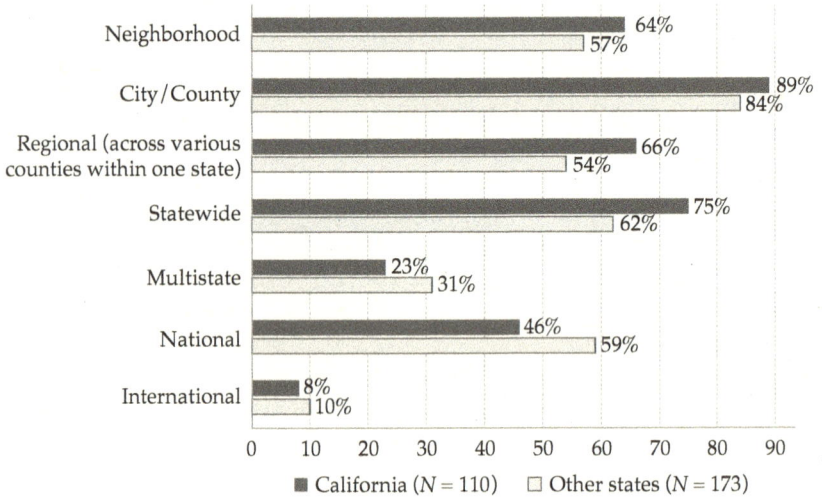

Neighborhood: California 64%, Other states 57%
City/County: California 89%, Other states 84%
Regional (across various counties within one state): California 66%, Other states 54%
Statewide: California 75%, Other states 62%
Multistate: California 23%, Other states 31%
National: California 46%, Other states 59%
International: California 8%, Other states 10%

■ California (N = 110)   □ Other states (N = 173)

Source: Author's calculations based on FCYO Field Scan 2019.

23 percent of California groups and 28 percent of groups elsewhere indicated that they always worked with older adults to change policies and systems, and most of the remainder indicated that they collaborated with adults most or some of the time. Although intergenerational tensions emerged in the course of campaigns, very few groups reported that they never or rarely work with older adults.

Youth organizing groups were particularly well connected to social movement and youth-service-provider networks locally and across the state; this was especially true in California, where groups had access to a comparatively robust civic infrastructure. Survey results indicate that most youth organizations were allied with other groups in their own neighborhoods. In dense urban areas, organizations like KGA tended to link up with community partners with similar agendas. However, such coalitions were less common in rural or less dense regions where groups tended to be more isolated.

Groups were very likely to join city- or countywide networks focused on school district, city, and county policies (see figure 2.6). For example, more than ten youth organizing groups participated in a coalition that mobilized in alignment with the 2020 George Floyd and Black Lives Matter protests, successfully convincing the Los Angeles Unified School District to reduce funding for school policing by $25 million.[45]

Often sharing strategies and useful lessons, two-thirds of California groups were part of alliances spanning two or more counties. For example, Loud for Tomorrow, located in the small semirural town of Delano in northern Kern County, collaborated with other youth, immigrant rights, environmental justice, and voting rights groups spanning multiple counties in the Central Valley.

About three-quarters of California groups networked with other groups across the entire state. Many were part of the YO! Cali network, which supported statewide campaigns and provided technical assistance and training. Staffed by experienced former youth organizers, YO! Cali disseminated approaches to youth organizing and hosted state and regional gatherings to facilitate networking and alliance building. Meanwhile, the Power California network coordinated intensive peer-to-peer young voter outreach efforts.

Some groups participated in national networks and alliances outside their state. Those in California were less likely to do so than those based elsewhere, perhaps because the well-networked groups there did not need to look outside of the state for allies. Finally, fewer than 10 percent of California groups belonged to international networks. Research on first-generation immigrants and refugees shows that immigrant organizations can mediate transnational relations between home and host countries.[46] However, very few nonprofit youth organizing groups prioritized immigrant community members' homeland ties. Taken together, these coalitional efforts aided second-generation youth in building their networks, furthering their ability to exercise political power largely on behalf of their communities in the United States.

Chapter Summary

As an adolescent participant of Kids First in the 1990s and later as the executive director of KGA in the 2010s, Lian gained organizational experience during a period of tremendous growth for the youth organizing field. Since Lian's early days of organizing, elders of prior movements guided youth organizing groups, enabling their power and numbers to grow. Recruiting mostly from predominantly low-income immigrant communities of color, these groups in California and across the country prepared members to demand that governments adequately and justly serve their communities. Intergenerational organizing and dense networks among organizations facilitated shared practices and overlapping campaigns that furthered the political incorporation of immigrant and refugee communities.

Over the past few decades, the field of youth organizing has onboarded numerous cohorts of young second-generation residents to social movement and ongoing political struggles. As powerful agents of adolescents' political socialization, this assemblage of civic associations has enhanced their members' capacities to lead in the short and long term, in times of greater opportunity as well as in times of adversity. The next chapter shows how adolescent group membership corresponds with later political engagement in early adulthood, while also including young people's assessments of what they gained from their youth organizing experience.

= Chapter 3 =

Finding Power:
The Developmental Roots
of Civic Leadership

"**I**'VE HAD so much practice talking to people who are in power," said Halima Musa. "I just show up and support the youth who are trying to learn how to become leaders in the community." At just twenty years old, Halima had already become a guiding force for her younger peers in the San Diego neighborhood of City Heights. When teenage members of Mid-City CAN (MCC) sought a seat on their community review board to oversee policing practices, they turned to Halima, a former high school member of MCC, for mentorship. Drawing on her own experiences, she guided the racially and ethnically diverse group of teenagers, helping them to understand the review board's functions and processes, strategize meetings with key stakeholders, and deliver compelling testimony before the city council.

Born in a Kenyan refugee camp to parents who had fled violence during the war in Somalia, Halima had developed a deep commitment to improving the community she has called home since she and her family resettled in the United States. Her involvement in youth organizing throughout adolescence helped her build an extensive network, not only in City Heights but across California. One of her many formative experiences as a high school student was when she represented MCC at a weeklong camp called Sisterhood Rising, which provided training and promoted well-being among girls and other female-identified youth organizing group members statewide. "I'm able to see what other girls in other organizations in California are working on," she said, "and then bring back those ideas and use them in my community." Halima stayed connected with the young women leaders she met at the camp, especially through social media, where they shared community news, personal updates, and viewpoints.

Halima began her community leadership journey as a shy seventh grader. While she benefited from attending a fairly well-resourced

47

https://doi.org/10.7758/gert1126.1457

public school outside of her community, she developed her civic capacities outside the classroom—initially through City Heights Youth for Change (CHYFC), which primarily involves East African youth, and later through MCC, which engages diverse Latinx, East African, Southeast Asian, Southwest Asian, North African, and African American youth. Her experiences with these groups "made me more open to actually using my voice," she claimed. "Now I realize that when I start speaking, I think about what I'm saying before I actually speak."

As a ninth grader, Halima took a leadership role in MCC's halal chicken campaign, initiated in 2013 to add culturally appropriate food choices to the public school menus in her neighborhood. She wrote a carefully crafted proposal and presented it to the school board. Although she was shaking as she spoke, she made a case for the benefits of halal food for all students, not just those of Muslim heritage like herself. The campaign showed her how school boards work and the importance of negotiation, strategy, and persistence. "Low-income communities are not at the top of the priority list of people making the decisions," she said. "You have to show up more than once to be heard and be seen."

As someone who learned to challenge the status quo, Halima also became a proactive LGBTQ+ ally. "Some of my friends are not aware of having the privilege of being cisgender, so they don't understand that you can't just say stuff. . . . I'm calling out people all the time for that," she explained. She also sought to educate Bantu elders about the general harms of homophobia, though not always successfully. Furthermore, during the 2020 racial unrest, while she advocated for police reforms, Halima educated community members about police murders of LGBTQ+ individuals. "I know that there [are] people actually dying just for having that identity."

After graduating from high school and enrolling in a local community college, Halima remained highly active in her community, seeking to make a difference in both public and private settings. Halima credited her adolescent youth organizing experience for developing her ability to stand up for what she believes is right. "It's all because of the organizers and the people pushing me to go past my comfort zone that I learned who I am as a leader and how I can impact my community," she asserted.

In this chapter, I show how Halima's leadership development and ongoing political activism reflects that of other youth organizing group members across California. Survey findings suggest that youth organizing groups, more than other types of adolescent civic groups, accelerate the political incorporation of young second-generation immigrants. As agents of political socialization, these organizations expand their members' capacities and deepen their motivation to remain politically engaged in early adulthood. The participatory patterns I identify cannot be explained solely by members' individual interests or personality traits. Rather, I argue that the transformative political socialization these adolescents collectively experience contributes to their comparatively high levels of political participation in early adulthood. Using young people's self-reports, I show how members benefit from the developmental supports, critical civics education, and extensive guidance in taking civic action that these groups provide. My evidence comes from multiple waves of surveys and semi-structured interviews, further detailed in the appendix (see table A.1).

Pathways of Political Incorporation

Entering the political sphere can be difficult for second-generation adolescents. As discussed in chapter 1, second-generation youth are less likely than their peers of nonimmigrant parentage to learn about U.S. politics from their parents, and many attend schools that lack the resources to support robust civic engagement.[1] However, political participation among the second-generation varies significantly. As May Lin and I have argued, these young people generally follow one of three main political pathways.[2] A large proportion exhibit depressed engagement, or fairly low levels of political participation compared with those of peers of nonimmigrant parentage (commonly referred to as the third-plus generation). Another sizable proportion of the children of immigrants displays a moderate level of participation, generally comparable with that of the third-plus generation. A third small but important segment exercises civic leadership, meaning that their participation notably exceeds that of the third-plus generation.

Adolescent Civic Groups and Political Incorporation Pathways

As agents of political socialization, youth civic associations provide young people with invaluable experience relevant to participating in politics. However, not all civic groups are created equal—at least in the extent to which they impact young people's political development and trajectories. High school associations that involve public speaking, community service, and group collaboration (such as student government, service groups, and drama clubs) tend to increase members' political participation in their young adulthood.[3] While such groups may be apolitical, they nonetheless are public-oriented and thus encourage skills and values that can spur political participation. However, these public-oriented groups do not typically focus on preparing adolescents to interject their voices into policy processes or impact government elections. This is where grassroots organizing groups enter the picture, by enhancing members' abilities to influence public debates.

For my argument, I draw from a 2011 representative survey sample of 2,200 18-to-26-year-old youth who had previously attended high school in California. In this telephone survey, I asked study participants about their organizational involvements in high school. More than 52 percent of respondents had not been involved in a civic group with political relevance, and 42 percent had been part of a public-oriented group like student government, debate, community service, and other organizations that typically remain apolitical. Only 6 percent of respondents had belonged to a youth organizing or other explicitly political group.[4]

I also gathered data on survey respondents' political participation in early adulthood, asking whether respondents in the previous year had gotten involved in community work, expressed an opinion on a social or political issue, engaged in protest activity, or registered to vote. My statistical analyses examine the link between prior group membership in high school and these different types of political participation, while accounting for other confounding factors.[5]

Figure 3.1 illustrates the results. As a point of comparison, the first set of (dotted) bars illustrates the average likelihood of participation in early adulthood among California residents of nonimmigrant parentage (the third-plus generation who compose 46 percent of the population), regardless of their prior group memberships in high school. The remaining solid bars illustrate the patterns of political participation among the second-generation (54 percent of the population), disaggregated by their prior high school group memberships.

Group memberships, or the lack thereof, map onto one of the three aforementioned political incorporation pathways. The lighter bars show the average likelihood of adult involvement for second-generation young adults lacking prior participation in a relevant adolescent civic group. These young people were the least likely to become involved in their community, voice a political opinion online, engage in protest activity, and register to vote. They tended to display depressed engagement in early adulthood, possibly reflecting a growing sense of political apathy and skepticism that scholars identified among an earlier cohort of young adults.[6] Unfortunately, prior research suggests that this pattern of depressed engagement is likely to continue as these young people age.[7]

The children of immigrants who had joined public-oriented, typically apolitical, civic associations as adolescents (represented by the third set of bars) were likely to evince moderate participation as young adults, at similar levels to their nonimmigrant peers. In other words, student

Figure 3.1   Political Participation of Young Adults by Group Membership as Adolescents, 2011 (*N* = 2,200)

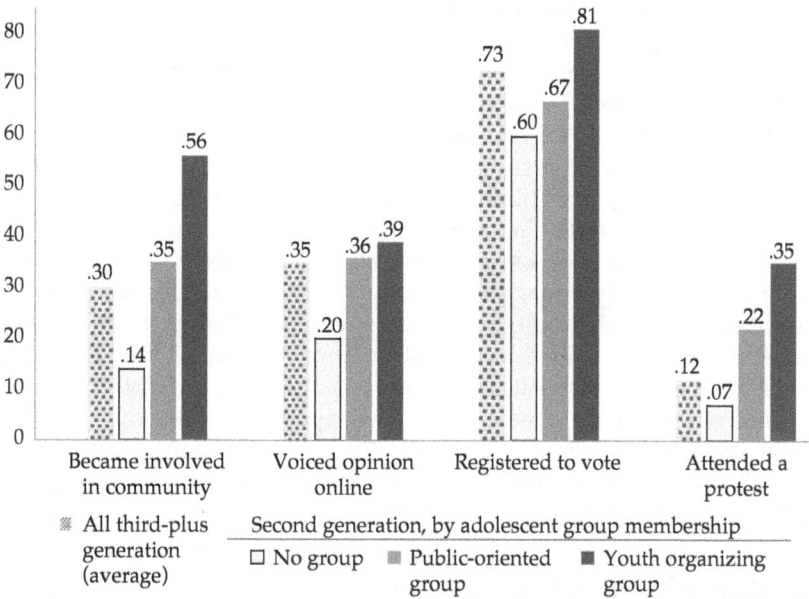

government, community service, and other public-oriented groups possibly enable a significant segment of the second-generation to "catch up" to their nonimmigrant peers, at least when it comes to the political activities measured in this analysis. Notably, young adults from immigrant families who had previously been involved in public-oriented groups were more likely to protest as adults than their peers from nonimmigrant parentage. This finding could be partially attributable to political conditions: The children of immigrants may have had more opportunities to protest on behalf of immigrant rights and in support of the federal or state Dream Acts that had been up for debate within the year prior to when the survey was conducted. In general, these findings support earlier research that highlights public-oriented youth associations as agents of socialization that encourage political participation.[8]

The small percentage of the second generation who had been involved in adolescent youth organizing (represented by the bars on the right) demonstrated greater likelihoods of political participation in early adulthood when compared with similar third-plus generation and all other second-generation peers. Additional survey analyses further confirm that the alumni of youth organizing groups pursue a distinct political trajectory from that of their peers.[9] In fact, through interviews with survey respondents and informal observations, I found that many alumni members of youth organizing groups resembled Halima, sustaining their civic momentum after they were no longer in high school. They actively shaped public debates on college campuses, in grassroots organizations, and within established political institutions.

However, my cross-sectional data do not permit me to make causal claims about the relationship between adolescent youth organizing group involvement and adult political participation. Arguably, the young people who joined such groups were possibly already inclined to become—and remain—politically engaged in young adulthood. In this view, such groups serve as self-selection mechanisms rather than provide formative experiences with long-term political impacts. While acknowledging these potential predispositions toward engagement, my objective is to explore whether, and in what ways, participation in these civic groups shapes young people's capacities for political participation. Accordingly, the following pages examine both self-selection mechanisms and indicators of a transformative political socialization.

A Deeper Look at Experiences in Youth Organizing Groups

To better understand youth experiences in these groups, I leverage data from the Youth Leadership and Health Study. Specifically, I analyze surveys collected from 520 second-generation members and 180 semi-structured interviews.[10] These data highlight three types of programming activities that enhance members' agency in the public arena: (1) developmental supports helping young members to make the transition to adulthood amid harsh economic and social inequalities; (2) a critical civics education that unpacks interlocking, compounding social inequalities and policy reforms; and (3) practical guidance in taking civic action so that members can participate in grassroots or nonpartisan voter outreach campaigns. To be clear, not all youth organizing groups offered the same programming, and quality varied across organizations and even within an organization. However, as shown in chapter 2, these groups were highly networked and thus overlapped substantially in their programming.

Why Youth Join

To contextualize the role of youth organizing groups on members' leadership development, I asked respondents to indicate the reasons

Figure 3.2   Reasons for Joining a Youth Organizing Group (*N* = 520)

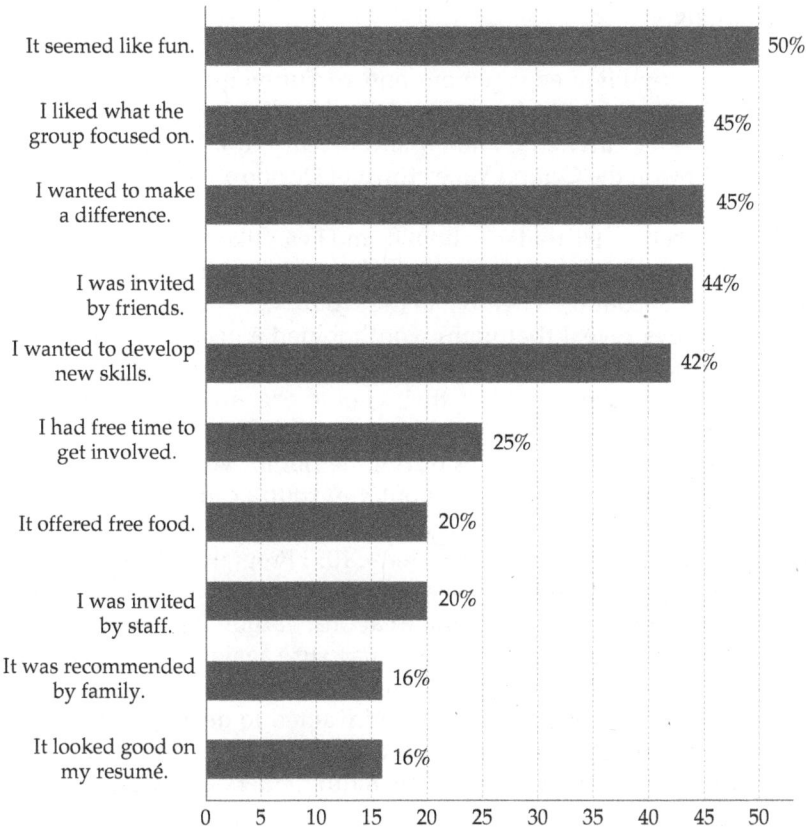

Reason	Percentage
It seemed like fun.	50%
I liked what the group focused on.	45%
I wanted to make a difference.	45%
I was invited by friends.	44%
I wanted to develop new skills.	42%
I had free time to get involved.	25%
It offered free food.	20%
I was invited by staff.	20%
It was recommended by family.	16%
It looked good on my resumé.	16%

Source: Author's calculations based on the Youth Leadership and Health Study Survey, 2016.

why they had joined their respective organizations in both surveys and semi-structured interviews. Overall, findings suggest that these youth organizing groups do not simply recruit low-income young people with an interest in politics. In fact, many members initially become involved for social reasons. In the survey, respondents were allowed to select more than one reason for joining; the most common reason given was, "It seemed like fun" (see figure 3.2). For example, Jennifer from Alianza in the Eastern Coachella Valley attended a meeting after seeing a presentation by a peer in her ceramics class; she stayed because she enjoyed the experience and it was "a safe space." Interactive group activities often incorporate humor, play, and ethnic and youth culture, building bonds among young people and contributing to their sense of belonging.

During adolescence, peer networks begin to play an important role in determining civic engagement and recruitment.[11] Survey results indicate that 44 percent of members joined organizing groups because their friends had invited them. Nineteen-year-old Edgar joined Loud for Tomorrow in the Central Valley town of Delano after being recruited by another student in his drama club: "We did a play together, so we were kind of close. He told me about it, and I was like, 'Okay, I'll check it out.'" Another 16 percent were recruited by a sibling, including Halima, whose sister encouraged her to join the group.

The surveys reveal that many youth joined a group because they wanted to make a difference (45 percent); the same percentage (45 percent) joined because they liked their chosen organization's focus. For example, Arely, a Salvadoran American, joined the Labor Community Strategy Center in Los Angeles during her junior year in high school after hearing other students talk about the group's campaign to demilitarize the school police. The goal was to end the school district's participation in the U.S. Department of Defense 1033 Program, which provides schools with surplus military weapons, including an armored vehicle, grenade launchers, and automatic weapons. "I didn't think it was fair that the school police had those weapons to use against us," Arely said.

Low-income youth self-select into youth organizing for other reasons: 42 percent of respondents had wanted to develop new skills, while 25 percent joined a group because they "had free time"—an option disproportionately selected by ninth graders. Some groups that serve communities with relatively high rates of food insecurity offer youth snacks or meals. Indeed, 20 percent of respondents said they joined their group because it offered free food. Another 20 percent said they were invited by staff. Additional factors beyond the predefined survey options likely influence adolescents' motivations to join their youth organizing group. These include gendered reasons—particularly given the overrepresentation of young women in these groups—as well as English-language speaking ability and personality traits.

Notably, the youth who join organizing groups often have different motivations than those who join public-oriented groups like student government or community service groups. Adolescents who join public-oriented groups are disproportionately high academic achievers, and many also join such groups to enhance their résumés and college applications.[12] In comparison, those who join youth organizing groups appear to care more about community uplift than individual achievement. Furthermore, while some members of youth organizing groups are high academic achievers, a significant percentage are not. Halima admitted that she "didn't do so well" academically, which for her meant that she had received mostly Bs and Cs at her fairly competitive high school.

Overall, the research findings suggest that social motivations, peer or network invitations, and the alignment of a group's focus with personal interests often spur adolescents to join youth organizing groups.

Indicators of a Transformative Political Socialization

Regardless of their reason for joining youth organizing groups, members tend to remain politically active as they transition to adulthood. Indeed, I contend that these adolescent groups (to varying degrees) facilitate members' transformative political socialization and ongoing civic leadership. My evidence comes from in-depth interviews, as well as survey questions asking young leaders to rate how much their group involvement affected their personal development, civic awareness, and capacity for civic action: Did it have no impact, very little impact, some impact, or a lot of impact? Such self-reports are obviously subjective, arguably suffer from social desirability bias, and are less valid than tests measuring growth, awareness, and abilities. However, the range of responses shows that participants were not reluctant to express negative opinions about their experiences—indicating a degree of honest evaluation. Accordingly, I feel confident in both the survey and semi-structured data, which suggest that these organizations offer beneficial, structured opportunities for peer-to-peer learning and hands-on experience in nonpartisan political processes.

Developmental Supports

Youth organizing groups often find themselves compensating for the failures of other institutions to meet members' developmental needs and stresses relating to poverty, immigration concerns, or other issues. To this end, these groups offer and encourage activities that promote well-being, and they often secure additional resources to help members achieve their personal goals and thrive. Because adolescent brains are marked by resilience and the potential for significant growth, targeted interventions like these can significantly impact members' developmental outcomes.[13] As such, youth organizing groups can play a vital role in their members' personal and civic lives. Moreover, age-appropriate developmental programming keeps adolescents engaged in campaigns and civic issues more generally.

Figure 3.3   Self-Reported Impact of Joining a Youth Organizing Group on Personal Development (N = 520)

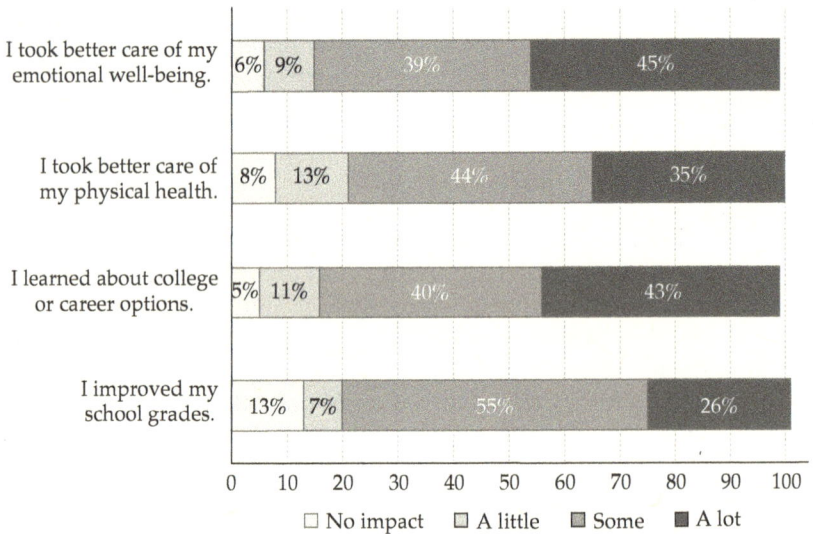

I took better care of my emotional well-being. 6% 9% 39% 45%

I took better care of my physical health. 8% 13% 44% 35%

I learned about college or career options. 5% 11% 40% 43%

I improved my school grades. 13% 7% 55% 26%

0 10 20 30 40 50 60 70 80 90 100

☐ No impact   ☐ A little   ▨ Some   ▪ A lot

Source: Author's calculations based on the Youth Leadership and Health Study Survey 2016.

Promoting Well-Being   Over the course of the 2010s, youth organizing groups increasingly focused on healing and wellness. Many groups adopted healing circles to help youth process emotional hardships or address internal conflicts. They also incorporated peer or staff-led mindfulness exercises, meditation, breathing exercises, forward stance (a form of tai chi), and other culturally informed activities to support members' mental and physical health. Some also reminded members of the importance of physical exercise, encouraged healthy diets, or distributed nutritious snacks. "We don't eat [Flamin'] Hot Cheetos here," a fifteen-year-old from Fresno's CFJ once said to me.

This attention to wellness appears to have had an impact, at least as self-reported by members (see figure 3.3). In surveys, 45 percent of second-generation members indicated that they took a lot better care of their emotional well-being as a result of their involvement in youth organizing groups, while another 35 percent reported taking a lot better care of their physical health. As noted elsewhere, young people who took part in healing or self-care practices were significantly more likely to report positive outcomes.[14] Chapter 5 further discusses how healing and wellness activities contribute to participants' political socialization.

Academic and Professional Development   With varying levels of frequency and intensity, many youth organizing groups offer programming encouraging career exploration, job readiness, higher educational attainment, and academic achievement. For example, Brotherhood Crusade in South Los Angeles occasionally invited professionals to discuss their career trajectories, and other groups helped members prepare their résumés. Meanwhile, well-funded groups like RYSE in Richmond provided robust tutoring and academic guidance counseling. Funding constraints, however, limited some groups' developmental supports to informal guidance or referral services. Halima's organizing group, for example, did not directly provide academic tutoring or guidance on college and career options. Instead, the staff referred her to the East African community center for tutoring.

Career and academic supports, when available, can fill educational service gaps in under-resourced schools and low-income communities. About 43 percent of survey participants said that they learned a lot about college and career options through their youth organizing group, and 26 percent said that their group helped them improve their grades by a lot. Indeed, the alumni of youth organizing groups tend to exhibit high rates of four-year college enrollment and employment.[15] In short, youth organizing groups grant members access to programming resources that can help them thrive and develop their leadership capacities.

Critical Civics Education

Apart from offering developmental supports, youth organizing groups politicize their members by helping them make sense of the social inequalities and policy debates affecting their communities. Groups typically adopt critical civics curricula that use popular education techniques to encourage members to reflect on their own lived experience, family migration stories, and ancestral roots.[16] Additionally, as members frequently attested, political education workshops that help students analyze community problems often "make learning fun" or "teach you things you don't learn in school." Earlier research suggests that some youth may be apathetic or cynical about politics.[17] However, a critical civics education likely counters such tendencies by exposing members to historic and contemporary examples of how young people have made a difference.

Political Education   As part of this critical civics education, groups regularly offer political education workshops that exposed members to a range of social issues and political processes. Rocio Aguayo, a then twenty-four-year-old staff member and former adolescent leader of the

San Bernardino–based Inland Congregations United for Change, shared one example from her organization's curriculum. To introduce young people to government budgets, a youth facilitator divided participants into groups that must agree on a budget at the federal, California, local county, local city, or school district level. The facilitator then shared a summary of the agency's most recent budget and handed out play money in large denominations (millions or billions) along with additional spending guidelines. The facilitator tasked youth participants with determining their spending priorities and revising the agency's budget. According to Rocio, this activity opened students' eyes to the size of government budgets, typically provoking spirited debates about local funding needs. At the end of the workshop, the facilitator explained how residents, including youth, could have a voice in shaping budget priorities going forward. For youth organizing groups, these introductory exercises typically serve as a stepping stone to more nuanced discussions of budgetary issues, funding sources, and community involvement.

As part of this civics education, groups sometimes guide members in gathering data on local concerns and possible solutions. For example, the young black, Latinx, and Southeast Asian adolescents involved in the Los Angeles County–based Brothers, Sons, and Selves coalition designed and administered (with the technical assistance of staff and researchers) a survey on how youth of color experience safety and justice across multiple contexts.[18] The adolescents analyzed the data they collected from more than 3,000 young residents, interpreted the findings, and leveraged them in their successful campaign efforts to defund the Los Angeles Unified School Police Budget by $25 million.[19] This youth-led survey shows how carefully designed youth participatory action research projects can enable group members to deepen their analysis of community problems and secure broad-based support for campaign demands.[20]

Perhaps unsurprising given how youth organizing groups engaged with community concerns through original research, workshops, and hands-on campaigns, about two-thirds of young leaders reported learning a lot about issues impacting community health and well-being (see figure 3.4).[21] A slightly smaller share—60 percent—said that they learned a lot about how government decisions impact their community. For example, while at MCC, Halima learned about how the San Diego Unified School District's lunch options were possibly contributing to poor health outcomes: "We talked about how it was important for us to have fresh, organic, free-range chicken lunch options—halal options that are healthier for everyone, instead of the processed frozen chicken nuggets that were being served." Through MCC, she learned that the local school board was responsible for school menu options; she also learned how to approach the board to effectively update its menu.

Figure 3.4   Self-Reported Impact of Joining a Youth Organizing Group
               on Critical Civic Knowledge (N = 520)

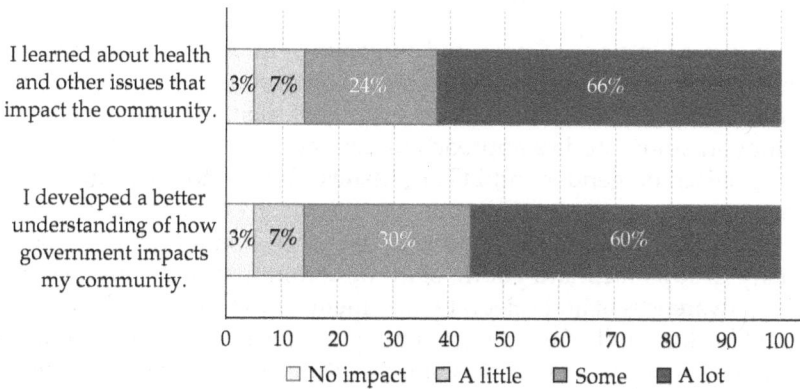

I learned about health
and other issues that   3% 7%   24%   66%
impact the community.

I developed a better
understanding of how   3% 7%   30%   60%
government impacts
my community.

0   10   20   30   40   50   60   70   80   90   100
□ No impact   □ A little   ■ Some   ■ A lot

Source: Author's calculations based on the Youth Leadership and Health Study Survey 2016.

Youth often recounted their excitement at learning about issues important to their communities. For example, Alisa, a seventeen-year-old Hmong American who assisted with developing and executing in-depth workshops on drinking water pollutants in her Merced County community, recalled that she "felt energetic and passionate about doing [this work]. It didn't feel boring or tedious. It wasn't like homework." Depending on the focus of their campaigns, youth developed expertise on topics as varied as the benefits and limitations of city sanctuary policies providing protections for undocumented immigrants, sex education in schools, the health effects of pesticide exposure, and how state and municipal taxes fund local social services and infrastructure projects. Over the years, I personally observed adolescents' proficiency on a wide range of issues as they eloquently and thoughtfully testified at government meetings and across various forms of public media.

As suggested by survey findings, some youth could better articulate their understanding of policy concerns than others. Often, the second-generation adolescent members who were most fluent in the technical nuances of a political debate had been with their organizations for at least one year and were generally older—juniors and seniors in high school. Additionally, some organizations provide more in-depth training on policy or electoral issues than others. In-depth interviews and observations reflected this variability, as not all interviewees could discuss issues in extensive detail. For example, one young man who had participated in an anti-gentrification rally understood that his group was "fighting evictions," but he struggled to articulate the specificity of their demands, admitting, "I forgot what it was for exactly."

Unpacking Diversity, Power, and Inequality   In addition to exposing members to policy issues, youth organizing groups often address the distinct experiences of different segments of their communities. Many adopt an ethnic studies approach in their curricula, layering on activities focused on gender and LGBTQ issues. One broad goal common to many groups is to counter mainstream society's erasure or misrepresentation of second-generation and non-white communities. As such, many groups facilitate youth, staff, or community-led activities that raise awareness of and celebrate their members' ethnic, racial, or immigrant backgrounds. Such programming can foster a sense of belonging and have a positive effect on youths as they develop their identities.[22] These activities offer valuable learning experiences, as 64 percent of second-generation youth reported learning "a lot" about their own racial or ethnic group—a finding reinforced by in-depth interviews. Fourteen-year-old Eve's reflection was illustrative: "Before I joined, I just really hated being Hmong because it wasn't cool." In her Central Valley–based group, however, she found out more about how and why the Hmong people fled Laos, and this encouraged her to develop educational workshops that she shared with predominantly Latinx peers. "How we came here as Hmong Americans isn't known well. I really just want my history known here," Eve explained.

In their goal of building multiethnic, multiracial solidarity, many youth organizing groups educate members about their migration backgrounds alongside the histories of established racial minority groups represented in their communities. In all, 56 percent of second-generation adolescent members said that they learned a lot about other racial groups in their communities (see figure 3.5). Youth organizing groups thus serve as a bridge linking immigrant and more established racial minority communities. MCC, for example, is a group with a particularly diverse membership, including sub-Saharan African, North African, African American, Latinx, and Southeast Asian students. Born in Mexico, Lupe worked alongside Halima on the halal campaign, and she appreciated how MCC enabled members to "counter the silence" around their identities by creating spaces for peers to share their family's migration backgrounds, ethnic cultures, and histories.

Youth organizing groups help members develop a greater awareness of social disparities and identity-based differences. For example, campaigns—especially those demanding more resources for schools and communities—require members to analyze how economic forces

Figure 3.5   Self-Reported Impact of Joining a Youth Organizing Group on Critical Civic Knowledge (N = 520)

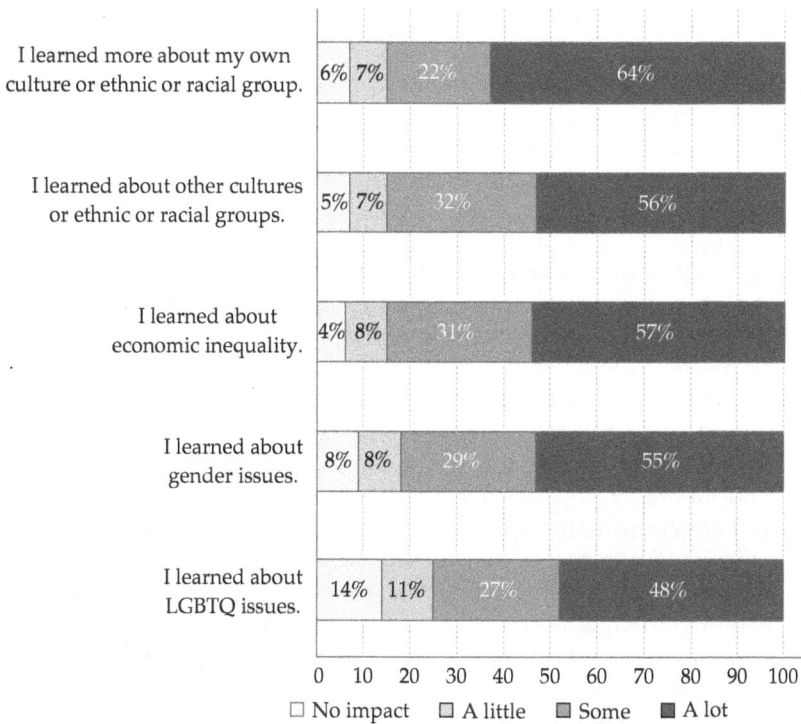

Source: Author's calculations based on the Youth Leadership and Health Study Survey 2016.

shape local opportunities. In surveys, 57 percent of second-generation members stated that they learned a lot about economic inequality. Meanwhile, 55 percent said that they learned a lot about gender issues, and another 48 percent said that they learned a lot about LGBTQ issues. Some groups introduced members to the concept of intersectionality, prompting them to consider how the interplay of multiple identities and systems of oppression shape lived experiences. Halima recalled that after she learned about intersectionality as an adolescent, the term stuck with her "because there [are] a lot of different parts that make up our identity." The concept of intersectionality helped her reflect on what it means to be a dark-skinned black woman, a refugee, and a first-generation college student. The concept also helped her recognize her privilege as a heterosexual, cisgender woman.

Guidance in Civic Action

As agents of political socialization, youth organizing groups train members to lead policy change and voter outreach campaigns. This often entails developing their basic civic skills and capacities to engage others in broad-based collective actions. Staff and older, more experienced adolescent members tend to scaffold learning opportunities for newer and younger members, a process that takes time but enables young people to help determine the course of campaigns.[23]

Acquiring Basic Civic Skills   Youth members from low-income immigrant families often need help developing basic civic skills that they might otherwise have acquired in public-oriented groups, skills related to public speaking, making presentations, and planning events. Halima, for example, was a quiet middle school student when she first got involved in City Heights Youth for Change. After years in the program, however, she had developed into a confident organizer with no qualms about speaking in public forums or sharing her views in videos, blogs, and social media postings. Facilitating meetings for younger youth to help them coordinate their own events also became second nature to her. Survey results collected from second-generation members of youth organizing groups reflect her growth (see figure 3.6). About 68 percent of survey participants reported experiencing a lot of improvement in their ability to communicate with others, and 57 percent mentioned improved public speaking. Another 52 percent indicated that they significantly improved their ability to plan events and activities.

Collective Action   Youth members gain leadership experience through group efforts to influence policy debates and educate voters. As shown in figure 3.7, 62 percent of respondents said that they learned a lot about how to impact policies. For instance, by attending or participating in meetings, public hearings, and rallies, Halima acquired strategies for gaining the support of elected officials, learning along the way that decision-makers needed to hear "what youth want directly from the youth." Again, Halima's progress was typical of other youth organizing group members. In interviews, study participants exhibited an emerging understanding of how to influence the local elected officials making decisions that affected their community—most often at the city or school district level, although occasionally at the state level. For example, members from ACT for Women and Girls in Tulare County spoke to state elected officials about the importance of providing comprehensive sexual health education and HIV prevention education across all California middle and high schools.

Figure 3.6   Self-Reported Impact of Joining a Youth Organizing Group on Acquisition of Basic Civic Skills (N = 520)

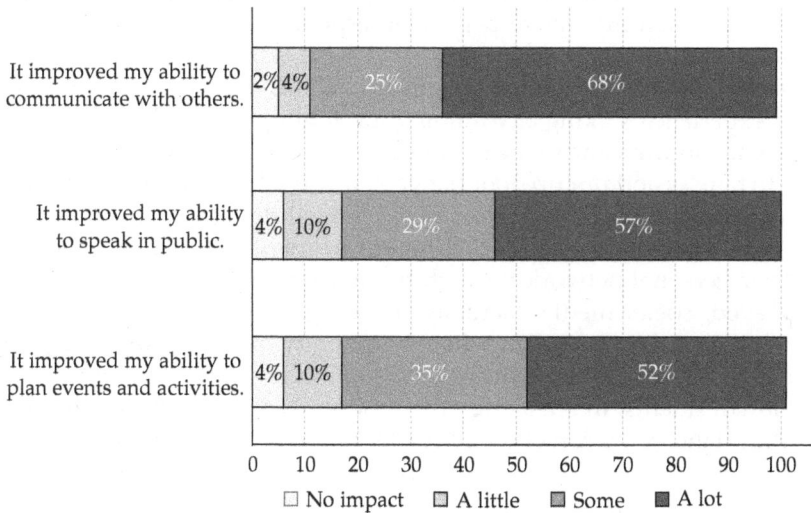

Source: Author's calculations based on the Youth Leadership and Health Study Survey 2016.

Figure 3.7   Self-Reported Impact of Joining a Youth Organizing Group on Capacities for Civic Action (N = 520)

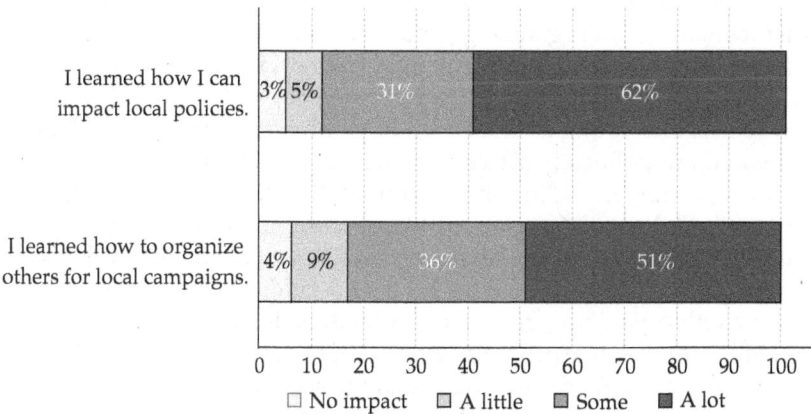

Source: Author's calculations based on the Youth Leadership and Health Study Survey 2016.

Adolescent members also tend to gain significant experience in educating broader constituencies—usually peers, teachers, local residents, or voters—and enlisting them to support their nonpartisan causes. Figure 3.7 indicates that 51 percent of respondents felt that they learned a lot about how to organize people in local campaigns. For example, Jocelyn, a Filipina American member of RYSE in Richmond, spoke of her experience seeking city funding for youth programs: "I went door to door and was canvassing in different community places.... [I would] go to houses and put up door hangers. It was a lot of going to Safeway, the Richmond BART [Bay Area Rapid Transit station], or the El Cerrito BART to get signatures from different people." She also reached out to her personal network through her Instagram account because, she believed, social media "actually has a big impact." Overall, youth understood that organizing their community meant conducting public outreach around an issue and, in some cases, gathering input from fellow residents. In engaging others, adolescents actively advance the political incorporation of their broader immigrant communities.

Chapter Summary

Through her connections to CHYFC and MCC, Halima experienced a transformative political socialization. She blossomed from a shy preadolescent to an outspoken young adult. After participating in multiple campaigns throughout high school, she remained motivated at the age of twenty to continue "doing the work to get more people involved and to inform them about issues that are important."

In this chapter, I suggest that Halima's experience was typical of members in youth organizing groups. I contend that adolescent organizing groups enable young members like Halima to experience a transformative political socialization, often expanding their leadership capacities. The young adult alumni of youth organizing groups tend to remain more politically active than their peers who were not members of such groups, including those with adolescent experience in public-oriented adolescent associations like student government. Survey and interview findings indicate that members benefit from the developmental supports, critical civics education, and guidance in civic action that their youth organizing groups provide, thus demonstrating the potential of comprehensive programming to engender a transformative political socialization. Arguably, these settings accelerate members' political incorporation as they acquire the capacities to weigh in on policy debates and educate voters.

Prior research has established that second-generation immigrants exhibit varying socioeconomic trajectories, and that parental resources and their parents' (or their own) legal status play key roles in predicting their economic prospects.[24] At the same time, immigrants' political incorporation does not necessarily align with their socioeconomic incorporation.[25] My research suggests that adolescent associational memberships are interventional mechanisms; by facilitating a transformative socialization, youth organizing groups aid their members in overcoming social, economic, and emotional challenges, cultivating their ongoing civic leadership. Obviously, the very factors that prompt young people to join activist associations in the first place also likely motivate them to stay involved later on in life. Nonetheless, organizational programming bolsters members' abilities to diagnose social injustices, exercise their own voices, and lead collective action.

In the next chapter, I look more closely at one subset of this population: undocumented youth activists. For these youth facing multiple layers of marginalization, intersectional frameworks provided them with the courage to take political action and build coalitions. The case of undocumented youth activists shows how adolescent experience in a local youth organizing group prepared members, upon reaching adulthood, to help define a national movement.

═ Chapter 4 ═

Youth Organizing, Intersectionality, and the Making of the Immigrant Youth Movement

ON JUNE 22, 2011, Irvis Orozco testified before the California Senate Education Committee on how the bill it was considering, the California Dream Act (AB 131), could change his life. An undocumented student who had joined his mother in the United States as an infant, Irvis gained admission to competitive schools in the University of California system. Yet, as he emphasized, the cost of college imposed a severe financial burden. AB 131 would provide critical financial support to undocumented students like himself.

Summarizing his story for legislators, Irvis said that his mother, facing financial hardship, had taken him out of high school when he was thirteen to pick tomatoes with her outside of Sacramento. "I begged her to let me go back to school and to finish," he said, and she agreed. As an openly gay leader in the undocumented youth movement, Irvis knew he was among many young immigrants with significant financial barriers to achieving their educational goals. Although they lacked U.S. citizenship, he and his peers felt emboldened to demand financial support for their education. "It is now up to us to stand up and tell you that we are unafraid and we are here," Irvis told the committee.

This was not Irvis's first appearance before state legislators; he had previously been involved in health-related campaigns as an adolescent. Having joined the California Center for Civic Participation in tenth grade, Irvis became familiar with policy debates around substance abuse, reproductive health, and health care access. Staff prepared members to weigh in on state legislative bills and present their views to decision-makers. The program, according to Irvis, covered "how to talk, how to dress, how the whole system of advocacy actually worked." Irvis believed that the work he and his peers completed—including a statewide survey

66

https://doi.org/10.7758/gert1126.4775

of young people on their health needs—helped make the case for the September 2004 passage of SB 1173, which further prevented the sale of tobacco products to minors.

At the California Center for Civic Participation, Irvis found mentors who helped him apply to college. He went on to attend the University of California, Davis, near his hometown of Woodland so that he could work part-time in the fields to pay for his education and support himself. On campus, he met others struggling to make their way through school with the stigma of being undocumented. "[We were] a little scared to open up about our status at the university," he recalled, "but we knew we might be able to get support." He and several peers started an undocumented student club called SPEAK (Scholars Promoting Education and Knowledge), which offered peer support for undocumented students and connected them to immigrant rights organizations, including the California Dream Network (CDN) sponsored by CHIRLA.

Surrounded by peers who were sympathetic to the challenges he faced as a gay, undocumented, and financially struggling immigrant, Irvis poured his heart and soul into organizing around the Dream Acts. Between 2010 and 2012, when the immigrant youth movement was at its peak, young leaders were openly talking about their multiple identities and deploying intersectionality in what social movement scholars refer to as a collective action frame. Collective action frames can help adherents make sense of their identities and related challenges, motivate them to participate in political activities, and guide their strategies.[1] Undocumented youth leveraged intersectional collective identities to build ties with groups organizing around LGBTQ rights, civil rights, education justice, and health justice. Additionally, Irvis and others served as mentors for younger cohorts, including 1.5- and second-generation youth.

Irvis shared a trajectory with many undocumented youth activists who overcame significant hardship to take on prominent leadership roles as college students. Some undocumented youth (usually those who overstay their visas) come from more affluent backgrounds, but most grow up facing financial challenges. Many of their parents work in the underground economy, without access to living wages, benefits, or worksite protections. As a result, undocumented youth tend to have higher dropout rates and lower college attendance rates than their counterparts.[2] Their precarious legal status presents other difficulties. During the first decade of the 2000s, undocumented youth lacked access to government IDs and driver's licenses, many faced difficulties opening bank accounts and obtaining credit cards, and their access to health care was poor (unless they were enrolled in a four-year university).[3] Against these odds, and thanks in part to a supportive immigrant rights civic infrastructure, these young people were able to successfully advocate for the California Dream Act and help shape the national dialogue around immigrant rights.

In this chapter, I profile California's undocumented youth activists involved in immigrant rights efforts in 2011 and 2012. As members of campus and community organizations, these young immigrants leveraged a broader social movement infrastructure to help define statewide and national immigration policy debates. My central argument is that the transformative political socialization that many of them experienced in adolescent organizing groups prepared them to take a place at the forefront of an immigrant rights movement informed by intersectional frameworks once they reached adulthood. The developmental supports, critical civics education, and guidance in civic action undocumented youth accessed as adolescents provided them with a foundation to lead campaigns that resulted in tangible policy changes for themselves and peers who encountered a blocked pathway to citizenship. I also highlight how young immigrants like Irvis continued their activism throughout the 2010s, leaving their mark on the broader field of youth organizing.

My findings are based on 410 surveys and 66 in-depth interviews primarily conducted just prior to the 2012 implementation of DACA. Additionally, occasional participant observations, informal conversations from 2004 to 2020, and secondary sources inform my analysis and understanding of the trajectories of these young leaders. This chapter demonstrates how to support the voice and political agency of a vulnerable young population.

Social Movement Infrastructure and Dream Organizations

Adolescent youth organizing groups provided Irvis and many of his 1.5-generation immigrant peers with a supportive social context in which they developed the capacity to become influential civic leaders. It would be an overstatement, however, to suggest that adolescent exposure to a transformative political socialization alone enabled undocumented youth to assume leadership roles in a national movement. Rather, as learning theory would suggest, adolescent youth organizing groups (and to a lesser extent, public-oriented groups) provided the scaffolding for these undocumented youth to acquire higher-level skills.[4] These groups also critically intervened in the lives of young people as they sought to navigate their precarious legal status and overcome challenges common to their low-income immigrant communities.

Undocumented youth leaders expanded their organizing abilities through college, community-based, and allied organizations, learning how to intervene in the public sphere as adults. Scholars have noted that resources can determine a social movement's success.[5] In this regard, undocumented youth had a variety of national, statewide, and local resources at their disposal. At the national level, Center for Community Change, the National Immigration Law Center, MALDEF, National Council of La Raza (now called Unidos US), and the AFL-CIO provided funding, legal expertise, political muscle, and other resources.[6] Meanwhile, United We Dream connected undocumented youth organizations across the country to help young people learn about and engage in federal immigration policymaking debates.

Moreover, California-based campus and community immigrant youth groups benefited from the state's comparatively robust civic infrastructure.[7] Low-wage sector unions, which were aligned with the immigrant rights movement, offered young activists political, monetary, and in-kind support.[8] María Elena Durazo, the first woman to lead the Los Angeles County Federation of Labor (who served from 2006 to 2014), often spoke out in support of the young activists and helped secure labor's support for the Dream Acts. Meanwhile, Latinx and AAPI civil and immigrant rights organizations also offered legal guidance, funding, and other support.

At the local level, undocumented youth activists participated in college- and community-based groups, including in regional Dream Teams—comprised mostly of college graduates and out-of-school youth—or at ASPIRE (a pan-Asian immigrant youth organization). While some immigrant youth organizations on college campuses were independent, most were part of the CDN. Started in 2003 to support the alumni of CHIRLA's Wise Up! adolescent youth organizing group as they entered college, CDN founded and coordinated immigrant student support and advocacy groups on college campuses around the state.[9]

One consequential college program was the Dream Summer, established in 2011 by the University of California, Los Angeles, Labor Center, a university research and training unit. This program brought together immigrant youth leaders from around the country for training and internships in well-resourced labor and nonprofit social justice–oriented organizations, strengthening participants' professional networks and ties to allied social movements. As a Dream Summer participant, Irvis received training from the late Reverend James Lawson, a civil rights movement veteran who at the time lived in Los Angeles. Irvis recalled, "I think that was very vital that we were trained in nonviolent protest. We saw a lot of connections between their [African Americans'] civil rights movement, the rights that they were fighting for, and what was happening with us. Reverend Lawson really connected the dots for us." Youth leaders like Irvis drew explicit parallels between the civil rights movement's racial justice claims for black Americans and their own fight for immigrant rights—in addition to LGBTQ rights and other causes.[10] Arguably, Dream Summer helped participants articulate to broader audiences. At the same time, the program also paved the way for many participants to later find employment in unions and in the nonprofit sector, as it exposed them to the professionalization of activism.

Who Were California's Immigrant Youth Activists?

In the first dozen or so years of the twenty-first century, undocumented youth activists often referred to themselves as Dreamers—immigrants who would benefit from the Dream Act. This chapter describes the activities of these youth activists in California in 2011 and 2012. Many of these activists no longer refer to themselves as Dreamers. The movement has since broadened its scope, and many see the term as drawing an unfair distinction between so-called "deserving" child immigrants and their "undeserving" and criminalized parents, who likely took great risks and made significant sacrifices to come to the United States.[11]

When the immigrant youth movement in California was most active, a distinct set of young immigrants were involved in advocating for federal and state Dream Acts. Table 4.1 shows the characteristics of undocumented members of immigrant youth organizations who completed the survey alongside a representative sample of 1.5- and second-generation youth (hereinafter referred to as the general population).[12] Survey results indicate that women outnumbered men, making up 58 percent of undocumented youth leaders. Additionally, 13 percent of activists identified as LGBTQ+, compared with 5 percent in the general population. Immigrant activists were disproportionately high academic achievers in high school, and 56 percent later attended or graduated from a four-year college or university, compared with 30 percent of the general population.

At the same time, survey results demonstrate that these immigrant activists were particularly likely to experience economic marginality. Nearly nine out of ten activists came from low-income backgrounds (determined by their eligibility for free and reduced lunch while in high school), compared to roughly half of all other children of immigrants in California. In addition, 68 percent of immigrant youth activists reported trouble paying their utility bills in the past year, compared with 20 percent of the general population. Moreover, paying for college caused significant hardship for many undocumented youth leaders; they did not qualify for any government financial aid at the time of the survey. A disproportionate number worked one or more jobs, earning under-the-table wages.

Table 4.1   **California Immigrant Youth Leaders' and Second-Generation Youths' Sample Characteristics, CYAS 2011–2012**

	Immigrant Activists	All Children of Immigrants[a]
Average age	21.3	21.1
Gender		
Male	42%	52%
Female	58%	48%
LGBTQ	13%	5%
Born in the United States	0%	67%
Socioeconomic background		
College-educated parent	18%	28%
Low-income background	89%	51%
Faced difficulty paying utility bills	68%	20%
College enrollment		
No college	10%	38%
Community college	34%	32%
Four-year college	56%	30%
Stopped out of college	72%	35%
Adolescent civic group membership		
Public-oriented group	48%	41%
Youth organizing	26%	5%
Neither group	26%	54%
Sample size	410	1,180

Source: California Young Adult Study, Immigrant Youth Survey, 2011–2012.
[a] Weighted results.

Irvis was among the 72 percent of college-going activists who needed to "stop out," or take a break from college at some point (compared with 35 percent of the general population), many for economic reasons.[13]

The Relevance of High School Youth Organizing Groups to the Immigrant Youth Movement

Survey results suggest that most undocumented youth activists joined immigrant youth organizations as young adults after obtaining relevant civic experience as adolescents. As noted in chapter 3, public-oriented groups like high school student government and community service organizations, while apolitical, can orient youth toward political participation in early adulthood. Survey results indicate that 48 percent of these activists were part of public-oriented group, compared with 41 percent of their counterparts in the general population. Another 26 percent were part of an adolescent youth organizing or other activist group.[14] In comparison, only 5 percent of the general population were part of similar groups. In sum, the alumni of youth organizing groups were highly represented among organizations fighting for the Dream Act.

Prior adolescent group membership corresponded with the roles these young people assumed within their young adult immigrant youth organizations, as demonstrated by multivariate logistic regression results further detailed in the online appendix. Figure 4.1 illustrates how prior group memberships predicted leadership within young adult groups, as determined by two questions about their activities within their young adult organization. Members of public-oriented groups (represented by light gray bars) and youth organizing groups (represented by dark gray bars) were more likely to help make decisions and conduct outreach for their organizations than those who had not joined civic groups as adolescents (represented by the white bars). Prior group membership seems to have enabled some undocumented youth to take on responsibilities within college and young adult organizations.

The survey results also indicate that among these immigrant youth movement activists, the alumni of adolescent youth organizing groups were particularly likely to engage in a range of political activities, as shown in figure 4.2. Compared with the alumni of public-oriented groups and those who did not belong to earlier groups, youth organizing alumni were more likely to have shared a perspective online and contacted broadcast or print media. They were also more likely to have signed a petition and canvassed, which typically entails going door to door to gather support for a cause. Moreover, alumni of youth organizing groups were significantly more likely than their peers to have contacted public officials, and they were especially likely to have participated in a public protest, something a typical undocumented youth fearing deportation might consider a high-risk activity.

Former members of student government, community service, and other public-oriented groups were not as politically active as those with youth organizing experience. Yet compared with those who had no prior group experience, these undocumented youth were significantly more likely to share an opinion online and attend a protest.[15]

Overall, survey results suggest that the alumni of adolescent youth organizing groups were exceptional in terms of their leadership and political activity. These findings do not account for talent, ambition, personality, or other unmeasured characteristics that likely contribute to civic group membership in high school and, later, to political participation.

Figure 4.1   Predicted Probabilities of Undocumented Youth Activists'
Organizational Leadership by Prior Adolescent Group
Membership ($N = 410$)

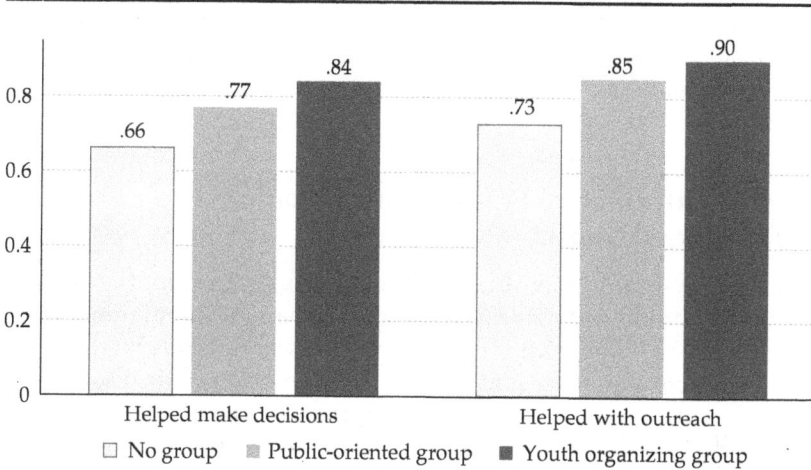

Source: Author's calculations based on the California Young Adult Study, Immigrant
Youth Survey 2011–2012.

Figure 4.2   Predicted Probabilities of Undocumented Youth Activists'
Political Activity by Prior Adolescent Group Membership
($N = 410$)

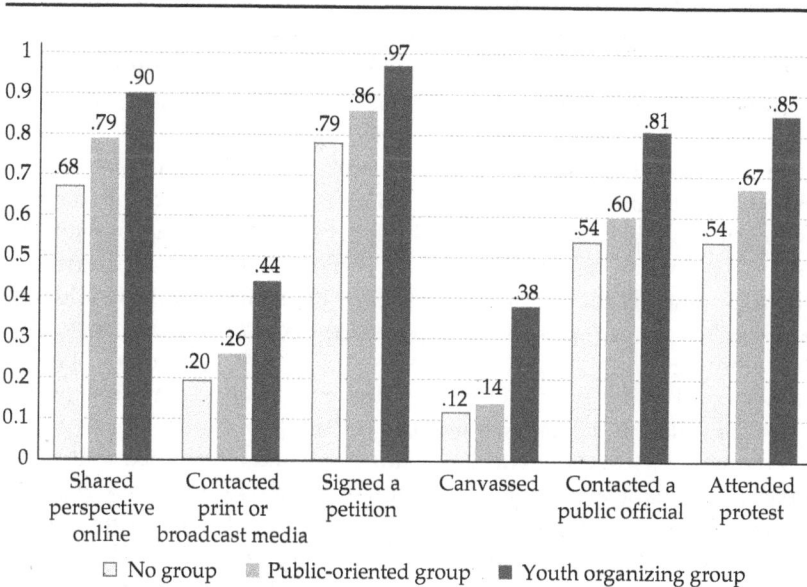

Source: Author's calculations based on the California Young Adult Study, Immigrant
Youth Survey 2011–2012.

Therefore, cross-sectional survey results cannot conclusively demonstrate that adolescent civic groups nurture subsequent civic group leadership and political involvement among undocumented youth. However, the following semi-structured interview findings offer insights into how civic organizations—and adolescent youth organizing groups in particular—offered members invaluable support, training, and experience relevant to leading a social movement.

The Transformative Political Socialization of Immigrant Youth

How did Irvis and other undocumented activists acquire the capacities to play prominent roles in statewide and national immigrant rights campaigns? My argument is that many adolescents in this highly marginalized population experienced a transformative political socialization. The following describes how immigrant activists benefited from the developmental supports, critical civics education, and guidance in civic action accessed through adolescent youth organizing groups.

Developmental Supports

Undocumented members of youth organizing groups disproportionately benefited from developmental supports that helped them overcome challenges and thrive in high school. These supports also propelled them toward college, where they accessed networks that further connected them to a larger immigrant rights movement.

Mentorship is one crucial developmental support for immigrants from humble family backgrounds.[16] Indeed, the alumni of youth organizing groups were especially likely to report having a mentor who helped them on their journey (for survey results, see appendix table A.2). In Irvis's case, his mother doubted that he could pay for or even benefit from additional schooling, given the legal barriers to employment he faced as someone without papers. However, his mentors encouraged him to pursue higher education: "They were pushing for us to build our résumé, but there was also a component on education. And basically, they were pushing us to go to college, especially as young people of color [and] as part of this social activism." Their encouragement proved vital as Irvis applied and was accepted into college.

His mother's fears about his undocumented status were not unfounded. Apart from financial barriers, undocumented status—and a lack of information about what supports undocumented students were entitled to—made accessing higher education more challenging.[17] Though AB 540, the California law that allowed immigrants and students born in other

U.S. states to pay in-state tuition for state colleges if they attended high school in California, was adopted in 2001, in the 2010s, many undocumented youth remained unaware that they were eligible. This lack of awareness deterred many from attending college.[18] Eighteen-year-old Dora was resigned to not attending college before she found out about the law: "I really did want to go to school," she said, but then "the college counselor told me about how much I was going to pay, so I was like, oh man, I guess I wasn't going to go." However, after she joined CHIRLA's Wise Up! club at her high school and learned that she qualified for tuition as an in-state resident, she changed her mind. Staff at CHIRLA helped her and other undocumented members apply for this nonresident tuition exemption, also guiding her through the college application process. This experience was common among youth in my study. As survey results (shown in the appendix) indicate, the alumni of youth organizing groups were especially likely to have learned about AB 540 while still enrolled in high school.

The alumni of youth organizing groups also received encouragement and guidance on course requirements and the application process, which was typically offered to all members regardless of their legal status. This additional support was extremely helpful because students attending overcrowded and under-resourced schools typically received less assistance from school personnel. Myrna, a former member of Californians for Justice (CFJ) recalled, "College counselors come in and sign you up for classes, but they don't put an emphasis on taking the A through G," referring to the courses needed for admission to a four-year institution. The CFJ staff, by contrast, encouraged Myrna and her peers to enroll in college-preparatory coursework and assisted them in applying for scholarships, stipends, and other resources to help her pay for college.

Critical Civics Education

As adolescents, the alumni of youth organizing groups obtained the tools to recognize the structural roots of social inequalities. This early exposure to a critical civics education facilitated young adult leaders' analysis of immigrant rights issues and their articulation of empowered identities.

Political Education   Youth organizing groups introduced undocumented activists to social issues and analytical tools of which they would not have otherwise learned. Although Myrna joined CFJ because of the free food, she quickly got "hooked" because the group leaders were discussing issues that did not come up in her classes: "It was like, why are we not learning this at school, you know? It's stuff that's affecting us, like the school-to-prison pipeline, like globalization." Myrna said the group focused on "trying to improve the California educational system for students of color, LGBT students, low-income students, and immigrant students [who are] pushed to the margins." This broad-ranging political education raised her awareness of real-life concerns and helped her make sense of the community's challenges.

Other adolescents also experienced this growing awareness. Through his involvement in a San Francisco youth organizing group seeking to improve race relations and address local environmental issues, twenty-year-old Eugenio said he "learned about immigration, gentrification, environmental racism, and other social justice issues." As a cofounder of the immigrant youth organization at his state university, Eugenio looked into "the political causes" of community concerns, enriching his understanding of how residents dealt with displacement and other challenges.

Working on campaigns focused on health, education, and neighborhood concerns, youth like Myrna and Eugenio only touched on immigration policy. This was not the case for the alumni of CHIRLA's Wise Up! youth organizing group, who were well represented among immigrant youth activists. Based in Los Angeles, Wise Up! engaged teens in campaigns pushing for in-state tuition exemptions for undocumented students through AB 540.[19] In the process, members developed a robust program to demonstrate how immigration laws shaped and could potentially ameliorate their predicament. With chapters in LAUSD high schools serving many immigrants, the group sought to educate undocumented peers and their families about AB 540, the Dream Acts, and other immigrant rights efforts, ensuring that their members were well-versed in immigration laws and debates.

At Belmont High School's Wise Up! club, one of the largest chapters in LAUSD, Ivan recalled "learning everything" about immigration laws because his role was "building awareness of the Dream Act, immigration reform, and unjust laws" through presentations to students, religious organizations, and other community agencies. Lunchtime club meetings at Belmont High often entailed communicating policy updates and information about AB 540 and undocumented students' rights. Given their early understanding of immigrant rights policy debates, Wise Up! alumni often found themselves providing valuable immigrant rights civics lessons to their less experienced peers.

Identity and Empowerment   Wise Up! helped adolescent members overcome the stigma of being undocumented, an experience they found especially empowering. The group regularly hosted discussions to help members process their feelings about their legal status. According to Jaime, a leader of the University of California, Berkeley's undocumented youth organization R.I.S.E. (Rising Immigrant Scholars through Education), Wise Up! delivered "that support that you were unable to find in other areas" — support that allowed him to "connect with the other students in other schools and create this community feeling." For Jaime, sharing his experience of being undocumented, learning about college options, and discovering ways to change policies as an adolescent "defeated that sense of fear."

During the 2000s, Wise Up! was unique among youth organizing groups in centering undocumented identities. Most groups primarily attended to racial or ethnic identities during this period, treating other identities as secondary. For example, groups tended to incorporate ethnic studies and other identity-based workshops into their programming in order to raise political consciousness. At the statewide conferences Irvis attended while in high school, he learned about the injustices experienced by Mexican immigrant farmworkers, the histories of African Americans and Arab Americans, as well as other contemporary struggles. Ixchel, whose youth organizing group collaborated closely with labor organizations, vividly recalled learning "a lot about the struggles of farmworkers, about labor struggles. It got me questioning what we were learning in history class." And demonstrating that ethnic pride can provide racialized populations with a sense of self-worth and agency, she asserted, "In high school, I became a proud Chicana," an identity she appeared to continue to celebrate as a college student.

In the 2000s, youth organizing groups rarely discussed intersectionality or encouraged members to think about overlapping identities. However, a handful of interviewees did learn about different types of diversity and embrace intersectional thinking. Jason, an undocumented and queer alumnus of InnerCity Struggle (ICS), noted that members often discussed different sources of diversity during campaign development and programming. And at the group's annual retreat, he and his peers received more intensive training. "We went down the list and talked about all the oppressions," he said. "We would play video clips and discuss: Who is the target group? Who is the group in power?" As a queer youth, he saw "how homophobia interlocks with all these other oppressions, and how they fuel each other, and it's okay that you're queer, because it's natural." Through this enlightening experience, Jason and his peers learned valuable lessons that helped them feel comfortable in their own skin: "It's okay to be ourselves. . . . We've been taught all these things are wrong, and we finally see the real picture."

For Silvia, another alumnus of ICS, intersectional awareness not only fostered pride in her own identities but also instilled in her a commitment to addressing social justice in intersectional ways. "[If] you're going to fight against one type of oppression," she explained, "then you have to fight against all kinds of oppression." As public intellectuals and theorists in their own right, young leaders shared their own interpretations of intersectionality as part of a generally widespread, although not universal, practice in 2011 and 2012. Groups such as ICS exposed undocumented adolescents like Jason and Sylvia to lessons about interlocking oppressions, and this education prepared them to fold intersectionality and queer inclusivity into their immigrant rights activism as young adults.

Guidance in Civic Action

By 2011, when this research was initially conducted, the immigrant youth movement was widespread and fairly visible across California. Interviews with alumni members reveal that their adolescent groups helped them develop basic civic skills useful for conducting public outreach, coordinating activities, and interfacing with decision-makers. Irvis's trajectory provides an illustrative example. As a young adult, Irvis was responsible for hosting and implementing statewide conferences for undocumented youth, at which leaders discussed strategies for advancing the federal Dream Act and statewide immigrant rights policies. These conferences politicized undocumented youth leaders, established networks among student activists, and provided vital support to a movement with undocumented youth at the forefront. Irvis was well prepared for this role, having participated in California Center for Civic Participation's tobacco campaign as a high school student, where he recalled learning "how to coordinate events, to challenge people to get involved, and get them to not lose hope." In high school, Irvis had also learned how "to do grassroots organizing — how I can get support from the people that are affected the most and get them to stand up for what they need" — and to serve as a bridge between the grassroots and elected officials: "I learned not to be afraid to speak to people like the assembly speakers that I met. I have a voice and I can talk about how my community is really affected by different problems." Irvis's story shows how civics experience during adolescence can prove vital for later organizing work.

Basic Civic Skills   The undocumented alumni of youth organizing groups, like their peer alumni of public-oriented groups, became comfortable speaking in public, gained experience in planning events, and learned how to run meetings. For example, I interviewed Ernesto, an eighteen-year-old in his first semester in community college, when he was an active member of his Dream organization. Ernesto vividly recalled how he and his peers ran the highly organized Wise Up! lunchtime meetings at Huntington Park High School, a mostly Latinx school with a sizable undocumented student club. He and student leaders were tasked with preparing and executing a tight agenda for the group's half-hour meetings. After introductions, they would provide information about the group for newcomers, update members on the Dream Act campaign, and cover relevant campus or community activities for the week. Soon after graduating from high school, Ernesto continued to build on these organizational skills, running the meetings of his community college organization.

"I was able to get to know people that I wouldn't normally get to know," recalled Ixchel of her adolescent experience supporting local labor organizing campaigns. "I liked that I developed relationships with [the] administration," she added. Ixchel's experience was representative of the alumni of youth organizing and public-oriented groups who benefited from the confidence and networks gained from prior collaborations with adult authority figures.

Organizing and Collective Action   Adolescents applied their civic skills to a series of high-profile political activities. Between 2009 and 2011, undocumented young adults spearheaded meetings with elected officials and organized public demonstrations demanding a pathway to citizenship and other rights for Dreamers.[20] The alumni of youth organizing groups discussed how they drew on their prior campaign efforts to aid their leadership in the immigrant rights movement and share their experience with their peers. As a former member of ICS, Jason was among the high school students who challenged school board members and elected state officials over school discipline policies, school overcrowding, and lack of access to college prep courses at his school and others in low-income areas. The disagreements arising at these meetings provided a valuable lesson as he continued to intervene in policy debates: "What is important is having relationships with authority figures, and it's okay to challenge them," explained Jason. Once in college, Jason leveraged his prior experience working with decision-makers in guiding his peers as they met with university leaders, local elected officials, and congressional representatives to demand policy changes.

Through youth organizing groups, adolescent immigrants practiced conducting broad public outreach and mobilizing people to support their cause. Joel, a Bay Area resident who had once organized a student protest to save a magnet program at his high school, noted that his organizing school group offered lessons in "how mass mobilization of the people who are being affected can influence someone with power." And Lourdes, a native of South Los Angeles who belonged to a similar group there, helped lead a walkout at her school to protest the war in Iraq, which "definitely prepared me for planning Dream actions," she claimed. Lourdes became recognized across the country as she helped coordinate national organizational efforts around the Dream Act, occasionally traveling out of state to train other undocumented youth leaders.

Former Wise Up! members who had advocated for immigrant rights as high school students were especially prepared to help peers in Dream organizations execute campaigns. In high school, Wise Up! prepared Oracio to educate others about immigrant rights. "I could go give presentations about AB 540 and the Dream Act," he asserted, and "talk about immigration reform, how it affects you and other people." He also spoke at community events and went door to door to speak to voters, and later, as a community college student, trained his peers to do the same. Another Wise Up! member, a Salvadoran immigrant named Edwin, recalled that the group taught him "how to conduct legislative visits and how to tell your story in a meaningful powerful way." Edwin drew on this experience to train his college peers on what to expect during legislative visits in Sacramento. Norma, another Wise Up! member, learned how noncitizens could obtain political power by "educating people and getting them out to vote" as well as through "mass protests and rallies." Having worked on the Dream Act in high school, she brought her peers up to speed on campaign efforts when she attended community college. Norma's experience also taught her to take the long view. New or young activists typically expect to see immediate change.[21] Yet Norma understood that campaigns are not won overnight. "I was able to have faith that some type of legislation was going to pass," she claimed, "maybe not, you know, today or tomorrow, but in the future if we work and organize."

These examples show how youth organizing groups boosted the civic capacities of undocumented adolescents, enabling them to guide their peers as they participated in a national social movement. Notably, most undocumented former members of high school youth organizing groups held leadership positions in college and community Dream organizations, and some like Irvis even helped found these young adult immigrant rights groups.

Intersectional Collective Action Frames of the Immigrant Youth Movement

During campaigns for the federal and California Dream Acts, youth leaders leveraged their dense networks and interconnected infrastructure to frame their movement in intersectional terms.[22] Their analysis of their own lived experiences as undocumented immigrants, LGBTQ+ people, women, and people of color motivated their critique of the broader social structures underpinning the challenges they faced. Predisposed to thinking about their multiple identities in politicized ways, undocumented students with prior adolescent youth organizing experience were well positioned to promote their own understandings of intersectional frameworks within this youthful movement. Moreover, even those undocumented youth activists without prior organizing experience had likely taken college coursework in sociology, ethnic studies, gender studies, and related disciplines that would have exposed them to the concept of intersectionality.[23]

Ultimately, the immigrant youth movement's call for leaders to "come out of the shadows" fueled the widespread adoption of intersectional language among activists. Initiated by LGBTQ+ undocumented leaders in Chicago, the public campaign urged undocumented youth to openly discuss their legal status as a way to combat their precarious legal situation and to humanize their experiences for broader audiences.[24] For some activists, declarations of legal status were accompanied by disclosure of a queer identity in public demonstrations, online venues, and mainstream media.[25] Youth leaders popularized the phrase "undocumented and unafraid, queer and unashamed." Such public pronouncements from 2010 to 2012 raised public consciousness of how interlocking identities and systems of oppression shaped the lives of undocumented activists across the country, with implications for the critical civics education of the younger 1.5 and second generations.

Undocumented and queer people in these groups encouraged other members to take intersectional stock of their multiple identities in order to understand their challenges and privileges. For example, Samir, an undocumented leader from the Pacific Islands, explained how immigration laws and homophobia heightened the marginalization of queer undocumented youth:

We can't [legally] have jobs, so we already have these financial issues. Once you come out to your family—and if they don't respond very well—then there is that chance of losing your bed, a place to sleep. There's a lot more you can lose because you can't really take care of yourself financially when you're undocumented.

For Yohanna, a twenty-four-year-old community college student and single mother, an intersectional frame helped her reflect on her identities and experiences: "I've learned through the movement that we're not only one thing; we're not only Dreamers. I'm a single mom, a queer. I'm undocumented. I'm a woman of color. I'm all these things."

Leaders widely shared their intersectional analyses through social media and taught the concept in workshops, and thus intersectionality became what Robert Benford and David Snow might recognize as a multipurpose collective action frame.[26] At the height of their immigrant youth movement from 2010 to 2012, undocumented activists leveraged intersectionality to (a) make sense of their own multiply marginalized identities, (b) inspire action, and (c) build inclusive organizations and bridge social movements.[27] The intersectional frameworks pervasive in the immigrant youth movement—as well as other progressive millennial movements, including the Black Lives Matter movement[28]—significantly informed the curricula and campaigns of adolescent youth organizing groups.

Apart from sensitizing immigrant youth leaders to the ways in which power and privilege operate, intersectional frames also helped spur these young people to action. They developed what Benford and Snow call vocabularies of motive.[29] According to Roman, an outspoken movement leader, intersectionality gave participants the language, experience, and identities to say: "We're fierce and we're leaders and our voices matter and our identities are important." The campaign to reveal one's undocumented status in particular facilitated the deployment of intersectionality as a motivational frame. As Yohanna reflects, "Once you decide to come out as undocumented, you might as well come out [as] all the things you are. So you live kind of a free life, in a way." Awareness of one's identities, according to Yohanna, "helps people 'get over' the daily challenge of feeling ashamed, of feeling little in the world." Having acquired the conceptual tools to meet that daily challenge, young immigrants were then prepared to "drive forward in the movement."

Finally, intersectionality informed strategies for addressing multiple and overlapping forms of oppression both within and outside of youth organizations. Undocumented youth leaders ensured that their organizations attended not only to immigration-related issues but also developed programming around other identities, building deliberately inclusive groups. Noting that leaders should "walk the talk of intersectional work," Roman, twenty-seven, helped to develop and conduct an intersectionality workshop that sought to "get people to think about their identities and share how they have affected them." While the workshop brought out deep emotions among participants, it contributed to a "better understanding among the people in the room, so that people could step into the space with their whole selves, their queer selves, not just their undocumented selves," said Roman. In a similar vein, Allen, an ethnic Chinese leader, underscored the need to raise awareness about undocumented AAPI experiences. Undocumented immigrants make up a much smaller proportion of the AAPI population than of the Latinx population, which can lead to relative silence around the distinct challenges of this former group.[30] Allen explained: "There are a lot of Asian immigrants, but they're not talking about it, and they're not doing anything [politically], and it's not talked about in the media. As with the rest of America, Asian immigrants see us [the undocumented] as criminals." Intersectional frameworks thus guided leaders to incorporate workshops and other activities that helped ensure that the movement, though dominated by Latinx youth, also was inclusive and addressed the needs of diverse Asian immigrants.[31]

Organizations also adopted various practices to ensure that LGBTQ+ members felt welcome. For example, email and other announcements from one group explicitly indicated that gatherings were queer-inclusive, and various groups sought to address homophobia by educating members rather than publicly shaming them. They also urged straight allies to speak up in support of LGBTQ rights so that the burden of combating homophobia did not always fall on queer members.

Aware of how multiple systems of oppression negatively affect their communities, undocumented youth connected with other social movements beyond immigrant rights. Mateo, twenty-three, said that he and his peers felt prompted to "build those bridges with other organizations already working with the grassroots." Indeed, the Dream Summer in 2011 (and the 2012 Queer Dream Summer) helped cement those bridges by placing members within allied organizations.[32] For example, Irvis's Dream Summer internship was at the Asian Resource Center in Sacramento, where he offered training sessions on the relevance of cross-racial solidarity and immigrant rights.

Subsequent Youth Organizing Efforts

After the immigrant youth movement waned following President Barack Obama's DACA announcement in 2012, Irvis and many of his peers maintained ties to grassroots youth organizing groups, either introducing or reinforcing intersectional frameworks in the training of subsequent 1.5- and second-generation immigrant adolescents. In fact, with DACA, some of these young immigrant activists secured jobs in nonprofit youth organizing as the number of groups in this field grew over the course of the 2010s (see chapter 2).[33] Accordingly, I witnessed some of them take over the helm of youth organizing groups. Others assumed influential positions at YO! Cali and Power California—two intermediary groups that provided training and technical assistance to youth organizing groups across the state, aligning inclusive approaches to organizing and voter outreach. Meanwhile, other alumni joined labor and social movement organizations that worked alongside youth organizing groups, strengthening networks among allied organizations. As millennials and early adopters of social media, they also contributed the strategic use of digital technologies within this civic infrastructure.

Arguably, the years after the height of the immigrant youth movement saw an expansion of programming fostering the transformative political socialization of second-generation youth. The next chapter will feature one case in Orange County, where young people made significant strides in dismantling the school-to-prison-to-deportation pipeline.

PART II

LOCALIZED POLITICAL CONTEXTS AND THE TRANSFORMATIVE POLITICAL SOCIALIZATION PROCESS

IN PART I of this book, I provide an overview of youth organizing groups that carry forward the legacies of past movements by engaging low-income second-generation immigrant adolescents in grassroots campaigns. As agents of political socialization, these groups offered their members developmental supports, exposed them to a critical civics curricula, and provided them with hands-on experience in civic action. Taking an intersectional approach to their programming and campaigns, these groups propelled many of their adolescent members toward high levels of political engagement as young adults. Drawing on evidence gathered across California, I contend that in participating in these programs and contributing to their campaigns, members experienced a transformative political socialization that further enabled them to shape contemporary policy debates, voter mobilization efforts, and social movements.

In part II of this book, I elaborate on the key elements of youth organizing groups' programming that engender a transformative political socialization. I feature groups from different regions of California, describing aspects of their programming in greater depth while offering an overview of the geographic contexts in which they operate. As Edelina Burciaga and Lisa Martinez argue, immigrant social movements respond to their localized political contexts, specifically the extent to which their host communities are hostile or accommodating toward newcomers.[1] The subsequent chapters demonstrate some of the ways youth organizing groups make local adaptations to their programming in response to their localized political contexts. I follow the lead of other immigration scholars who study civic associations and subnational patterns of immigrant political incorporation.[2] Specifically, I attend to the roles of local demographics, histories of resistance, and the availability of immigrant-serving civic infrastructure in shaping how youth associations prepare their adolescent members to take on public leadership roles.

Selecting groups to feature proved a difficult task, as the 110 organizations included in this book have unique histories, campaign focus areas, curricula, and staffing configurations. As further detailed in the appendix, I opted to feature geographically diverse groups with well-developed programming related to a key component of the transformative socialization process. At the same time, I also made sure to select groups whose featured programming was similar to that offered by other groups across the state but still incorporated local adaptations. My intent is to demonstrate the richness of the organizational practices while also recognizing the importance of localized political contexts.

The opening chapter in part II features the efforts of Resilience Orange County (ROC) in Santa Ana to support members' developmental growth and capacities to participate in contentious politics by focusing on healing and self-care. Emotional wellness became a growing element of programming in the 2010s as youth organizing groups responded to the mounting mental health challenges voiced by their members. Santa Ana is a predominantly low-income Latinx immigrant city within a larger, wealthy county known for its tough-on-crime and anti-immigrant narratives. Given this context, ROC adapted their program to attend to the emotional hardships young people were experiencing as a result of to their families' legal and economic precarity.

In chapter 6, I turn to one of the most progressive places in the country: Oakland, California. This ethnically and racially diverse city boasts a long history of civil rights and social movement activism led by people of color, and grassroots youth organizing there engaged members in a critical civics education that carefully attended to issues of identity and diversity. I show how two organizations—Asian Youth Promoting Advocacy and Leadership (AYPAL) and Youth Together (YT)—adapted their curricula to facilitate coalitions among diverse newcomers from around the globe and more established black residents.

Chapters 7 and 8 describe in greater detail how grassroots youth organizing groups enhance their members' capacities for civic action. In chapter 7, I highlight how InnerCity Struggle (ICS) in the predominantly Latinx Eastside of Los Angeles developed members' basic civic skills and prepared them for collective action around bold, intergenerational grassroots campaigns. ICS seized opportunities that arose through the region's robust civic infrastructure and decades of coalition building. In chapter 8, I turn to a very different localized political context—the

Central Valley, a region of the state where, in 2018, prominent elected leaders vocally supported President Trump and his anti-immigrant and racist rhetoric. Grassroots youth organizations across this vast region adapted their strategies and campaign goals to a context in which youths' voices faced significant opposition. Lacking access to an extensive and supportive intergenerational civic infrastructure, organizations trained their adolescent members to exercise their political power through widespread voter education and mobilization.

The concluding chapter highlights lessons learned from youth organizing for youth-serving institutions (including schools) that can empower young people to collectively and inclusively advance their community's interests in the political arena. It briefly features COVID-19 youth organizing efforts by Future Leaders of America (FLA) in Santa Maria, a semirural city where the children of immigrants exercise a growing political influence, despite the drastic economic inequalities that characterize the larger Santa Barbara County area in which they reside. Young people in FLA, like those in other groups, pivoted to respond to layered crises their communities faced in 2020 and in the early months of the second Trump administration as I finalized this book. In sharing these illustrative cases that span distinct social geographies and unfold within an evolving national political climate, I hope to shed light on both the diversity and continuity of organizational practices. My research demonstrates the possibilities that arise when youth-centered spaces support adolescents' transformative political socialization.

═ Chapter 5 ═

Healing, Self-Care, and Fighting the School-to-Prison-to-Deportation Pipeline in Orange County

D URING A difficult period of her middle school years, Citlali Ruiz, a student in Santa Ana, got into a physical fight with another girl. "We were just being bullies to each other," she explained. The principal intervened and called her aside, telling her that because she was undocumented, she could face grave consequences if city police charged her with assault. Citlali clearly understood the principal's warning—throughout her childhood, her parents had cautioned her, "Don't do anything bad, because if you get involved with the police, you're going to get deported." Naturally, then, she was relieved when the principal did not report the incident to the authorities. "I was suspended for three days," she recalled, "and when I came back, I knew I couldn't get in any more trouble." While Citlali was put on probation, the other girl, who had a history of fighting, was expelled and placed in an alternative educational program. "I never saw her again," Citlali said, "but she had papers, so there was a difference between me and her. She wasn't going to get deported."

While she was lucky enough to avoid such consequences, Citlali, the daughter of an Indigenous Zapotec Mexican mother and non-Indigenous Mexican immigrant father, learned how easily a student might get caught up in the school-to-prison-to-deportation pipeline. Unlike some youth who do not learn about their undocumented status until they are going to college, Citlali was well aware that she could be deported. Immigration officials had taken away others in their community, which instilled in Citlali's family a sense of fear not only of U.S. Immigration and Customs Enforcement (ICE) but also of the police, who could report undocumented people to ICE.

This fear of the police, coupled with the threat of deportation, can have negative consequences for mental health.[1] Additionally, Citlali's

89

https://doi.org/10.7758/gert1126.4776

family situation presented additional challenges. "I had to take care of my two younger siblings because my parents were working jobs from 9 a.m. to 8 p.m.," she said, and her parents were also going through a divorce. "That was a lot for me to deal with, and so I just wanted to rebel." Citlali admitted that she was an angry child, and this anger manifested itself in harmful behaviors to herself and others. Given her mental state, she wasn't sure she was going to make it through high school when she first enrolled.

During her sophomore year, however, Citlali was fortunate to come across Resilience Orange County (ROC). Through self-care and healing practices, the group taught Citlali how to cope with her stress and anger. Activities that focused on her emotional wellness helped her stay out of trouble, improve her relationships with her family members, and develop the emotional bandwidth to participate in contentious grassroots organizing. Like other youth organizing groups, ROC prompted a transformative political socialization, in part by attending to adolescents' developmental needs. Founded by former members of Orange County Dream Team Alliance and participants in the broader immigrant youth movement discussed in chapter 4, ROC staff attended to the multiple stressors experienced by young people in their communities. ROC's members came from mixed-status families or were undocumented themselves, many struggled with poverty, some had experienced violence or criminalization because of their gender, and some identified as LGBTQ+. In response, ROC addressed their developmental needs by adopting intersectional, culturally relevant, and age-appropriate approaches to build adolescent members' emotional resilience.

Citlali said that these processes prepared her to "walk confidently with all these identities: being undocumented, being a woman, being Indigenous, being the first to graduate from high school." Benefiting from ROC's programming, members acquired the emotional capacity to campaign against the criminalization of immigrants and other young people and encourage government decision-makers to engender a more representative democracy—one that considered the needs of noncitizen residents. In other words, a politicized approach to healing advanced youths' collective efforts to improve the broader well-being of their community.

Like other grassroots organizing groups, ROC functioned as an influential agent of adolescents' political socialization. Citlali and her peers participated in a critical civics curriculum that attended to issues of diversity and inequality while providing members tools to analyze policy concerns. A key component of these curricula focused on ensuring that members understood the link between local school discipline policies and the high deportation rates among adolescents in Orange County, also known as the school-to-prison-to-deportation pipeline. As scholars have noted, school discipline, policing, and immigration enforcement combine to racially profile, track, and surveil students in ways that introduce them to the criminal justice system or, if they are undocumented, to the deportation apparatus.[2] ROC sought to disrupt this school-to-prison-to-deportation pipeline and thus guided students as they engaged in civic actions aimed at decriminalizing local youth and their families.

ROC's programming adapted to the localized political context of the city of Santa Ana and, more broadly, Orange County. As a predominantly Latinx and midsize city with a growing immigrant-serving infrastructure, Santa Ana remains somewhat of a haven for immigrants; however, it is located within a larger county with a history of anti-immigrant and xenophobic politics.[3] Mindful of this, ROC attended to its members' concerns about the possibility that they or their families could be deported as it encouraged members like Citlali to develop a public voice.

In this chapter, I begin by describing the school-to-prison-to-deportation pipeline and Orange County's localized political context, along with ROC's origin story. However, I primarily cover how ROC addressed members' developmental needs through programming focused on adolescents' well-being. To do so, I draw on interviews with youth members and staff focus groups, but I also reference statewide data to discuss how ROC's approach mirrors that of other youth organizing groups statewide. I argue that participation in healing and self-care activities contributes to youths' transformative political socialization.

The School-to-Prison-to-Deportation Pipeline

In the 2010s, youth and community organizing groups across the country coordinated efforts as they sought to tackle the school-to-prison pipeline, defined by Mark Warren as "an interlocking system of policies and practices that push students of color from low-income communities out of school and into the juvenile and criminal justice system."[4] This pipeline reflects a history of white supremacy in the United States, which has criminalized young people of color, especially black males. From the 1980s to the 2000s, federal, state, and local policies (including those supported by California's voters) further increased the proportion of youth of color behind bars. For example, in 1994, California voters approved Proposition 184 (known as the Three Strikes law), which augmented sentencing for multiple offenses. Then, in 2000, voters approved Proposition 21, which further increased sentencing and gave prosecutors the discretion to send minors to adult court.[5]

For some youth, schools functioned as on-ramps to the prison system. As a result of school discipline policies implemented in the 1990s, schools in high-poverty, non-white neighborhoods grew to rely on suspensions and expulsions, a school police presence, student searches, surveillance, ticketing, and on-campus arrests to manage student behavior.[6] In California, students were commonly suspended if they "disrupted school activities or otherwise willfully defied the valid authority of supervisors, teachers, administrators, school officials, or other school personnel."[7] These zero-tolerance policies took students out of the classroom for short or extended periods of time, undercutting the primary goal of the educational system.

As someone who had previously been suspended, Citlali also witnessed other students experience overly punitive discipline. For example, during her junior year she saw officers tackle a fellow student who walked of a meeting at the principal's office. According to Citlali, the boy had failed to bring homework to school three times, and the principal wanted to "write him up right away and expel him because he was in a gang," Citlali said. "It was super traumatic and horrible to see because this was in front of a lot of students during lunch. I was like, 'I cannot believe this is happening in front of me.'" Citlali never saw this student at school again.

This anecdote is a vivid example of how the school-to-prison pipeline affects students of color from high-poverty backgrounds. Scholars have noted that punitive school discipline policies both directly and indirectly contribute to mass incarceration. Such criminalization especially affects young men of color.[8] Analyzing 2011 CYAS survey data (described in chapter 3), Jeff Sacha, Robert Chlala, and I found that boys who had been suspended or expelled were four times more likely to have a criminal record in early adulthood compared with students with similar academic performance and demographic backgrounds but no record of punitive discipline.[9] Teachers' biases and stereotyping play a role as well, as they may perceive students of color as threatening.[10] Similarly, they may punish LGBTQ+ students for not abiding by gender norms and expectations.[11]

For undocumented immigrant students, the pipeline can also lead to deportation. The federal Secure Communities 287(g) program allows municipal agencies and school police to jail and detain immigrants, including minors.[12] This program strengthened ties between federal immigration enforcement and local law enforcement, including school police.[13] Fear of police violence, incarceration, and deportation can have broad negative implications for youths during the transition to adulthood.[14] In the latter half of the 2010s, the vocal anti-immigrant sentiment shared by then President Trump and his followers heightened youth anxiety about deportation.[15]

Criminalized in Orange County

Situated just southeast of Los Angeles County, Orange County can be a somewhat inhospitable localized political context for engaging second-generation youth in grassroots civil and immigrant rights campaigns. With its history of segregating Mexican and black residents in schools, pools, and other public facilities, Orange County has been relatively unwelcoming to immigrants, particularly those from Mexico and Central America.[16] For example, in 1994, the Orange County–based political advocacy group California Coalition for Immigration Reform cosponsored Proposition 187, which would have denied undocumented immigrants access to public schooling, health care, and other services. Approved by voters, the statewide measure was challenged in court and never implemented. Also in Orange County, Jim Gilchrist of Aliso Viejo cofounded the Minuteman Project, an anti-immigration group prominent between 2005 and 2009 that formed a volunteer border patrol after asserting that the federal government was failing to stop illegal crossings.[17]

Orange County leaders became early adopters of the Secure Communities 287(g) program in 2006, which prompted law enforcement agencies to screen inmates for immigration violations and refer undocumented immigrants to ICE.[18] The county was also the last in California to terminate its 287(g) agreement and did so only because it violated the 2017 Senate Bill 54, also known as the State Sanctuary Bill or the Values Act, which restricted state and local law enforcement's communication with federal immigration authorities.[19]

Orange County's thirty-four distinct municipalities vary in the extent to which they welcome immigrants.[20] Some municipalities grew substantially during the late twentieth century as a result of white flight, or the exodus of middle-class white residents out of Los Angeles's urban centers into less racially diverse suburban communities which they perceived as safer.[21] Some also experienced an influx of middle-class Korean and Chinese residents, as well as Vietnamese and Filipino residents of diverse class backgrounds.[22] Others, such as Santa Ana, Orange, and Anaheim, became increasingly segregated low-income, predominantly Latinx communities.[23]

By the early 2000s, anti-gang hysteria had gripped the nation, amplified by sensational media coverage and divisive political rhetoric.[24] This was especially true in Orange County. As local demographics shifted, conservative white residents—fueled by stereotypes linking Latinx communities to criminality—pressured law enforcement to implement aggressive tough-on-crime measures.[25] Beginning in 2006, local city governments authorized the arrest of gang members for a range of activities, many benign: littering, wearing clothes with "gang colors" (for example, blue or red), running late-night errands, being out after a 10 p.m. curfew, or gathering with family members.[26] During informal conversations and interviews, I heard firsthand how these policies impacted the region's youth. For example, Citlali recalled how her boyfriend and a companion were pulled over and searched by police when they were walking home after a study session. "[They] were just wearing red shirts, riding bikes, and they had their hoodies on," Citlali said.

Confrontations with the police and immigration enforcement agencies can add to the layers of stress that young people experience in low-income immigrant communities.[27] Given that Orange County is a more hostile localized political context for immigrants than places like Los Angeles and the Bay Area, ROC adapted its program with an eye toward addressing the emotional hardships youth experienced as they or their immigrant families are criminalized. To this end, the group sponsored activities that promoted members' well-being, while at the same time engaging them in campaigns to dismantle the school-to-prison-to-deportation pipeline.

ROC's Origin Story

ROC's founders were high school students during the mid-to-late 2000s, when Orange County had vigorously adopted tough policies on crime; collaboration among school administrators, law enforcement, and ICE was at its peak; and the county was implementing its 287(g) agreement. As undocumented youth or the children of undocumented immigrant parents, ROC's young founders drew on firsthand, often traumatizing experiences with immigration and police agencies to define their campaigns.

Abraham Medina, ROC's founding executive director, is a prime example. With some guidance from a high school teacher, Abraham organized a campus protest to educate peers about a 2005 bill granting driver's licenses to undocumented immigrants, which then Governor Arnold Schwarzenegger was threatening to veto. Realizing how the bill would benefit him and his family, Abraham joined with other leaders to protest. "Over a hundred students showed up in the science lab at Santiago High School, and I got in trouble," Abraham recalled. After being admonished by a vice principal for allegedly bringing together students from rival gangs for the protest, Abraham sought to continue his activism on campus, with limited success. "They kept us in the office at lunchtime, so we couldn't talk to people," he said.

Following their attempts at activism, Abraham and his friends became the target of police harassment on campus. Certain Latinx boys, and sometimes girls, were singled out: "During lunch, if we were hanging out with four other people, campus police would take us into a room and take a picture of us," Abraham said. "They would ask us if we have any gang ties at school." He eventually realized that the school was cooperating with local police to implement a broad anti-gang injunction prohibiting association among alleged gang members. A high-performing student, Abraham nonetheless felt like the school and law enforcement were treating him like a suspected criminal based on his activism and wardrobe.

Later, Abraham and other students formed the Alliance of Orange County Student Uprising, staging a 2006 school walkout in coordination with national protests against H.R. 4437, also known as the Border Protection, Anti-Terrorism, and Illegal Immigration Control Act, which would have further criminalized undocumented immigrants. In Santa Ana, four to five hundred police officers met the thousands of students who walked out. Political scientist Alfonso Gonzales likened the scene to a war zone "where police had full riot gear, 'non-lethal' weapons, armored vehicles and contingents of officers mounted on horseback."[28] Police arrested several dozen participants, some of whom were subsequently deported.[29] Luckily, Abraham escaped severe consequences.

In the years following the 2006 marches, Abraham and other undocumented youth activists continued their immigrant rights organizing efforts. Some joined the Orange County Dream Team and took part in the surveys and interviews featured in chapter 4. Notably, Orange County youth leaders played an important role in broadening the conversation beyond the Dream Act. By 2011, a cadre of undocumented youth leaders and citizen allies had formed Resistencia, Autonomía, Igualdad y Liderazgo (RAIZ) and started developing strategies for dismantling the school-to-prison-to-deportation pipeline. The next year, Abraham found employment in the nonprofit Santa Ana Boys and Men of Color (SABMOC) coalition, which is dedicated to violence prevention, leadership development, and systems change efforts.

With overlapping memberships, RAIZ and SABMOC worked on shared campaigns around youth criminalization, beginning with the successful coalitional fight to end discriminatory checkpoints for driving under the influence and the impounding of unlicensed immigrants' cars. These leaders also joined a statewide coalition to push for the passage of AB 899, which prevented the Orange County Probation Department from identifying undocumented youth for ICE referrals and thus nearly severed the prison-to-deportation portion of the pipeline. In 2016, the young leaders established ROC. While they benefited from the support of some elders in the community, technical assistance from organizers from Los Angeles and the Bay Area, and ties to the University of California, Irvine, young leaders were at the helm of their organization.

Since its origin, ROC spearheaded multiple campaigns to counter the criminalization and deportation of immigrants and youth. In doing so, its young founders engaged in intersectional praxis by drawing on their own lived experience as young residents of a low-income, non-white, immigrant community to make sense of and demand change in the institutions that produced hardships for local residents. As this work entailed engaging younger cohorts in political struggle, founders understood that they could further their adolescent members' affective capacities to lead by attending to their emotions and well-being.

Transformative Political Socialization and Youths' Healthy Development

The rise in mental health concerns predates the COVID-19 pandemic.[30] For members of ROC and other youth organizing groups, a number of challenges can compound emotional distress. They may experience emotional hardships related to poverty, neighborhood or interpersonal violence, contact with the criminal justice system, racist treatment, and a broken immigration system. For some, normative gender expectations, homophobia, and transphobia exacerbate stress.[31] Additionally, young people's involvement in political work can further elevate their stress, especially when they encounter hostile opposition to their agenda.[32]

Over the course of the 2010s, adolescent leaders placed increasing emphasis on their emotional well-being, and many of their organizations responded by expanding programming to assist them in managing multiple stressors. By 2019, 65 percent of California groups, including ROC, offered healing and self-care activities at least once a month. As an illustrative case, I describe how ROC's healing, self-care, and wellness programming formed part of the transformative political socialization process within youth organizing. I focus on curricula, practices, and activities aimed at promoting mental health, healthy relationships, and positive behaviors at the individual level and among group members. Activities and curricula often linked to and reinforced campaigns that advanced community well-being more broadly. Through this programming, participants came to understand individual and community well-being as inextricably connected.

In prioritizing well-being, youth organizing groups expanded members' emotional bandwidth and motivation to participate in political campaigns.[33] As evidenced by interviews and observations, groups tailored their activities to adolescents who were navigating their identities, relationships with their families and peers, attendance at under-resourced and sometimes unwelcoming school environments, and other challenging circumstances. To this end, groups typically implemented curricula or hosted workshops that encouraged adolescents to reflect on their identities, emotions, health-related behaviors, and relationships. Many also facilitated healing circles, mindfulness practices (such as meditation and breathing exercises), and physical activities like stretching, yoga, and forward stance (a spiritual form of tai chi used by some progressive organizations). Staff typically reminded students to take breaks, eat healthy food, and exercise regularly. Occasionally, some groups incorporated social and recreational activities such as movie nights, hiking, and beach outings, which can contribute to positive developmental outcomes.[34] However, youth organizing groups tended to place a lower priority on and had fewer resources for recreational activities compared with apolitical youth programs.

Youth organizing groups did not intend for their wellness-related activities to be a substitute for much-needed professional mental health services and quality health care. These groups' activities had distinct aims from self-care or wellness initiatives that utilize neoliberal logics to frame health care as primarily an individual's responsibility,[35] or those that depend on costly health and beauty products.[36] Instead, staff recognized that their members faced multiple sources of stress and often operated on the assumption that addressing physical and mental well-being can counter both current and historical forms of oppression. Staff aligned with, and in some cases invoked, Audre Lorde's contention that "caring for myself is not self-indulgence, it is self-preservation, and that is an act of political warfare."[37]

Youth organizing groups often embraced healing and self-care practices rooted in ethnic traditions, emphasizing Indigenous or non-Western cultural interpretations of health and wellness. By drawing on these cultural practices, the groups sought to reconnect members with their own traditions or introduce them to those of others within their community. As such, programming countered stigmas and negative stereotypes about marginalized groups while highlighting their resilience and collective resistance. These activities can have salubrious effects. Quality interventions, including those acknowledging youths' multiple identities, can stimulate neurobiological adaptations and behaviors that better equip young people to handle future adversities.[38] Moreover, healing and other wellness activities can give youth a sense of radical hope, empowering them to imagine and take action toward creating a more just society.[39]

ROC programming demonstrates how youth organizing groups promote their members' mental health, healthy behavior, and positive relationships, thereby facilitating youths' leadership in political campaigns. By featuring this particular group, I highlight themes that emerged from interviews with youth in organizations statewide. At the same time, I observed ROC making local adaptations to their programming in response to Santa Ana's demographics and Orange County's political dynamics by addressing youths' concerns regarding criminal justice and immigration enforcement.

ROC's Introductory Healing and Wellness Curriculum for Young Women and Men

ROC's founders took the mental health of youthful members seriously. As undocumented youth or children of undocumented Mexican immigrants, they knew how federal immigration laws and local law enforcement contributed to personal stress and even trauma. They also had experienced the failed campaign for a federal Dream Act, which took a heavy emotional toll.[40] ROC's founders believed that by engaging members in healing and wellness activities that target an adolescent age group, they could mitigate some of the challenges that might otherwise inhibit young people's political participation.

Accordingly, ROC introduced members to healing, self-care, and other wellness strategies through its programs—Joven Noble, which means "noble young man" in Spanish, and Xinachtli, which means "germinating seed" in Indigenous Nahuatl; these programs were geared toward young men and women, respectively. They incorporated the curriculum written by the National Compadres Network, a nonprofit that initially sought to rehabilitate Chicano youth exposed to gang violence. Both the Xinachtli and Joven Noble curricula addressed gender-specific concerns in safe spaces for members who had experienced violence and the impact of the criminal justice system on themselves or close family members. The curricula respond to an understanding that adolescent boys and girls exhibit different mental health and wellness outcomes influenced by cultural notions of femininity and masculinity, the specific stressors they encounter, their coping strategies, social relationships, and personal resources.[41] Designed by Mexican Americans who had studied with Indigenous elders, the curricula exposed participants to Mesoamerican Indigenous cultural history (particularly Nahuatl) and traditional healing and self-care practices, including herbal remedies, sweat lodges, and healing circles. Overall, the National Compadres curriculum aimed to help young men and women appreciate their ancestral heritage, encourage community service, and provide youth with strategies to attend to their physical and mental health.

ROC staff modernized the Xinachtli and Joven Noble curricula. Recognizing that the original National Compadres curricula did not reflect the fluid, nonbinary, and transgender gender identities of some members, staff incorporated discussions about diverse genders and sexualities. Lessons addressed the social stigma and marginalization experienced by individuals who do not conform to dominant gender norms or identify as heterosexual. When appropriate, staff would introduce immigration-related and other concerns into group dialogues. Dulce, a founding staff member who played a role in shaping the curricula, noted: "From the beginning, we wanted the program to take an intersectional approach to helping the youth reflect on their life stories, and to get them to think about how different systems of oppression impact them." This meant creating the space for members to examine a variety of issues: their gendered experiences as Latinx (and sometimes queer or trans) young people whose lives are shaped by poverty, their status as racialized minorities, and a broken immigration system. Yet, she added, the overall purpose of the introductory curriculum remained fairly stable:

> Xinachtli and Joven Noble are about learning about your anger, learning about yourself, [exploring], "Where does your anger come from? What are some of those boundaries you have with yourself, with family, with others, with partners? What are some of the shields that you carry with you?" A lot of that part of self-discovery involves [asking], "Who is my community? Who is my family? What are my roots? What is my name? Who am I?"

Early in these programs, young people were introduced to physically sitting or standing in a circle in order to share stories, generate meaningful dialogue, and build community. Indigenous cultures have long used circle communication to address conflicts within groups.[42] Moreover, circles can facilitate shared leadership, contributing to a less hierarchical form of communication.[43] Recognizing the historical roots of circle communication, participants in Xinachtli and Joven Noble used it for several purposes. In healing circles, members shared personal experiences in a safe space, received affirmation from their peers, and built relationships and bonds within their organizations. Distinct from what might be considered group therapy, ROC healing circles included ceremonial practices, such as burning medicinal herbs like sage or copal (tree sap from the copal tree native to Mexico). During these circles, facilitators typically set participant guidelines for active listening and turn-taking.

The Xinachtli curriculum recognized that adolescent Latinas in high-poverty communities with gang-related problems may become victims of violence or may be at risk for early childbearing. The curriculum includes units on women's rights and reproductive health. Often using circles to facilitate open communication, facilitators engaged participants in discussions about sexual abuse, dating violence, and gender norms that constrain women's abilities to make choices about their future. Instructors also provided young women with strategies for setting healthy boundaries in romantic and other relationships. Citlali appreciated the program's gendered focus: "I think it's really important to have that separate space for male-identified and female-identified folks who don't have the same struggle. We don't go through the same thing. There's different levels of struggle and pain, and I feel like male-identified folks are more privileged than women-identified folks."

Xinachtli allowed young women to reflect on the daily impact of sexism on their lives. As Citlali noted, young men do not experience "being cat-called, nor being harassed [while] having to walk at night or having to just walk down the street in the middle of the day." She added, "I hear a lot of men, to this day, be like, 'women need to do this, women need to get married.' It's this whole patriarchal thing. As a man, you're never going to have to go through this." Citlali thought that discussing these issues apart from the young men was essential: "I don't think we're able to be in the same space just because they are not able to relate to our pain."

Sixteen-year-old Reina, a U.S.-born daughter of Mexican immigrants, concurred. She felt more comfortable sharing some personal topics only among women: "We know what to say and how to handle the situation, whereas men don't know how to respond to something that's happening, or they just simply don't say anything, which is not wrong, but I'd rather be in a circle of women." Along with discussions of sexism and harassment, Xinachtli invited conversation about body image, reproductive health, dating concerns, or other relationship issues. Reina also appreciated the safe space the program provided to reflect on her sexuality: "Ever since then, I've tried to figure myself out and try to figure out what I really want." Eventually, Reina, who identified as bisexual during the time of our interview, explained that she felt comfortable sharing her self-exploration with staff and members: "I came out to them." It was helpful that the program introduced her to young queer and trans role models along with immigrant rights activists.

Meanwhile, Joven Noble supported the development of healthy masculinity, placing a particular emphasis on keeping one's word, or the notion of palabra: taking responsibility for one's actions. Targeting young men who had been involved in gang violence, units discussed how to "learn and practice ways to express themselves, communicate with words, not violence."[44] The curriculum also explored healthy relationships (including safe sex) with women, the precursors to domestic violence, and its physical, emotional, and legal ramifications. ROC's version of Joven Noble incorporated programming that sought to combat homophobia and transphobia. One aim of Joven Noble was to counteract gendered socialization that encourages boys to be stoic, even in the face of abuse and violence. As one organizer pointed out, changing youths' mindsets can take some effort, given that families, peers, and dominant gender norms limit young men's emotional expression. This was the case for nineteen-year-old Rogelio, who initially joined the program at age sixteen:

> At first when I heard about healing, it was when people would talk about, "Oh, you need self-care." I'm like, "What do you mean you need self-care? Life is rough, just deal with it." But at the same time that was my bad, toxic mentality. That's how I was taught through my peers and at home as well.

The oldest of three siblings and the only one without papers, Rogelio grew up hyperaware that he or his parents could be deported, but he did not discuss how this made him feel. The program helped Rogelio come out of his shell:

> Well, you're not going to believe it, but I'm really shy. So, I wasn't used to talking about my feelings. I used to not tell people what I was thinking. I used to keep everything to myself because I was being the man in the house because my dad's always working, so I feel like I have to be the man in the house. I had to keep all that emotion inside of me so I wouldn't portray it to my siblings.

Being more open about his deep fears and concerns about his precarious legal status made him feel better, said Rogelio, who found comfort in knowing others understood and empathized with his situation.

Meanwhile, Samuel, the U.S.-born sixteen-year-old son of an undocumented Mexican mother and U.S.-born Mexican American father, reflected on gendered socialization and the benefits of the gender-segregated program. Samuel attended middle and high schools with prevalent gang activity, which can cause anxiety and mental health challenges for young men.[45] Samuel, along with his peers, had accepted this reality but never discussed it openly:

> I think that's why I really learned a lot, because it's men in the circle, young men. It's like we're young men of color talking about problems that we would never talk about. And it's just so empowering seeing people talk and not be afraid to say whatever they want to say.

Through Joven Noble, Samuel and his peers created a space to respectfully discuss peer pressures, relationships, sexual health, immigration issues, sexuality, and other personal topics. Samuel talked about the temptation to join a local gang to find connections, camaraderie, and protection, crediting Joven Noble for helping him choose a different path: "I'd probably have ended up with the wrong crowd to be perfectly honest with you."

Xinachtli and Joven Noble helped members develop crucial communication skills necessary for later programming, including explicitly political and organizational work. As participants took on increasing responsibilities in implementing campaigns, circle communication continued, and some of the lessons learned in this introductory curriculum continued to be incorporated into everyday programming.

ROC also offered other activities to enhance members' well-being—for example, guided meditation, mindfulness, or breathing exercises. Such activities can reduce stress and enhance physical or mental health.[46] On occasion, youth were invited to decompress through arts and crafts, or they played "silly games" that brought them joy. The group also organized peer-facilitated conversations about emotions. The following section elaborates on how healing and wellness strategies became ritualized practice in ROC and other groups.

Supporting Emotional Relief and Ongoing Growth

Like many California groups, ROC regularly set aside time for healing circles or brief check-ins in which participants quickly shared how they were feeling. Data gathered from members indicates that these activities may have freed up their emotional energy so that they could focus on their campaigns, school, or other matters. Young people often said that the circles contributed to self-understanding and emotional growth, and they appreciated the invitation to share their emotions. As eighteen-year-old Allen noted, "It helps you and it helps others because we would debrief in a circle and we would just let it all out. It's basically just trying to get out whatever that's bothering you, whatever hurts you, and not just saying 'it doesn't matter.'" Fifteen-year-old Ernesto in particular was a fan of ROC's regular circle discussions. Anxious and sensitive, Ernesto confessed that without ROC, he would "probably be stuck at home in bed." The regular group check-ins, healing circles, and other activities helped him process his emotions, "even just something small, because that's what happens to me. I overthink everything, so I take everything to heart." ROC's activities helped him "heal from those little things." When he joined ROC, Ernesto said, "I really doubted myself. My self-esteem wouldn't be the best." The circle discussions improved his outlook and contributed to his personal growth, he explained: "I started to affirm myself even more that everything will be okay. I'd say I'm more of a positive person now." Samuel echoed this sentiment, saying circles made him feel "better, like immediately ten times better. I don't feel sad or anything, I just feel like I could go around and just do whatever I want, but in a good way, not in a bad way. I feel more confident in myself every time I do it." Positive testimonials aside, organizers at ROC and elsewhere insisted that healing is a process, and individuals do not recover from harm overnight.

Processing Difficult Public Events

Across the state, organizing groups commonly scheduled healing circles after an emotionally difficult or traumatic event to help young people make sense of violence, injustice, or uncertainty that directly or indirectly impacted their communities. For example, youth organizing groups hosted healing circles after instances of local and nationally publicized police violence (the murders of George Floyd, Sandra Bland, and Adam Toledo); mass shootings affecting youth or communities of color (Parkland High School, Pulse nightclub); hate crime incidents; the murders of individuals youth knew; and local ICE raids. Coincidently, ROC was founded the year that Trump was elected to his first term as president. His administration exacerbated an already polarized political climate that, in conjunction with social unrest and racial animus, took a toll on young people, especially those residing in low-income, immigrant and non-immigrant communities of color.[47] As a group serving undocumented youth and adolescents from mixed-status families, ROC held regular healing circles to respond to Trump's election, his anti-immigration policies, and his intention to end DACA, a program that benefited many members.

For Citlali, these healing circles were especially comforting, the "thing that I needed," given that—on top of worrying about her own and her family members' increased likelihood of deportation under the first Trump administration—she was facing other personal challenges at school and at home. Similarly, Samuel, whose mother was undocumented, also found comfort in the healing circles: "I was scared of the whole Trump situation. I was just scared because I didn't know what was going to happen, especially when they announced the recent ICE raids."

While ROC used healing circles to discuss Trump's policies or other challenges facing members, they also made sure that members would not emerge from conversations feeling despair. ROC organizers frequently reminded members that if they worked collectively, they could support each other and effect positive change. In the face of adversity, therefore, healing circles also motivated young people to continue their civic and political engagement. As sixteen-year-old Reina noted, "I've learned to be patient with things that are going on and I know that the change is going to come, that change will come. I've learned to be hopeful for everything that we do here, for everything that we fight for." Reina's words, along with psychological studies, illustrate how healing circles and related political activities can instill radical hope and foster, in the words of Bryana French and colleagues, "a sense of agency to change things for the greater good—a belief that one can fight for justice and that the fight will not be futile."[48]

Dealing with the Stresses of Contentious Political Participation

ROC's founders participated in the earlier Dream movement, as well as in subsequent immigrant rights organizing efforts. In doing so, they learned that participation in contentious politics could be emotionally draining and at times heartbreaking. After the federal Dream Act and other initiatives that would have led to citizenship for themselves or their loved ones failed to pass, young activists faced a future defined by the precarity of their status in this country. Campaign losses have the potential to lead to despair and bitterness.[49] And successful or not, campaign work can also lead to burnout.[50]

Youth organizing staff believed that healing and other self-care practices could help young people cope with the everyday battles of grassroots organizing and prevent burnout. Organizing can be contentious, and young people are sometimes reprimanded for standing up to authorities. Healing and self-care practices can help young people process and recover from such experiences. Abraham explained that youth members had to learn to cope with the anxiety, stress, frustration, and disappointment of a campaign, saying: "If we're going to engage youth in advocacy or systems change, we need them to be resilient because otherwise, some of the youth will burn out or become involved in some unhealthy coping mechanisms." ROC's leaders, like those in other groups, sought to help their adolescent members develop healthy responses to emotional hardships, while also engaging them in grassroots organizing efforts to challenge the systems and practices that contribute to stress and trauma.

Rogelio, a two-year ROC veteran when I interviewed him in 2018, had contributed to a highly collaborative and successful sanctuary city campaign. On top of a busy high school schedule, he had also worked to register and educate voters, organize protests against Trump's decision to end the DACA program, and support other initiatives. The campaigns for sanctuary status and voter education were a success, but the work took a lot of time, and his efforts were not always met with approval or appreciation. At the time of the 2018 interview, when immigrant rights campaigns faced headwinds at the federal level, Rogelio understood that organizing could be exhausting and take an emotional toll:

> A lot of the work kills one's emotions. . . . It's a lot of hard work, so if you don't take care of yourself, you're going to burn out. [You're] not going to be motivated to continue this work. . . . It's really tough. And if one isn't able to balance it out, one is just going to feel like, "Wow, this is too much."

For Rogelio and many other youth, healing and self-care practices sustained their commitment to organizing. Like other groups, ROC set aside time for deep breathing, guided meditations, or physical stretches during the heat of campaign work. Rogelio appreciated these down times when they paid attention to physical tension and emotions. Another important component of healing, he added, entailed debriefing—one to one, in small groups, or in large circles—where members would say a few words about how they felt about campaign developments or other things that were going on in their lives. "There's always a role for healing in the movement," Ernesto noted. He also added:

> You're always bound to feel something about some sort of experience or information. And so here at ROC, we always check in on each other. If something was really heavy, they'll check in on us and ask what we're feeling. If we're feeling some sort of way, if we're feeling really over-whelmed, we'll step out for a bit and really breathe, and we'll talk it out and everything.

Building Community and Supporting Collective Well-Being

Although adolescent peer networks can sometimes encourage unhealthy behavior (such as smoking, drug use, or gang involvement), social networks can help reduce illness and disease.[51] Social ties formed through school- and community-based organizations tend to have a positive (albeit modest) impact on indicators of well-being.[52] As evidenced by interviews with members of youth organizing groups across the state, healing and self-care practices fostered strong ties as participants learned more about each other's personal lives. Healing and wellness activities can strengthen relationships among participants.[53] They can also prevent social isolation and provide protections against hostile political and social environments.[54]

Hence, healing circles and similar sharing activities contributed to a community of care in which participants received peer-to-peer consolation and encouragement and were often bonding experiences.

For example, sixteen-year-old Samuel noted the benefits of mutual exchanges in healing circles: "What everybody said there really affected me, but it was also good because they didn't have to carry that burden. I was able to talk, too, so that I wouldn't have to carry that burden on me. So people would say they'll be there for me." Samuel also underscored the sincerity of the group, explaining that when members promised to check in on each other, "they actually do go through with their word," building a culture of care in which everyone felt an obligation to reciprocate: "Dang, these are people down for me," said Samuel, "then I should be down for them."

Close bonds within groups like ROC are particularly important for young people who lack other adequate support networks. Rogelio's undocumented aunts and uncles returned to Mexico as a result of economic and social uncertainty during the Trump administration. Lamenting the loss of his family network, he believed that ROC's healing circles and other activities helped generate a new social support system:

> I think healing is building family. Personally, not having blood family here is rough because I felt like they were the ones who were supposed to be my support group. But building family here at ROC, with these awesome people, is where I feel at home. I feel accepted. And even though they're not blood family, I still feel very connected. You're able to feel wanted and just . . . accepted in this world because it's really tough.

While peers are not the same as family, for Samuel and others, healing activities eased the pain and difficulty of disruptions (including the deportation or incarceration of family members) and other challenges.

Through sharing hardships and building bonds, young people learn to accept and appreciate one another. In the case of fifteen-year-old Otilio, hearing from his LGBTQ+ peers made him sympathetic to their experiences. "I learned how much prejudice they had to go through," he said, "and if they were trying to come out, I told my friends, 'I'll be there for you.'" The two queer ROC members interviewed as part of this study confirmed that healing practices allowed them to be open about day-to-day challenges associated with their queer identities, a sentiment echoed in interviews with many other queer and trans youth across the state who took part in the broader study. As this data and other research indicate, peer-to-peer bonds might be particularly beneficial for the mental health of young people undergoing personal challenges.[55]

While peers offer social support, staff often played important mentorship roles in many quality after-school programs.[56] Youth organizing staff counseled individual members when they had a concern or problem.

For example, nineteen-year-old Alicia—who said she was often "freaking out because there are so many things in my head"—turned to a young staff member who was a mentor: "She helps me and makes it better. I definitely have learned a lot of things from her." Seventeen-year-old Angel also trusted the wisdom of his slightly older mentors: "If you have problems, you can talk to them. They will give you answers. It may not be the thing you want to hear, but it'll be the one thing you need to hear." In sum, these practices and an attentive staff provided vital support for these youths facing a variety of stressors.

Linking Healing to Restorative Justice

Like many youth organizing groups, ROC sought to work on group dynamics after misunderstandings, tensions, miscommunication, disrespect, or other negative experiences by applying principles of restorative justice to their healing circles. Initially based on Indigenous traditions of conflict resolution, restorative justice consists of a deliberative process of bringing offenders, victims, and other community members together to resolve crimes and conflicts.[57] The practice now has been adopted internationally to address juvenile delinquency and school misbehavior; it replaces courts or formal school disciplinary procedures with the goal of repairing harms, building community, and improving relationships.[58] ROC repurposed healing circles to teach youth how to address conflict constructively, especially for members (including Citlali) who had a history of getting into physical altercations. Staff and youth shared that "harm does happen," and that that harm should have constructive consequences (for example, apologies and other agreed on actions).

Besides addressing the victim's well-being, restorative justice interventions aim to promote the offender's growth.[59] In interviews across California, youth said that groups used healing circles to address a wide range of incidents involving two or more members, including school disagreements, cliquish behavior, bullying, homophobic remarks, and body shaming. Allen, for example, described a restorative justice circle at ROC that was prompted when another member used a homophobic slur: "Others were just trying to correct the person, telling them, you know, 'that's not right, what you said.'" The offender realized why his comment was hurtful, Allen said, and "he started regretting what he said." Ideally, the process repairs the harm and educates the offender and the rest of the group. Allen added, "the healing circle was just trying to talk about what just happened together as a group, and not leaving anyone behind." And Alicia, a two-year veteran who had once been an offender, spoke highly of the process as well: "I feel accountability could be very unhealthy and very toxic, but I feel accountability can happen in a really healthy way, right?" Noticing that Alicia was creating tension among members, staff encouraged the hurt parties to speak honestly about how they were feeling. Alicia recalled the outcome:

> This last summer they held me accountable in a very transformative way. We sat in a circle, they shared what they felt and how they'd been feeling, [and] it was very beautiful to me. Easily they could have just called me out on social media and made a big scene . . . easily. But no, they were willing to sit in circle, and they were willing to express how they'd been feeling, and I think for me it's been enough.

Alicia believed that the discussion improved relationships among the . group and is now using lessons about the process with her non-ROC friends and family members. The group accountability structure she learned in the healing circles helped her become a better communicator. Arguably, restorative justice and other community-building activities also contributed to groups' abilities to stay united as they engaged in collective political action.

The Challenges of Addressing Youths' Emotions

Youth organizing staff recognized that attending to members' mental health and well-being can be difficult. First, responding to their emotional needs and trauma can be overwhelming for staff. Given their intense involvement in members' daily lives, young staff often say they may become emotionally exhausted. While ROC encouraged its staff to engage in self-care and take time off as necessary, they sometimes found it difficult to take these necessary breaks because they felt responsible for successfully training leaders, guiding campaigns, and attending to youths' well-being. They thus often put themselves at risk of burnout.

Second, when not carefully facilitated, healing circles can potentially further traumatize young people and exacerbate emotional hardship, as interviewees and other California informants noted. This happened with youth who were survivors of physical or sexual abuse, had experience with the criminal justice system, or had suffered other forms of trauma. Staff rarely possessed the clinical training to address such trauma, and they often tried to refer youth to culturally sensitive therapists and other trauma professionals. However, such supports were rarely available at a reasonable cost in these high-poverty communities. In worst-case scenarios, staff reported instances of abuse to Child Protective Services, which did not necessarily guarantee a successful resolution because the child welfare system grapples with inadequate resources and intersects with the criminal justice system.[60]

Third, groups like ROC can struggle with finding enough time to adequately implement healing and wellness practices alongside other aspects of programming, including other developmental supports (such as tutoring, college readiness sessions, and workforce development training sessions). After all, attending to young people's emotions and other developmental needs represents just one facet of the often time-consuming work needed to support adolescents in leading well-coordinated and strategic grassroots campaigns. Achieving the right balance across different program activities can be difficult, requiring staff to continuously assess members' needs and capacities in relation to campaign demands.

Emotional Well-Being and Sustaining Civic Action

As agents of adolescents' transformative political socialization, youth organizing groups incorporated a range of healing, self-care, and wellness activities into their programming. They offered curricula, coordinated healing circles, engaged members in breathing or other exercises, practiced restorative justice to address conflicts, and hosted other activities that promoted emotional well-being. These interventions can contribute to socio-emotional learning and neurobiological adaptations that enhance resilience.[61] They can also make the process of political organizing enjoyable as adolescents strengthen their networks of support and develop a sense of community. Grounded in youths' cultural identities and connected to campaigns to challenge systemic inequalities, youth organizing groups' approaches to wellness can also inspire hope.[62] As such, healing, self-care, and wellness practices are an important component of building adolescents' affective capacities to lead.

This chapter featured ROC in Santa Ana as an illustrative example of how groups set aside time to attend to members' mental health and well-being. Adapting to the localized political context of Orange County, ROC centered the healthy development of young people who were growing up in a county with a history of criminalizing youth and immigrants. ROC's programming enabled members to reflect on their gendered experiences as adolescents, process difficult events, resolve interpersonal conflicts, and deal with stress in healthy ways. Healing and self-care activities helped young members feel better about the challenges and hardships they encountered, large and small, and strengthened ties with mentors and peers.

As ROC prompted members to attend to their own well-being, they also promoted the well-being of the whole collective through restorative justice and community-building activities. Importantly, ROC linked healing and wellness activities to their campaigns; the group sought to dismantle the school-to-prison-to-deportation pipeline, which contributed to the emotional hardships and trauma that some Santa Ana youth experienced in the first place. ROC's work demonstrates how healing and self-care, when tied to political action, can contribute to broader community change.

Healing, self-care, and other wellness activities can help young people maintain their commitment to fighting for change in their communities. During the COVID-19 pandemic and 2020 racial uprising, Citlali, twenty-two years old and no longer a member of ROC, remained deeply involved in politics. While supporting her family through illness and financial struggles, she coordinated mutual aid efforts and organized protests in support of the Movement for Black Lives. To avoid burnout and mitigate stress, she relied on the healing and self-care strategies she had learned as an adolescent. "I had to make time for myself," she said, which sometimes meant disconnecting from digital media and stopping work after intense flurries of activity. When she was really overwhelmed, she would do breathing exercises. Having developed a tight network of friends, she also participated in online healing circles in which fellow organizers discussed how they were managing their heavy workload and coping with illness and the loss of loved ones. "I felt stuck, like I wasn't doing enough," she recalled, but "connecting with community helped." Throughout the challenging pandemic and racial reckoning, healing and self-care played a central role in the online youth organizing gatherings I observed and discussions I had with youth leaders. "Sometimes you need to take a step back to take care of yourself, but fighting to make things better is also part of the healing process," Citlali said, echoing the words of many others I spoke to across the state.

The next chapter elaborates on the critical civics education curriculum that exposes 1.5- and second-generation youth to intersectional understandings of power and inequality. Like ROC members in Santa Ana, Oakland youth gained an awareness of complex group histories as they learned to form political coalitions.

= Chapter 6 =

"Know Yo' History, Know Yo' Self": Youth Organizing and Critical Civics Education in Multiracial Oakland

D AVID PHAN's mother worked in a nail salon and had no formal education. His father was a deliveryman whose primary education was disrupted by the war in Vietnam, his native country. Neither David's parents nor his grandmother ever told him about the circumstances that caused them to leave Vietnam or about the challenges they faced on arriving in the United States. Rather, he learned about how and why his family and other Vietnamese refugees came to Oakland through workshops led by AYPAL. After this education, he came to see himself not simply as an American but as a Vietnamese American, claiming, "I'm more proud of my identity and my culture." AYPAL workshops, David added,

> helped me a lot in terms of just being more proud of my background, having respect for my culture and for myself. Learning your history also makes you want to make things better for your community, you know? After learning all that we have been through, not just during the war, but also here in Oakland, it makes you want to continue working to improve things.

One interactive exercise that AYPAL used to expose members to the experiences of first-generation refugees made a particular impression on David. The exercise split participants into small groups representing a family unit, and then gave each group a scenario in which they had to flee their war-ravaged country:

> For example, you might have to make your way from one end of a lake to the other to escape. So what do you do? And they give us three options.

The title of this chapter comes from a phrase coined by AYPAL leaders.

https://doi.org/10.7758/gert1126.2146

> The first one is you swim. The second one is you try to dig out a path and try to get out the other end. Or number three, you figure out [that] since people have a small boat, half of the family can go on the boat and half of them can stay and wait for more help. And then after we made all those decisions, we hear what happens, whether some people may have died from drowning or people may have been killed if they stayed on and they didn't go over to the other side.

The exercise was followed by a group discussion about the challenges their parents and grandparents might have actually experienced as they fled their home countries:

> That was really, really impactful for all the youth to understand that, and it was really empowering and really emotional. I still think about it to this day, because it's still relevant. So I think that's really important to understand the history even though it's bad. It's good to understand and use it as a way to uplift each other and say, "Hey, we're really resilient."

AYPAL workshops covered different refugee experiences—for example, the genocide in Cambodia, the secret war in Laos, and the war in Vietnam. In addition, members learned about the Filipinx, Chinese, Korean, Samoan, and Tongan American experiences, while other workshops covered the experiences of other racial or ethnic groups, immigrant rights issues, gender roles, and LGBTQ+ identities.

AYPAL is not the only group that addresses members' ethnic or racial group histories and identities in preparing members for civic leadership roles. Youth Together (YT), also located in Oakland, similarly centers members' identities and communities as part of its critical civics education. But unlike AYPAL, which primarily serves ethnically diverse groups joined under the single panethnic racial category of Asian American Pacific Islander, YT prioritizes building bridges among racially diverse non-white groups. This chapter features AYPAL and YT as two illustrative cases of how youth organizing groups variously incorporate identity, power, and privilege as part of the transformative political socialization process.

In this chapter, I examine how a critical civics education introduces 1.5- and second-generation youth organizing group members to issues of diversity while also shaping their understanding of social and community issues. Through interactive workshops like the one David described, youth organizing encouraged members to take pride in their multiple identities and promoted solidarity as they tackled shared concerns. Groups prompted their members to analyze their similarities and differences with other racialized groups, a process that lends itself to coalition building. Moreover, programming on gender and LGBTQ issues introduced members to intersectional understandings of power, privilege, and racial and other inequalities. In sum, their programming oriented their members toward a multiracial democracy; that is, groups encouraged cross-racial understanding and solidarity in addressing issues of shared concern while also being attentive to other forms of power and privilege.[1]

The Bay Area: An Immigrant Gateway with a Civil Rights History

As with other youth organizing groups, local demographics and political dynamics informed AYPAL's and YT's curricula. Oakland is part of the greater San Francisco Bay Area, a historic gateway for immigrants and refugees, particularly those from Asia, Mexico, and Central America.[2] The region also has a sizable community of African and North African migrants. New migrants from the Global South settled alongside more established African American residents, eventually outnumbering them in some neighborhoods.

While demographics have shifted dramatically over the past several decades, African Americans have had an important influence on the culture and politics of the region. Drawn to the region's growing shipbuilding industry during World War II and postwar manufacturing jobs, their population grew significantly between the 1940s and 1960s. Redlining and other racist housing practices, however, often confined African Americans to certain moderate-to-low-income neighborhoods in San Francisco, Oakland, Richmond, and Berkeley, areas where future immigrants would eventually settle because they were relatively affordable.[3] The demographics of residents younger than thirty reflect this history of migration and urban succession: Latinx youth compose the plurality (30 percent) by a slight margin in the most populous counties of Alameda, San Francisco, Contra Costa, and Santa Clara. Ethnically diverse Asian American Pacific Islanders (AAPIs) make up 28 percent of the population. Meanwhile, white youth make up 27 percent, and the remaining identify as black (6 percent), Native American (2 percent), or some other race (7 percent), with this last group including individuals of multiracial, North African, and West Asian ancestry.[4]

Economic inequality, which has grown increasingly extreme since the 1990s, characterizes this racially and ethnically diverse region.[5] The tech boom (concentrated in the Silicon Valley), alongside the expansion of other industries like biotechnology and business services, contributed to a rapid increase in both high- and low-wage jobs.[6] During this growth, the immigrants, refugees, and African Americans who dispro-portionately occupied the lower ends of the economic spectrum expe-rienced economic hardship, particularly as housing costs skyrocketed.[7]

In Oakland, with its relatively high concentration of both established and newer youth organizing groups, racial and class disparities are visible and pronounced. The city is split between the hills—idyllic, quiet neighborhoods (such as Montclair) with mostly affluent residents—and the flats, where people of color are often crowded in substan-dard housing. Poverty has long been a problem in the flats—but the tech boom and corresponding housing shortage exacerbated racial economic disparities and the displacement of racially diverse lower-income residents. This heightened social and economic inequality can exacerbate ethnic and racial tensions, particularly in communities experiencing an influx of new immigrants.[8] As such, youth organiz-ing groups have had to be mindful of how economic disparities might contribute to prejudice and tensions, particularly among the groups most impacted by economic hardships.

Legacies of Multiracial and Inclusive Organizing

While the Bay Area is home to many new arrivals from all over the world, it also has a decades-long legacy of multiracial, LGBTQ-inclusive, and leftist politics that have helped define the local context in which youth organizing groups orient their members to political activity. Racial justice, immigrant, LGBTQ, and feminist movements in the area have worked independently on their own campaigns, as well as supporting each other's causes or collaborating on shared issues.[9] For example, the AIDS activism of the 1970s and 1980s included prominent activists of color working within or alongside the local women's and gay libera-tion movements.[10] Furthermore, Oakland's Black Panther Party, seeking to promote racial and economic justice for all oppressed peoples, relied on multiracial solidarity to form alliances with similar organizations, such as the predominantly Mexican American UFW and the radical Red Guard Party, a Chinese American organization. And finally, the local move-ment against the war in Vietnam was also multiracial.[11] These early multi-racial organizing efforts paved the way for the 1980s Rainbow Coalition and other multiracial political efforts.

In the 1960s, and to varying degrees throughout the rest of the twentieth century, the region's college campuses were a hotbed of progressive sociopolitical activities. As part of the Third World Liberation Front, for example, students at San Francisco State and the University of California, Berkeley, staged widespread and successful demonstrations in the late 1960s that resulted in the establishment of ethnic studies programs.[12]

Racially diverse students also supported efforts to free Black Panther activists Huey P. Newton and Angela Davis from jail.[13] These students strove to raise awareness about the various plights of people of color in the United States, including the incarceration of activists. In doing so, they also connected U.S. wars abroad to domestic racial and economic issues—a theme that remains important to understanding U.S. migration today.[14]

This multiracial, anti-imperialist organizing overlapped with the 1980s and early 1990s sanctuary movements, which demanded asylum for victims of political violence and an end to U.S. government interventions in Central America. As a result of this activism, San Francisco, Oakland, and Berkeley eventually declared themselves sanctuary cities, vowing that refugees would be safe from detainment and deportation.[15]

Writing about Bay Area youth organizing at the turn of the twenty-first century, Andreana Clay notes that the youth she observed were "expected to organize in the shadow of previous social movement activists."[16] Clay's observation demonstrates the lasting impact these local movements have had on Bay Area youth organizing groups. Established by movement leaders of an earlier generation, these groups largely serve newer waves of immigrants and refugees. Exceptions include groups that primarily target African American and Native American youth.

Bay Area Youth Organizing in the Twenty-First Century

Bay Area youth organization groups advance a transformative political socialization that encourages its members to learn from the legacies of twentieth-century and contemporaneous movements. In the 2010s, Bay Area groups continued to incorporate local twentieth-century movements into their curricula. Groups also borrowed from strategies of local immigrant youth and Black Lives Matter efforts. In doing so, they tailored their workshops and related activities to ethnically diverse local demographics.

This chapter primarily leverages data gathered from two Oakland groups: AYPAL and YT. Founded in 1998, AYPAL initially sought to address gang activity, truancy, and substance abuse issues among low-income AAPI youth, while YT was founded in 1996 in response to interracial violence. While AYPAL targeted ethnically diverse AAPI adolescents, YT explicitly sought to ensure racial diversity among its members. As further detailed in the appendix, my analysis primarily relies on forty-eight interviews, twenty-four from each group. I focus on these two groups that have regularly updated and refined their curricula to incorporate contemporary youth members' experiences and perspectives; yet issues of identity, diversity, and social inequality are a key component of many adolescent youth organizing groups, as evidenced in other chapters of this volume and prior studies on these groups.[17]

Centering Race and Ethnicity in Critical Civics Education Programming

In addressing race and racial differences in their programming, most youth organizing groups seek to counteract negative stereotypes about, and retell the histories of, racialized minorities in ways that motivate members to challenge racial hierarchies. Most do not merely attend to the experience of one racialized group in isolation. Rather, they tend to adopt what Natalia Molina and colleagues call a "relational approach" to racial dynamics. That is, members learn to understand racialization processes of non-whites not only in "relation to whiteness, but also to other devalued and marginalized groups."[18] To this end, youth organizing groups typically conduct peer-facilitated interactive workshops and informal discussions that explore the experiences of racialized groups in the United States.

The curricula of youth organizing groups tend to overlap. Many groups introduce members to key concepts like the "isms and phobias" (racism, sexism, xenophobia, homophobia, and transphobia) as well as other critical terms related to societal structures (such as white supremacy, patriarchy, and imperialism). Additionally, curricula include technical terms relevant to campaigns that can vary widely (for example, gentrification, local control funding formula, community benefits agreements, environmental impact reviews, stay of deportation, and sanctuary cities) and explanations of government decision-making processes. In my observations over the past couple of decades, I noticed that curricula evolved as adolescent members integrated their own lived experiences, contemporary events, and concerns from their schools and communities, as well as elements of youth culture, into lesson plans. The popular education approaches to the civics curriculum, though not entirely defined by members, allow them to play a significant role in codesigning workshops, discussions, and interactive activities.

At AYPAL and YT, peer-to-peer activities played an important role in how members understood each other's ethnic backgrounds. "It's impactful to learn from your friends about their histories and all they have gone through. It sticks with you, not like the stuff you learn at school," said David. In both groups, the curriculum prompted young people to collectively explore their own racial or ethnic groups' struggles as well as those of their peers of different backgrounds. AYPAL youth organizer Aian Mendoza described the curriculum as follows:

> At the core, it gives young folks a starting point for social justice and political education, and with that, a strong understanding of themselves and their histories. It's easier to understand those connections between white supremacy [and] capitalism when you're able to connect it back to yourself and your family. Once they are able to see that it's personally able to affect them in their own lives and how it's affected them, the folks around them, and their broader communities, then it's easier to understand other people's struggles. It's not just me, it's the larger BIPOC [black, Indigenous, and people of color], queer, undocumented community that's being affected by injustices.

At YT, members familiarized themselves with and adapted curricular units for audiences that vary in age from thirteen to eighteen and come from different demographic compositions. Tony Douangviseth, YT's executive director and the son of Lao refugees, explained, "It's not just one subset of folks that we need to organize, and so our programming has a theme around 'know yo' history, know yo' self,'" which echoes a refrain attributed to AYPAL, a longtime partner in coalition campaigns and other efforts. Speaking to YT's curriculum, he added:

> We start by focusing [on the fact] that people come from all of these ethnic backgrounds, and that's how we start to build solidarity across all these demographic groups. We really have them understand our different journeys, the past and the present, and let them know that they're gonna shape the future. . . . So we start out with . . . African American history or the black history. We also do units on SWANA [South Western Asian North African], Latinx, and [AAPIs]. We use the curriculum that recognizes the diversity within these groups. At the same time, our curriculum is about how systems of oppression, including xenophobia and immigration laws, impact folks of color and highlight the importance of solidarity work, how we need to show up for each other.

In exposing each other to similarities and differences across various racial or ethnic histories and struggles, AYPAL and YT members (along with those of many other groups) learned to leverage an understanding of diverse ethnic or racial group experiences and structural analyses of inequalities to build informed, multiracial alliances. Zakiya Luna describes this approach as embracing "sameness among differences" and "differences among sameness"—the former recognizing commonalities among ethnicities and the latter attending to their differences (including power differentials). According to Luna, the same-difference strategy differentiates a larger collective from external others and subsumes internal power differences to emphasize shared political goals.[19] In this vein, AYPAL and YT developed panethnic collective identities, as well as a broader identity as people of color. This same-difference logic, according to Luna, facilitates solidarity by framing people with similar ethnic characteristics as united through their differences from an other group. Luna argues that same-difference is about the cognitive comfort that derives from a sense that one belongs to, and is recognized by, an imagined community.

Meanwhile, the same-difference strategy also allowed groups to expand their ranks, build political power, pool resources, and ultimately resist marginalization. Yet in highlighting similarities, there is a danger of overlooking internal differences and possibly ignoring tensions or reproducing certain forms of privilege among these differently marginalized groups. Consequently, AYPAL and YT steered members away from homogenizing different immigrant, refugee, and other racialized groups by using a difference-in-sameness strategy that recognizes how youth can experience inequality differently than their peers. This included drawing attention to differences among ethnic groups that were similarly racialized (for example, Salvadoran versus Mexican, Vietnamese versus Lao). This difference-in-sameness logic avoided glossing over intergroup tensions and prompted continual questioning about power differentials in an effort to avoid reproducing internal inequality.[20]

While youth organizing groups shared this general strategy vis-à-vis identity, the depth and specificity of their curricula varied. For example, AYPAL's members could often articulate differences in the experiences of diverse AAPI ethnicities, as well as a broad understanding of the experiences of other racial and ethnic groups. Meanwhile YT members tended to be well-versed in their own ethnic and family histories, while also being able to share a general analysis of the experiences of black, Latinx, AAPI (and sometimes SWANA) panethnic groups in the United States.

Interestingly, few white students participated in California's youth organizing groups, AYPAL and YT included—in part because these organizations tended to serve racially and economically segregated communities. For example, during the 2019–2020 school year, white youth made up 8 percent of the public high school students in Oakland but only 1 to 3 percent of students in some of the high schools from which youth were recruited.[21] As such, organizing groups rarely included programming on whiteness or how to grapple with power dynamics among white and non-white youth. Rather, the consistent objective of the workshops in YT, AYPAL, and many other groups was to instill ethnic pride and to promote solidity among groups experiencing various forms of marginalization in an ethnically and racially diverse context.

The Development of Racial or Ethnic Pride as a Politicizing Process

When David joined AYPAL in the eighth grade, he was a typical adolescent whose friends "liked to hang out, shoot hoops, and eat." He wasn't thinking too much about his Vietnamese background, but AYPAL changed that: "I feel it was so impactful for me to learn about my culture, you know? It's not just, 'oh, we're Vietnamese, and we eat phở.' There's a lot more to our history, our culture. So, having that knowledge and having the information to kind of talk about my culture made me proud of it." Like David, members of California's youth organizing groups tended to develop ethnic pride and a desire to invest in their communities.

Curricula typically inspired members to promote their ethnic community's culture and social well-being. For example, Jared, a Mien American AYPAL member whose parents fled the U.S.-backed war in Laos, became highly motivated after learning about the area's history of AAPI activism:

> The Chinese, they've been here for like two hundred years. And you know, the organized Japanese have been here for like fifty to a hundred years, and they're organizing. Filipinos, same thing too. But you know, Mien, we've only been here thirty-four years. Like [the] first generation, they're just trying to survive. It's really the youth that are really getting involved and being politically conscious. . . . I really want to keep the Mien culture going, the Mien language going.

Additionally, Jared also wanted to address issues of educational equity and community violence that affect Mien and other Oakland youth.

As the children of immigrants, many of the young people in this study did not necessarily start out with much knowledge about their own racial or ethnic group's history and political struggles in the United States. Take, for example, Adriana, a YT member whose parents emigrated from Mexico and settled in the racially diverse Fruitvale neighborhood of Oakland. "I was born here. I felt like I grew up American," she explained. Adriana never reflected much on her Mexican heritage, even though she spoke Spanish and occasionally connected with family members in Mexico. To some degree, this may have been a function of her age; she joined YT when she was fifteen. Adolescents develop a more complex sense of self as they grow older.[22] At the same time, U.S. cultural representations may have also shaped Adriana's views of her ethnicity. "A lot of Mexicans, the way that we see ourselves, is very jaded," she asserted. Mexicans typically occupy the lower ends of the socioeconomic spectrum, and despite being the largest ethnic category in California, they remain largely invisible in mainstream culture. Mexicans have long been the targets of labor exploitation, racial profiling, and other forms of racial exclusion.[23] Since the mid-2010s, Mexicans have endured escalating hostility, following Donald Trump's vitriolic rhetoric criminalizing immigrants. Dehumanizing or negative public discourse about an ethnic or racial group can affect how members perceive themselves and their community.[24]

Adriana developed a greater awareness of her ethnic background and the racial exclusions Mexicans face after she joined YT and participated in workshops about the history of Mexico and Mexican Americans in the United States. "I learned more about Indigenous people and how a modern-day Mexican came to be, how we are a mixed people of European descent and indigenous descent, and that's when I wanted to do a deep dive into understanding my roots," she said. Adriana also recalled learning about colonization, economic disparities between the United States and Mexico, and immigration policies that block pathways to citizenship for families like her own. Additionally, she was inspired by the Mexican artistic tradition and by the history of the UFW and Chicano resistance, so she started to read more about these subjects on her own and bolstering her ethnic pride. "I'm so proud of being Mexican!" she exclaimed.

Salvador, a Mexican American YT member, developed a similar sense of purpose by becoming more aware of his ethnic group's history, culture, and contributions. He learned about, and occasionally met, elders who had long fought to protect the rights of the Latinx community. Salvador claimed that these experiences gave him "a lot self-pride—a lot of cultural pride, and a whole different identity for myself and a different way of thinking." He added: "I think about how . . . I will contribute to social justice, or to a better world." Having once been on the verge of dropping out of high school and joining a gang, Salvador became inspired to make a positive difference. "YT taught us a different way to fight—with our mind, with our voices, with our actions and not with violence," he explained. Salvador's experience aligned with research finding that interventions celebrating the identities of minoritized people can positively alter the trajectories of at-risk youth, channeling their energy to community uplift.[25] As such, ethnic studies curricula support positive racial identity development, help develop a sense of purpose, and inspire hope among second-generation youth whose communities continue to experience the lasting impacts of slavery and colonialization.[26]

Promoting Cross-Racial and Panethnic Solidarity

Building power often requires young people to cultivate multi-ethnic and multiracial alliances. To this end, programming that takes a relational approach, highlighting both shared struggles and distinct histories, can help strengthen bonds of solidarity among diverse youth.

Emphasizing Shared Struggles

Groups oriented their curricular activities toward developing multi-ethnic and multiracial understanding. "AYPAL did a really good job in making sure we had solidarity with all the other people of color," David recalled of his experiences as a member. Beyond the extensive curriculum about Southeast Asian experiences, David also learned about the history of Chinese Americans and Filipinos from his peers at AYPAL, while staff and guest speakers gave presentations on the history of African Americans and Latinxs:

> We talked about the history of racism against black people; we talked about our Latino brothers and sisters, and did a lot of racism workshops. We talked about how we can be a better ally or how can we throw away those stereotypes and prejudices we have about other groups, so we can be able to come together and support each other.

Youth and adult-led discussions, workshops, and activities centering other cultures—and the challenges they face—facilitated racially diverse political coalitions.

Interviews with AYPAL and YT alumni members suggest that ethnic studies workshops and activities allow youth to comprehend how other groups share the race-related struggles of their own groups. Like many of his peers, David could articulate how different ethnicities experienced similar inequality and oppression. For example, he spoke about how Latinx, black, and AAPI youth in his neighborhood attended under-resourced schools, lacked easy access to healthy food, and encountered housing instability. Through workshops, youth also deepened their understanding of group differences, facilitating informed alliances. In other words, they developed more nuanced understandings of how non-white groups might vary in terms of power and privilege. As a high school student, for example, David learned about the legacy of slavery and anti-black racism that continues to uniquely affect black Americans, and about the harm done by stereotyping AAPIs as perpetual foreigners or model minorities. And while he understood that some Asian immigrants also face blocked pathways to citizenship, he knew that broken U.S. immigration policies disproportionately tear apart Latinx families. Thus, the curriculum of AYPAL and YT instilled within members a relational understanding of race, encouraging their members to think about how contextually defined racialization processes manifest in overlapping and varying ways.[27]

As part of the transformative political socialization process, youth organizing groups encouraged members to share their understandings of overlapping political struggles. Youth leaders often took what they learned about their own background as a reference point for connecting with others. Hao, a Vietnamese American AYPAL member, clearly articulated the link between learning about her own identity and understanding the experiences of others: "The most important thing that I learned would be the history of my family . . . because knowing my history definitely puts a lot of things into perspective. It gave me a better understanding of other people in my community. And I thought it would be beneficial to learn about everybody." Hao eagerly participated in AYPAL's peer-to-peer and other ethnic studies workshops, which enhanced her understanding of her diverse Oakland community: "I realized how America had an impact on how some groups were affected by wars, some were torn apart, or not torn apart. And others didn't have [to experience] wars, but they had another thing happen [to them]." Indeed, AYPAL's curriculum outlined how U.S. wars and economic interventions connected to the enslavement and displacement of people from Asia, Latin America, and Africa and their eventual, sometimes forced, migration to the United States. Its approach reflected that of 1970s movement leaders who sought to create collective identities among diverse AAPI ethnicities. According to Christina Mora and Dina Okamoto, these earlier civil rights activists emphasized the ways in which imperialism and its colonial manifestations have had lasting economic, political, and cultural implications for ethnically diverse AAPIs.[28]

Besides providing in-depth information about different AAPI backgrounds, AYPAL's curriculum also offered structural explanations for the marginalization of AAPIs, Latinxs, and blacks relative to whites, illustrating why people of color have a shared vested interest in collectively addressing racial inequality. As Charlene, a Filipina American member, explained, AYPAL members discussed how "there are so many parallels in the experiences of [AAPI] folks, blacks, and Latinx. All of our communities deal with colorism, so that the lighter skinned you are, the more opportunities you get." She later added that at AYPAL meetings, members would share poverty-related issues faced by their families, and this allowed her to understand that in Oakland's lower-income flatland neighborhoods, "people of all races were stressed out by the high rents and not always having food to eat." Group discussions also covered shared concerns across racial lines, and members often agreed on the necessity of multiracial alliances to work toward mutually beneficial solutions. Charlene echoed the perspective of many of her peers, saying, "Unity is needed to fight police brutality, fix the immigration issues, get better jobs, and damn, just about everything. We need those coalitions, not just on one issue, but all of the issues that affect our communities." To this end, AYPAL youth joined a broad range of multiracial coalitions to address a range of shared concerns. For example,

AYPAL members actively supported the Movement for Black Lives and the push to hold the Oakland police force accountable for unjust policing practices. Adolescent members also turned out to support diverse coalitions to address access to translation services and other immigrant rights causes.

Like the youth in AYPAL, YT members took part in and contributed to a critical civics curriculum that deepened their own and others' understandings of race and ethnicity while highlighting commonalities across different groups. And similar to AYPAL members, those in YT developed their appreciation of their own ethnic backgrounds as they sought out connections with those from other backgrounds. Celia's experience was typical: "The program was really good for [reminding me] about who I am and where my family comes from, where my roots are, and they've also taught me how to communicate with people from other cultures." Celia developed ties to other Latinx ethnicities, especially through discussion spaces explicitly reserved for Latinx students, which helped her learn from her peers about their experiences:

> Both my parents are from Honduras, and we have our traditions, but it was just really important to learn about other Latino cultures and experiences. Because a lot of the Youth Together participants were Mexican, our upbringing, our values, and traditions were things that we always discussed as a group. So in having these discussions and being able to sit with them face-to-face, we were able to kind of draw out all the similarities and differences. I feel like there was just a common struggle and a common understanding of what it meant to be a person of Latinx descent in the U.S.

While Celia had many Latinx friends growing up, she did not know much about the specificities of their histories or culture. It wasn't until she joined YT that she noted similarities in how they were perceived and treated in the U.S. context. Adriana, who was quoted earlier, reported similar responses to YT programming. As a Mexican American who had previously assumed that most of her Latinx peers were of Mexican descent, she recalled, "I didn't know anything about Central Americans or about South America. I learned so much more about Latino countries I had no idea about." In hearing from her peers, Adriana internalized the importance of being "inclusive to all Latinos."

Thus, in creating different affinity spaces for students whose ancestors hailed from different regions of the world—Latin America, North Africa and the Middle East, sub-Saharan Africa, and Asia—YT encouraged panethnic identity development. As such, its curriculum built on the work of earlier civil rights leaders, while at the same time responding to the contemporary demographic make-up and ethnic origins of current immigrants. Importantly, panethnic labels lend themselves to shared narratives around racialized identities.[29]

On the surface, it may seem like these affinity spaces could have contributed to the self-segregation along racial lines that already occurs in schools.[30] As Celia noted, "I know that during high school, in a way . . . people stuck to what they were comfortable with—like you had the Latinos stick with the Latinos, most of the Asians were with the Asians, and so forth." However, these separate spaces also served to build bridges. Research shows that a positive view of one's own racial group can result in more sympathetic and understanding views of other groups.[31] As Celia suggested, YT's activities sought to increase understanding of groups whose stories remained invisible within the dominant culture:

> We had these discussions where the U.S. education tends to erase the voices and narratives of black Americans and other individuals of different ethnic backgrounds. We talked a lot about the Asian Pacific Islander communities, since they are also a very well-represented demographic at Skyline [High School]. There were a lot of Chinese students as well, specifically Cantonese Chinese-speaking students. Then there were also a lot of Vietnamese as well. We hosted Poly events [reflecting the different Polynesian cultures]. So we made sure to touch the different ethnic groups that really represented Skyline and who we interact with on a daily basis. So we definitely tried to reassure our community that there are these individuals who are very active, in terms of all of these different movements and kind of just shift the narrative from this Euro-centric perspective.

By centering the backgrounds of second-generation and other non-white peers, YT members contributed to alternative or complementary narratives not always accessible to the children of immigrants. YT's program helped Jimmy, a 1.5-generation immigrant from Taiwan who was still adjusting to life in the United States, connect with and understand others. "I'm more aware," he explained, "because where I came from, which is Taiwan, we're not very diverse."

In YT, second-generation members educated their nonimmigrant (mostly black and mixed-race) peers about their own backgrounds. Dennis, a self-defined mixed-race African American man with some Native American and Chinese ancestry, appreciated the mutual exchange among members: "I learned history, and not just about myself but about other people and how it affects me. So when we talk about the Filipino community or the Latino community or any other community, we have been influenced by each other in so many different ways."

AYPAL and YT members grew to identify beyond their ethnic and panethnic groups, acquiring broader identities as people of color, or

BIPOC. As a Filipino American, Patrick noted how his peers at AYPAL helped him with "seeing past Filipino issues, seeing the broader people of color issues and how those issues affect us the same or differently." Meanwhile, one Nigerian American member of YT was committed to grassroots organizing with a focus on people of color. When it came to YT's campaigns, members generally understood that policy solutions (such as increasing funding for schools) were designed to benefit diverse residents. In this way, second-generation immigrant youth in Oakland learned to identify with peers of different races occupying the lower echelons of the economic ladder, coming to embrace multiracial solidarity as part of a transformative political socialization.

Sensitizing Members to Intergroup Inequalities

In developing their members' shared collective identities, AYPAL and YT also encouraged their members to recognize the varying experiences of non-whites. For example, AYPAL members developed a nuanced understanding of the challenges and histories of the ethnicities widely represented in their diverse AAPI membership. In addition to describing the longer historical context for Chinese and Filipinx migration to the United States, the curriculum made clear how U.S. involvement in late twentieth-century wars in Southeast Asia paved the way for the flight of Lao, Vietnamese, and Cambodian refugees to the United States, and more specifically to the historically African American neighborhoods of Oakland. Through interactive and informative workshops and activities, members educated peers about the circumstances behind each ethnic group's exit from its country of origin and its corresponding trajectory in the United States.

Cindy, the daughter of Vietnamese refugees, recalled learning about the secret war in Laos, the reign of the Khmer Rouge in Cambodia, and the distinct cultural traditions of peers hailing from those countries: "It makes you realize you can still be ignorant. I definitely was able to appreciate . . . Mien and Lao culture and Cambodian culture [through AYPAL] because I grew up very sheltered. As a person of color, I'm still privileged in a certain way compared to my peers." Cindy learned about the PTSD experienced by Cambodian refugees who survived their country's genocide and about the extreme cultural dissonance and loss experienced by Lao refugees from Indigenous mountain tribes. Cambodian and Lao refugees arrived in the United States with fewer educational resources, she learned, and received less U.S. resettlement assistance compared with Vietnamese refugees.[32] Cindy thus came to understand why her Cambodian and Mien peers experienced greater levels of gang violence, extreme poverty, and other hardships when compared with her Vietnamese peers.

YT's curriculum took a somewhat different approach, opting not to offer in-depth workshops on specific ethnicities, national origin, or broader racialized groups. Reflecting the organization's original mission to address anti-racial violence, Jairo, a Mexican American student, noted: "Getting people to understand that we have similar struggles was the number one [priority]." At the same time, members avoided homogenizing group experiences. "We would talk about our different histories, or different experiences, and we learned to see things from others' perspective, and what other people have had to go through in this country."

In this regard, a workshop on stereotypes, a longtime staple of the YT curriculum, was particularly effective. As Jairo described it, "We talk about stereotypes of different groups, and how they affect us, how we buy into these stereotypes about ourselves and each other." When asked to elaborate, he shared: "We talked about how people think that an Asian person would never struggle in school because they are always super smart, and they will all become doctors or dentists, automatically." In essence, youth facilitators unpacked for their peers what is referred to as the model minority myth.[33] Drawing on the experiences of some peers, the group "talked about how with Asian American students, if they weren't doing good at school, they might skip school, sometimes they become gang affiliated. They simply would give up. The school ignored them if they didn't fit the stereotype." Jairo then elaborated on how stereotypes could also discourage black and Latinx youth from pursuing college and careers that required a college education; while racist assumptions about criminality closed many doors for black youth, assumptions about the precarious legal status and work preferences constrained educational options for Latinx youth. Jairo gestured toward a way forward: "At YT, you learn to identify those different patterns, but you also learn to fight against them, or how to stand up for one another, how to educate more people about them, right?"

Notably, YT and AYPAL, like many other youth organizing groups across the state and country, maintained connections to the contemporaneous Black Lives Matter and immigrant rights movements. These grassroots groups prepared second-generation Latinx and AAPI youth to counter anti-blackness within their own communities.[34] Members also shared sympathetic viewpoints on the experiences of undocumented immigrants with their parents and ethnic communities. These conversations weren't always easy, sometimes leaving members frustrated. Yet the conversations compelled them, as adolescents who had developed strong moral convictions about justice, to serve as allies to those most affected by anti-black racism and immigration issues.[35]

At YT, these discussions sensitized African American and mixed-race nonimmigrant members to the plight of undocumented immigrants. For example, D'Andre, an African American YT member, noted:

> I definitely learned about Latinx students and the immigration stories they shared about getting here. Some were seven years old when their parents made the transition to Oakland or to the United States, and so I got to hear that and really be empathetic to those stories. You know, you become less biased, but also not make jokes about them.

While YT typically did not take the lead on immigrant rights efforts, members sometimes turned out in support of certain initiatives. For example, in 2017 YT members assisted 67 Sueños (an immigrant rights youth group) in staging a day-long workshop and strategizing how to keep undocumented immigrants safe under the Trump administration. Members of YT, AYPAL, and other youth organizing groups, thanks in part to their groups' critical civics curricula, tended to be better informed about local political efforts than the average adolescent, and hence other organizations could more easily recruit them to support allied causes.

Learning About Gender and Sexual Orientation

California's youth organizing groups prioritized racial or ethnic awareness within their curricula, but adolescent members also worked with staff to co-facilitate workshops, discussions, and other activities that raise awareness of issues of gender and sexual orientation. Topics included sexism, homophobia, and transphobia, which typically prompted members to reflect on their own experiences and their interactions with others. As scholars have long noted, an awareness of one form of oppression can translate into an awareness of, and eventual activism around, its other manifestations.[36] This phenomenon was visible among the youth organizing groups I observed.

Efforts to raise awareness about gender and sexuality heightened members' consciousness of how socially constructed identities can contribute to unhealthy or harmful behaviors. For example, David credited AYPAL with teaching him and his peers "how to be comfortable with our masculinity, but also be really respectful, and be an ally for queer folks, women, other people of color." AYPAL helped him stop sexist behaviors: "I was an idiot back then, like in ninth or tenth grade. I'm not going to lie. It took some time to change. I was pretty rude to girls, and I always thought that they were lower than me, and I would talk mean things, just mean." Like David, other young men in AYPAL, YT, and other groups noted that they grew to understand how casual behaviors and homophobic slurs could be hurtful, resolving to improve their treatment of those who did not share their gender or sexual orientation. As David explained, "People used to say 'That's pretty gay,' or worse. Growing up, that was a common thing to do. So I think coming to AYPAL, we did have some folks saying it's not right. So I was able to learn not to use derogatory terms."

Like many California youth organizations, AYPAL and YT offered gender-affinity workshops, allowing members with similar identities to reflect on the gendered expectations, norms, and stereotypes underlying their own attitudes and behavior, as well as those of others. In the early 2010s, these groups largely reinforced the gender binary, but by the end of the decade, adolescent members themselves promoted more fluid understandings of gender. Overall, participants reported that these gender-affinity spaces lent themselves to honest and sometimes difficult—yet constructive—conversations. David, who participated in these gender workshops at a time when groups had not explicitly challenged the gender binary, said that in the men's group, participants discussed how "for guys, you're taught that you always have to be confident, you always have to be hard, to be the alpha." He learned to see himself in a different way as a young man:

> So I think that being at AYPAL, I was able to understand where this behavior was coming from and I had to correct myself. I had to understand that this is not me, and I was just portraying a certain image that society told me to be, not what I want it to be. I had to challenge myself to not conform to negative expectations. I had to get over being afraid of being vulnerable, you know?

Young men at YT also participated in gender-segregated workshops and shared some of the same reflections in interviews. They discussed how gendered expectations could result in sexist and homophobic behavior, while also preventing them from fully expressing their emotions. This reluctance to open up could result in negative mental health outcomes. Everardo, a Latino member of YT, initially resisted this gender-segregated activity: "We're separating the women and the men. I was like, 'Wow, this is so sexist. Don't get me into this macho bull crap. I'm already getting enough toxic masculinity from my pop.'" But then, as the peer-led workshop proceeded, he realized it was the "complete opposite. . . . When we got down to it, it really was a workshop to tear down toxic masculinity." Everardo became sensitized to how gendered norms could be harmful to women and men alike and came to believe that these gender-segregated workshops helped "promote a healthier lifestyle for young men." Apart from lessons on toxic masculinity and gender relations, AYPAL, YT, and some other organizers also hosted workshops focused on how young men are criminalized and experience unfair treatment in school and police harassment.

Workshops for female-identified members typically covered different forms of sexism and how to combat them. Gender-segregated spaces invited young women to discuss gender stereotypes, ethnic and mainstream cultural expectations, sexual harassment and sexist treatment, definitions of feminism, and effective strategies to promote gender equity and challenge gender norms. For Nancy, a mixed-race Southeast Asian and black member of YT, gender-segregated discussions were very empowering, forcing her to question gendered standards of beauty that contributed to her negative body image and eating disorder. During one of these discussions, she found it liberating when she said out loud, "No, I don't need to look like that," referring to dominant beauty standards. Furthermore, discussions helped her defy gendered expectations of normative behavior: "These activities showed me that I was able to define who I wanted to be, and that the woman I was turning into was great. I didn't need to portray society norms," she said. While young women had their own safe space in which to share these issues in confidence, they also often summarized their discussions with young men, hoping to sensitize them to women's experiences and encourage them to act as allies in interpersonal battles against sexism.

Discussions of sexism in its many manifestations sometimes led to greater gender equity within organizing groups themselves, often at the instigation of youth members. Mindy, an AYPAL member, recalled that the girls in her group took action when they realized that the boys were not equally contributing to activities: "We noticed that they would always come late with food or not even participate, not talk during our meetings, nothing. And we finally addressed that." Mindy was pleased that the male staff heard and acted on girls' complaints, making it clear to the boys that "it's constantly the woman standing up and taking accountability for everything, being responsible for everything and them just sitting around." She believed that as a result of this reprimand, and occasional reminders about the importance of gender equity within AYPAL, her male peers gradually increased their contributions to the group.

Adolescent leaders also learned to become advocates for LGBTQ rights. Co-facilitated workshops provided overviews of LGBTQ movements to help demonstrate how activism contributed to greater inclusivity. Both AYPAL and YT staged regular workshops on LGBTQ+ identities that created a safe space for members who identified as queer, questioning, trans, or nonbinary and offered members an education in sexuality and gender identities rarely available in their schools.

As part of the regular curricula at these organizations, members helped facilitate discussions about the meaning and implications of terms like homophobia and heteronormativity (the pervasive cultural assumption that heterosexuality is the only normal or natural expression of sexuality). Facilitators often guided students on how to identify homophobic behaviors and terminology, as well as regular cultural practices that may not be inclusive of those not identifying as straight or heterosexual. Thuan, an AYPAL member, said that these workshops sensitized him to the experiences of his LGBTQ+ peers: "Before, I was really closed-minded about [these issues], but now I'm like more understanding. I have a lot of gay friends now, too." Interviewees sometimes spoke about how they learned to be allies of the LGBTQ+ community by speaking out against homophobic or transphobic behavior within their own ethnic groups and beyond: "AYPAL really brought . . . those issues out for us because we [were] really helping students pinpoint . . . the underlying issue and how can we alleviate that," said Aria, an AYPAL member. Members of YT also reported this growing awareness and ability to confront peers about homophobic or transphobic remarks. Staff also modeled how to confront prejudice in ways that educated, rather than alienated, new recruits.

Before gender inclusivity became a widespread practice in academic and other social circles, staff and experienced adolescent leaders devoted energy to making nonbinary and transgender youth feel welcome as members. By the mid-to-late 2010s, staff and older youth leaders increasingly operated from an understanding that dominant language practices privilege and naturalize cisgender bodies and experiences while erasing trans, nonbinary, and queer identities.[37] For example, through peer-to-peer education, members learned to avoid gendered language like "you guys," recommending the use of gender-neutral terms like "y'all," "folks," or "people" instead. By 2018, members normalized personal introductions that included gender pronouns (for example, she/her/hers, he/him/his, or they/them/theirs) in order to affirm the identities of nonbinary and trans peers. Sometimes youth members introduced the rationale behind this practice to new recruits by explaining that a person's perceived gender may not always conform to how they identify themselves. "That's where I got exposed to gender pronouns first, where people would share their preferred [ones]. It gave me more sensitivity about using people's preferred [pronouns] instead of automatically assigning them one or also using just the gender-neutral one—them, they, them—for when you don't know," said Kalauni, a YT member and Tongan American.

Youth leaders learned to reinforce the use of correct pronouns while recognizing that sometimes people inadvertently made mistakes. As

YT member Adriana noted, peers kindly corrected each other when they misgendered someone, for example by saying: "I'm sorry it's not 'she,' but it's okay. How do we improve from here?" Cisgender members, rather than trans or nonbinary individuals, commonly took responsibility for correcting misgendering when it took place. Queer and trans youth typically reported feeling safe in their youth organizing groups. Indeed, research suggests that using gender-affirming language and avoiding gender-based linguistic assumptions can have an inclusionary impact for queer and trans young people.[38]

Approaching an Intersectional Consciousness

By addressing questions of gender and sexuality, race or ethnicity, and immigration, youth organizing group members engaged in what might be considered multi-identity work.[39] Through workshops, informal discussions, and other activities about diversity, young people learned to think about how different elements of their identity shaped their own and peers' experiences.

These workshops, explained Sally—an ethnically mixed Cambodian, Malaysian, and Chinese member of YT—gave her the tools to succinctly describe how structural forces had shaped her life. The difficulties her father encountered during his resettlement process led to financial challenges throughout Sally's childhood. When asked what she learned at YT about her background, Sally responded:

> There's a stereotype that we're not book smart, we're street smart. I grew up around Southeast Asian folks who gangbang because that's the easy route. So, I think just with the lack of resources that they came with [to the United States], it wasn't easy for them to do better than what the street has to offer.

Her father was a young Cambodian refugee who became involved in gang life. Raised in a high-poverty community, Sally learned how to survive in a tough and sometimes violent neighborhood. At the same time, she said, "I do have my privileges." Reflecting an intersectional understanding of her identity, she recognized that her class background, race, skin color, and gender all combined to shape her experiences. Of her relative privilege, she said:

> I do come off as lighter skinned compared to my dad or many other Cambodian people I know. I am pretty light, and I do feel like because of my skin complexion, I don't feel like I would get discriminated against as much as someone who identifies as black; but being a woman, I do feel like people view me as vulnerable.

Sally represents one example of how curricula raising awareness of legacies of racism, colonization, imperialism, sexism, homophobia, and transphobia spurred youth organizing members to reflect on how their multiple identities overlap to shape their experiences. In other words, the critical civics curriculum prompted adolescent members to think about intersectionality, even though they themselves did not always use the term (or use it precisely as defined by academics). As one fifteen-year-old said to me: "I am oppressed by my intersectionality." Indeed, adolescent members varied in the extent to which they grasped the concept. As research indicates, younger adolescents typically think of their identities as comprising discrete elements, while older adolescents increasingly see their identities as intersecting.[40]

However they processed their various identities, second-generation immigrant youth in groups like AYPAL and YT typically took pride in their racial, immigrant, refugee, and gender identities. Within their respective youth organizing groups, queer, trans, and nonbinary youth typically experienced acceptance and received encouraging messages about who they were. Such identity positivity can serve as a strong foundation for future political action.[41] Arguably, these second-generation immigrants were incorporating into a political culture informed by black and Chicana feminist theory, as well as U.S.-based identity and civil rights movements.

Making Sense of Intersecting Oppressions and Building Solidarity

Like the AYPAL, YT, and other youth organizing group alumni I interviewed, David was guided by his early exposure to critical civics education that centered diverse ethnicity, gender, and LGBTQ+ experiences. Later, while attending the University of California, Davis, David became a leader in a group called Southeast Asian Student Coalition that conducted outreach at local high schools. This volunteer work allowed him to "teach a lot of high schoolers about stuff that I was taught when I was a teenager," he said. Specifically, David took responsibility for training others in "self-advocacy, college stuff obviously, but more about just being really confident in yourself, your history." During college, David also joined a fraternity, in which he found himself applying the lessons he had learned about sexism and homophobia at AYPAL. "I had to talk to the guys about respecting women's boundaries," he recalled. "I had a certain grasp of safety and not wanting women to be in a space where [dangerous] situations can happen. So I wanted to be there and support them and be able to keep a safe environment for them." Furthermore, David regularly educated his peers about sexist and homophobic behavior. "Not all the guys had the background I did. So sometimes I [would pull people aside] and I would talk to them about how some of the stuff they were doing wasn't cool," he added. David's commitment to addressing issues of diversity and inclusivity was further evidenced by the job he pursued after college, concentrating on food justice issues at a nonprofit in West Oakland. A regular voter, he remained civically active, volunteering for community and political activities, and the lessons he learned as an adolescent guided how he addressed issues of power and inequality in his personal, professional, and public life.

Youth organizing groups' critical civics curricula shaped members' thinking about diversity, inclusivity, gender and sexuality, and racial justice. Often co-facilitated by peers, workshops and other activities contributed to the transformative political socialization experienced by second-generation immigrant members. AYPAL and YT were among the many groups that engaged members in this manner, but the specific curricular content, as well as the extent to which youth members code-signed lessons, varied across regions and organizations. The localized political context in Oakland, with its long tradition of multiracial and inclusive social movement activism, shaped AYPAL and YT programming. Hence, these organizations' curricula and campaigns leveraged a collective memory of coalition building.

As I have shown, AYPAL and YT conducted peer-to-peer ethnic studies in distinct ways. Yet both adopted a relational approach, raising awareness of power relationships among community members. AYPAL and YT members grew in their understandings of the similarities they shared with peers from racially or ethnically diverse backgrounds, as well as their differences. Moreover, in exploring different forms of power and privilege, youth acquired an early exposure to intersectional thinking at a crucial time in their social development. Arguably, such interactive programming enables the second generation to challenge negative stereotypes and the invisibility they often experience in schools and mainstream society. Furthermore, in developing pride in their identities, youth are better equipped to counteract the loss of cultural roots and the erosion of ethnic ties.

A critical civics education expands adolescents' abilities to enact political solidarity. For example, in 2018, AYPAL and YT members actively participated in citywide multiracial campaigns to fight education budget cuts; in 2020, both groups participated in a successful citywide campaign supporting a ballot measure that lowered the voting age to sixteen for school board elections. Featuring one group in Eastside Los Angeles, the next chapter elaborates on how members benefited from extensive guidance in order to lead ambitious grassroots campaigns.

═ Chapter 7 ═

Building on the Legacies of the Chicano Movement: Guiding Youth to Lead Campaigns in the Los Angeles Eastside

About forty thousand people attended the Los Angeles March for Our Lives rally in front of city hall on March 24, 2018.[1] Although he was only a seventeen-year-old high school senior at the time, Brandon Najera, the son of Honduran and Guatemalan immigrant parents, confidently addressed the crowd on behalf of ICS, a community organizing group serving the Eastside of Los Angeles. Starting with remarks on gun reform and the Parkland, Florida, shootings that motivated the rally, Brandon quickly moved on to voice a broader vision:

> I do want to see the mass epidemics of school shootings end, but I definitely want to talk about the mass epidemics that we face here. The mass epidemic of criminalizing youth of color that leads to mass incarceration, the mass epidemic of youth suspensions across California, and of course the mass epidemic of gun violence that people of color face in their daily lives. I know that in my life I face many of these things.

Brandon feared neighborhood violence on a daily basis. Gang activity and drug dealing in the neighborhood made his walks from home to the middle and high schools dangerous, and moreover, he "was terrified" of the police because of racial profiling. Brandon said, "I could easily be taken to jail for something that I never did or could be pinned for something that had nothing to do with me." During his speech, he invited the crowd to empathize with his experience:

> How do you think I feel when I don't feel safe to walk down my own street to get home? How do you think I feel when I can't go home because

134

https://doi.org/10.7758/gert1126.8837

my street is closed and is swarming with police? How do you think I feel when I walk out of my own home and see a body lying there, just shot because of a drive-by?

As a three-year veteran of United Students, ICS's high school student group, Brandon was convinced that he could address the violence in his community through ongoing civic action. He participated in campaigns that changed school site and district discipline policies, increased youths' access to health services in schools, and contributed to statewide school climate and safety policies. These experiences taught him that strategic collective action could make a difference, and he invited the audience to join existing grassroots efforts. "It's our job to continue mobilizing and fighting to create change within our homes, our lives, our schools, our communities and in our nation," he told the crowd.

Reflecting on this momentous day, Brandon said: "People have to understand that the protest, that rally, was only one step. We've been organizing for a long time on the Eastside, and we continue to organize after this protest." Because of his experience in multiple grassroots campaigns, Brandon understood that change rarely comes from one single protest. Rather, success requires sustained engagement with the public as well as significant alliance building, ongoing engagement with elected officials, and policy negotiations. In high school, Brandon and his peers received significant guidance in leading such activities through ICS.

Based in the residentially dense, environmentally distressed, and predominantly Latinx Eastside of Los Angeles, ICS is embedded within a localized political context supportive of immigrant rights, civil rights, and the labor movement. The organization made strategic local adaptations to its programming by leveraging Eastside social movement histories and an expansive civic infrastructure to prepare Brandon and other members for civic leadership. Like their peers in other youth organizing groups, many ICS members experienced a transformative political socialization as a result of the developmental supports, critical civics education, and guidance in civic action they received.

This chapter further elaborates on the third component of the transformative socialization process: guidance in civic action that enables adolescents to play active roles in grassroots policy change campaigns. Brandon, for example, grew from a shy ninth grader into an outspoken civic leader thanks in part to the ongoing coaching and guidance from more experienced peers and staff. Before addressing the large crowd during the March for Our Lives event, he had honed his public speaking skills at numerous smaller gatherings. Research demonstrates that youth organizing groups facilitate members' involvement in grassroots campaigns.[2] I elaborate on this literature by demonstrating how second-generation immigrant youth engaged in guided opportunities to develop basic civic skills such as public speaking, communicating with adult authorities, running productive meetings, and hosting events. I also show how these youth become versed in collective action repertoires; they learned how to strategically engage broader audiences at large rallies and through targeted outreach to peer networks, older adult constituents, and media outlets. This transformative socialization process often entailed scaffolded opportunities for youth to gain the skills and experience to lead political actions.

I begin this chapter by showing how a localized political context welcoming of immigrant rights shaped the contours of ICS's training program. I then draw on twenty-five interviews with members, ten interviews with staff, news reports, and survey data to describe the various ways in which the organization prepared members to take civic action. I conclude by describing a decisive episode in which youth, informed by their intersectional politics, stepped forward on the civic stage and led a collective action.

The Legacy of the Chicano Movement and ICS's Campaigns

"Living in the Eastside, it's not really an obligation, but it was more like, how could I not be an activist, especially considering all that had happened around me?" asked Brandon. With roots in earlier twentieth-century neighborhood and labor activism, Eastside Chicano student activism has been making headlines since the 1960s.[3] The local Mexican American activists who adopted the politicized identity of Chicano may be best known for the 1968 East LA blowouts, when thousands of students walked out of school to protest their learning conditions. However, young Eastside activists of the late twentieth century tackled a range of other issues, including the war in Vietnam, civil rights, labor rights, poverty, immigrant rights, environmental justice, and LGBTQ rights.

Surrounded by polluting freeways and marked by dense, often substandard housing, the Eastside continues to experience high rates of poverty. However, decades of Chicano activism have fostered a robust civic infrastructure dedicated to serving and engaging newer waves of Mexican and Central American immigrants who settle in predominantly Latinx Eastside barrios.[4] While many upwardly mobile Chicanos have moved to environmentally safer areas, local organizations still benefit from the political influence of former activists whose networks span the city, state, and nation. These histories and connections helped sustain civic leadership among low-income, second-generation Eastside youth in the first two decades of twenty-first century. Indeed, having met a number of Eastside veteran Chicano activists, Brandon felt like he was building on this rich legacy.

Within this context, local community leaders established ICS in 1994 in response to the crack epidemic and gang violence devastating the Eastside. Initially, the group involved gang members and their families in resolving gang violence in local housing projects. In 1999, the organization began engaging in the type of grassroots campaigns that have come to characterize both ICS and the broader youth organizing field in the twenty-first century after Luis Sanchez, a University of California, Berkeley, graduate mentored by progressive social movement elders, joined the staff as a part-time organizer.[5] Sanchez went on to become ICS's executive director. He was succeeded in 2007 by Assistant Director Maria Brenes (also a child of Mexican immigrants, ethnic studies major, and University of California, Berkeley, graduate).

Sanchez and Brenes connected ICS to local and statewide civil, labor, and immigrant rights infrastructures in order to advance ambitious, often coalitional campaign efforts. These broad-based networks helped ICS achieve some notable campaign wins during the first two decades of the millennium. Among them were the construction of new schools to address extreme classroom overcrowding in the Eastside, the establishment of wellness centers at two local schools, and community benefits agreements guaranteeing local hiring practices at the newly expanded University of Southern California medical campus.[6] ICS also joined forces with Community Coalition (featured in chapter 1) and other aligned organizations to contribute regularly to campaigns at the local school district, city, or county levels, as well as occasionally to statewide efforts. Well-coordinated campaigns resulted in increased access to college preparation courses, a revamping of school district disciplinary policies, millions in additional funding for schools in low-income communities, and renter protections for low-income tenants, among other victories. As a group that organically bridged electoral participation and social movement-inspired political actions, ICS devoted significant effort to developing a broad political skillset among its adolescent members.

ICS adapted its programming to its localized political context, and it drew on its own organizational and community history to instill pride among its membership. With sixty to seventy core leaders operating at six Eastside schools, the group offered a robust locally adapted critical civics curriculum that addressed issues of diversity and offered an overview of policy debates. After-school meetings enabled students to access extensive developmental supports, including academic assistance, college advising, and healing and self-care activities. Members also received hands-on experience in campaigns, sometimes alongside ICS's Familias Unidas (United Families) parent group. A local social movement history that enabled Latinx and immigrant residents to increasingly exercise their political muscle bolstered ICS's grassroots efforts. As Hilda, the daughter of Mexican immigrants and a Roosevelt High School student, indicated:

> This organization allowed me to realize there's so much pride and beauty in our community, and nobody could take that away from you. We have so much history and we're so rooted in political organizing. We're just building off a past that we could continue growing upon in the future.

Similarly, Penny, a two-year member, noted: "I feel empowered because I know that we have gone through a lot of things and we're still strong. We still push forward. I like how our community just perseveres, and we don't give up. We're just *luchando* [fighting]."

Guiding Youth in Civic Action

Commentators have long argued that civic associations develop members' civic skills.[7] However, adolescent groups can have a profound impact on members' ability to lead political action efforts because their members are undergoing a period of significant neurological growth.[8] Because second-generation immigrant adolescents typically join youth organizing groups with limited experience in the public arena, organizers help new members to acquire basic civic skills. According to Barbara Rogoff, intensive learning can occur through guided participation, in which staff and experienced group members engage novices, often within a group context.[9] In observing apprenticeship programs, Jean Lave and Etienne Wenger find that mastering skills takes time and frequent opportunities for novices to practice their skills.[10] As agents of political socialization, youth organizing groups thus function like apprenticeship programs, offering a mix of group and personalized guidance.[11]

Ana Godoy, ICS's youth organizing coordinator, explained that staff incrementally engaged members in activities that developed their ability to take action in policy campaigns and mobilize others around political causes:

> Everyone participates first, then they shadow others, and then we'll start giving them roles. . . . We don't just throw them into a situation and expect them to figure it out on their own. We really are intentional about preparing them, making sure that they feel comfortable, that they get to practice and have all the information that they need.

Furthermore, Godoy stressed the importance of building an entire team of skilled core leaders who could take on different roles in the organizations' activities and campaigns. This took ongoing training, since students graduate and new members joined every year. Additionally, some youth moved in and out of the program because of other interests (like sports) or because of personal or family issues:

> So we make sure that it's not the same two to three [members] at each school doing everything for a campaign, but it's about teaching them the skills that it takes to be part of the whole process, and taking advantage of those pockets of opportunity for them to take on a new role. So it's . . . an evolution over time. They take that ownership, but we also sometimes have to challenge them and say, "You got this and you're ready for it."

Godoy explained that staff assessed the skill level of each core leader and then structured opportunities to expose members to different types of civic actions. "At any given time, it's important to have people ready to take on different roles," she added. In this regard, youth organizing groups are similar to adult community organizing groups, which create a distributive leadership structure that relies on continuous coaching.[12] However, adult and college-based groups often further enhance the civic skills of members who already have prior civic experience.[13] Here, I add to the literature by highlighting how youth organizing groups tailored their programming to bolster the ability of second-generation immigrant adolescents with limited prior experience in taking civic action by spending significant time imparting basic civic skills. Subsequently, these groups guided members to use these civic skills to strategically mobilize constituents to achieve political aims.

Supporting the Development of Basic Civic Skills

In youth organizing groups, staff help members acquire basic civic skills that adolescents might otherwise acquire in any apolitical, public-oriented group like student government or a community service group. Such opportunities tend to be more readily available to middle-class or more affluent students than to their lower-income peers.[14] In contrast, students who initially join groups like United Students tend to be like Brandon, who arrived at his first meeting with little experience with clubs or similar youth associations.

Members in these groups initially assume small roles in meetings and activities, usually within a safe, low-stakes context. Students shadow staff and experienced peers and then take on more responsibilities as they gain the skills to speak to larger groups, run meetings on their

Figure 7.1   Self-Reported Impact of ICS United Students on Basic Skills Among Novice and Veteran Members (N = 120)

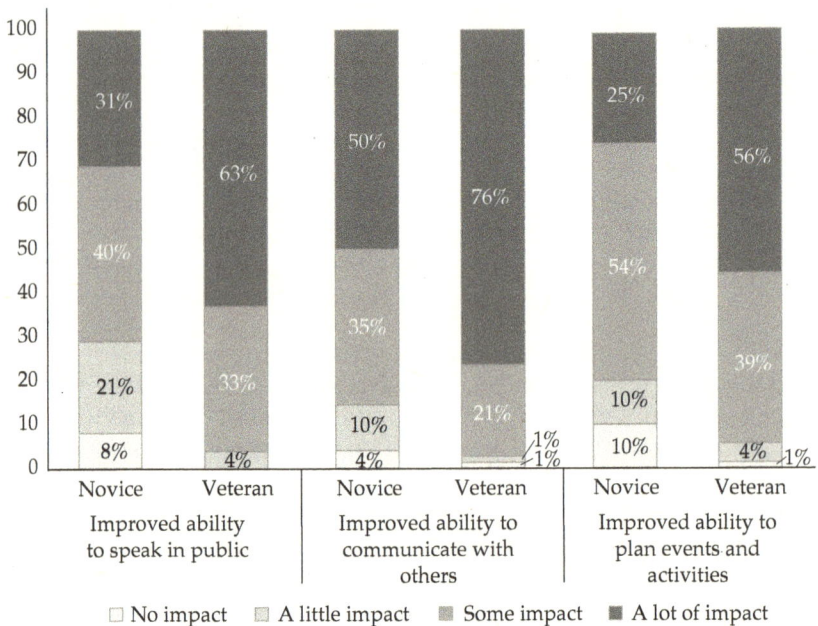

Source: Author's calculations based on the Youth Leadership and Health Survey 2014 and 2016.
Note: Percentages may not add up to 100 percent due to rounding error.

own, and plan events.[15] Surveys I conducted in 2014 and 2016 with core ICS leaders evidence members' progress. In the questionnaire, I asked members to rate how much their involvement in the group altered their civic skills: Did it have "no impact," "a little impact," "some impact," or "a lot of impact"? I divided members into two groups—novices who had been part of United Students less than a year (n = 48) and veterans who had been part of ICS for a year or longer (n = 72). While I acknowledge that such self-reports are subjective, may suffer from social desirability bias, and are less valid than tests of actual civic skills and knowledge, results suggest that members improved their skills as a result of practice gained and time spent in their youth organizing group (see figure 7.1).

For example, while 31 percent of novice members reported that United Students impacted their ability to speak in public "a lot," this percentage was twice as high (63 percent) for veteran members. Meanwhile, 50 percent of novice members claimed that their involvement had improved their ability to communicate with others by "a lot," compared with 76 percent of veteran members. Finally, while only 25 percent of novice members said that United Students had "a lot" of impact on their ability to plan events and activities, this percentage was more than double—56 percent—for veteran members. Importantly, as students developed their basic civic skills, they also expanded their capacity to use these skills to take strategic collective action or turn out the vote.

Finding a Voice and Using It

As the children of working-class immigrant parents, ICS members enjoyed few, if any, opportunities in early adolescence to speak their minds in public settings prior to joining the organization. Most recounted that United Students activities "forced" them to become more outspoken and communicative in groups, and Jesus's experience was typical in this regard. Before joining Garfield High School's United Students chapter in ninth grade, he noted, "I was super shy, you know, a very timid person." Through group activities, he learned to "step out of [my] comfort zone," speak up in meetings, and eventually give public presentations. By senior year, Jesus was a prominent school leader, modeling public speaking for younger members. Similarly, Sylvanna, also from Garfield High School, said that were it not for United Students, she would "still [have] been the shy girl," a bit of a loner who "wasn't really confident with people talking to me." Brandon, too, said he was "shy at first."

As Godoy, ICS's organizing coordinator, explained, many youth start out with "quiet voices" until staff "remind them that they have power in their voice." She added, "They just haven't either been given that push or the opportunity to speak up." Once newcomers attend a few meetings or events, the staff or older peers invite them to take on a greater role. "We give them the mic, or the megaphone, and we practice with them," said Godoy.

United Students members learned to take on public speaking roles by rehearsing in group meetings. Regularly scheduled activities required members to stand before others and share something about themselves, their campaign, or another topic so that they became comfortable speaking in front of people. "ICS offers up a lot of support, especially for speaking roles," Camila, a Roosevelt High School senior, noted. "Students had to make sure they understood the facts and the issues before speaking," she added. For Camila, learning the details about a given campaign issue and process wasn't the challenge; rather, she needed to increase her confidence: "It's a matter of practicing and communicating what you are working on," she said.

ICS organizers monitored the distribution of speaking roles and members' growth in order to ensure that all members developed their public voices. Once members gained sufficient practice, organizers invited them to speak in government meetings or before large crowds. Members also occasionally addressed county and city agencies or legislative sessions in Sacramento. As the stakes increased, staff provided youth with significant coaching. As Brandon explained, "Any time I give a speech, I have to come into the office and prepare. I would have to draft it, write it, and they're going to make sure that I'm going to practice and everything." Brandon was comfortable speaking at the March for Our Lives event not only because he had rehearsed this particular speech but also because he had previously spoken at school rallies, before the school board, and at other public events. He was among several members interviewed who had extensive experience and knew the exhilaration that comes from giving public testimony. After once seeing herself as a shy person, Gaby became a spokesperson for ICS's college access campaign and grew to enjoy such public roles: "Before, I wouldn't be able to do public speaking, but now that's one of the main things that I love," she said. "I love going up there, like without even getting shy, and informing my peers about the things that are going on."

Overcoming Unequal Power Dynamics

Youth organizing groups prepare low-income, second-generation immigrant youth to speak confidently to adult decision-makers while navigating unequal power dynamics stemming from differences in age, class, gender, sexual orientation, immigrant background, and/or legal status. Embedded within a larger civic infrastructure that includes adult organizations, ICS staff made concerted efforts to ensure that its young members gained the confidence to participate in intergenerational political settings. As suggested by prior research, second-generation youth often need places outside the family home to practice addressing elders because their parents rarely hold positions of authority and may not feel entitled to question, make demands of, or negotiate with authority figures.[16] In interviews, most United Students members said that their parents were not actively involved in politics, although some parents openly discussed concerns around the anti-immigrant rhetoric of the Trump administration with their children.

Within the context of United Students campaigns, adolescents gained practice in working and communicating with adult community members. As a starting point, adolescents participated in monthly organization-wide meetings with ICS's Familias Unidas parent members, in which youth and adults updated each other on campaigns and strategized. Sylvanna, introduced earlier, appreciated that ICS offered a safe space where "the parents actually believed in the students' rights." She had always thought most adults would not "listen to minors," but United Students members typically enjoyed being heard by the parents in attendance, who often praised the students for their efforts and made them feel that they were doing right by the community.

Youth experienced greater challenges communicating with teachers, the first of the various authority figures students might need to persuade to support a campaign. Mariana, a student at Mendez High School, said that ICS staff encouraged her and her peers to ask their teachers to allot class time for them to speak about their campaigns. Mariana was in eleventh grade the first time she had to coordinate with teachers. "I was nervous. Talking to the teachers was nerve-racking," Mariana recalled. Members planned their outreach strategy, deciding to approach a teacher before or after class and gauge their stance on United Students' campaign to extend the school's lunch break. Mariana recalled the basic script: "Hey Dr., Ms., or Mr. (last name), I'm with this program called InnerCity Struggle, and this is what we are trying to do. Here's some information. What do you think about it?" If the teacher was supportive, members would ask: "Can I give a presentation or do a survey during class?" According to Mariana, this approach generally worked and increased her confidence. She said that this experience proved invaluable during her senior year, as she helped lead a new ICS campaign to lower the voting age to sixteen in school district elections.

However, not all youth shared Mariana's positive experience; some members discussed conflicts with teachers. At Torres High School, for example, Steven worked on the "Student Bill of Rights" campaign aimed at reforming districtwide disciplinary policies, an unpopular effort with many teachers, who feared student demands would undermine their authority in the classroom:

> When it came to the Student Bill of Rights, where we were trying to make sure that the zero-tolerance policy didn't happen anymore, a lot of the teachers actually called me out, and they were just saying how they don't agree, and how this is going to make their job harder for them. So we did get a lot of backlash, and it was just a little awkward just because you assume that these teachers are here for you, but then when you hear that stuff, it's like, "Can I actually trust you as a teacher?"

During this campaign, students sought out staff advice on how to approach teachers. "It was definitely scary," Steven recalled. After some members expressed concerns that teachers might retaliate by giving them poor grades, the group decided to focus on outreach to teachers and others whom they thought would be supportive. Staff also offered to mediate between students and teachers who opposed the campaign, should any perceived tensions develop. Thanks to this support, Steven felt more confident approaching potentially sympathetic teachers.

Nonetheless, ICS staff held regular discussions about the best ways to effectively challenge teachers, school administrators, and other adults who opposed campaign efforts. According to Godoy, staff let the students know that "sometimes teachers and other folks will see eye to eye with us on certain issues, [but] sometimes they might need a little information to sway them over." She added, "And sometimes they just might not see eye to eye [with] us. And that's okay." When teachers or adult figures did not agree with the students, staff coached members to calmly share their viewpoint without telling adult figures that they were wrong, Godoy said. For example, they encouraged youth to initiate debate with phrases like, "Have you ever thought about it this way?"

Jason, a skater who felt negatively stereotyped by administrators, found Godoy's approach helpful. While Jason told me he personally preferred to avoid school administrators, he felt like he had learned an effective approach to speaking with them when necessary. "With administrators, sometimes you need to be calm, assert yourself, be confident, because otherwise they don't take [you] seriously," Jason said. When asked how he approached these encounters, he responded: "I tend to bring up my own experiences because those administrators, those adults . . . they don't always understand where I'm coming from, where people my age are coming from. I guess times have changed. Our generations are different, and they need to understand our situations are also different."

United Students members learned that winning over administrators and other adult decision-makers sometimes required persistence and preparation. As Brandon explained, "Sometimes you will talk to a principal and they won't take you seriously. . . . They assume you are a student who doesn't know much." United Student members held to a strategy that "knowing your facts" was important when meeting with authority figures. Thus when Brandon was advocating for a wellness center to administrators, he came armed with data:

> They couldn't deny any of the information that I said or any of the claims that I made if I actually had the proof and the information to back it up. That's kind of how I approach it, because sometimes, adults are not very keen on having that conversation. But administrators are much more open if you can actually prove that there is a disparity or need.

Beyond speaking to authority figures at their schools, United Students members gained experience in approaching other decision-makers, most often school board and other district officials. Some members mentioned directly speaking with local city council members, county leaders, and state elected officials; one even spoke to Governor Gavin Newsom. Summarizing an important lesson he learned regarding speaking with elected officials, Jesus noted, "It's okay to challenge them."

Running Meetings and Organizing Events

Members of apolitical public-oriented student groups acquire the capacities to organize events, preparing members for broader civic and political participation.[17] Yet when compared with members of apolitical groups interviewed as part of this broader study, those of youth organizing groups typically received significantly more coaching and guidance. Mentorship and supervision gradually enabled members of youth organizing groups to run meetings and coordinate activities and events, sometimes involving large numbers of people, in the service of promoting nonpartisan campaigns.

At ICS, members acquired techniques for coordinating effective meetings and events. Rafael, a member of the United Students at Roosevelt High School, said staff "were just there to supervise. We basically ran most of it." Indeed, many staff members confirmed that they tried to stay in the background during lunchtime club meetings, intervening only when the conversation got sidetracked or when members conveyed incomplete or incorrect information. They also ensured that novice members did not just sit on the sidelines. "Sometimes it means making sure that they take on little pieces of the work, whether it's an icebreaker, facilitating a break-out group, or making a presentation during part of the agenda," explained Godoy.

During his three years with United Students, Brandon recognized his peers' growing leadership abilities:

> A lot of students start out by not knowing how to make an agenda, [to] think through what you want to come out at the meeting. They don't know they need to debrief after a big meeting. We did learn how to run meetings. The site organizer made sure we came prepared, set up snacks, brought the sign-in sheet, and had the presentation ready to go. [Staff] taught us how to facilitate meetings. . . . Facilitating the meeting meant you showing up on time, setting everything up, having everything ready to go. You know the contents of what you are going to talk about. You know when you are going to talk. And you know what you are trying to achieve by the end of the presentation and what you want folks to take away.

Gradually mastering facilitation and coordination skills, members eventually took charge of lunchtime meetings and played active roles in after-school Coordinating Committee meetings involving all six Eastside United Students chapters.

During Coordinating Committee meetings, members planned school or community events and activities, with occasional guidance from staff. Events could include anything from an informational classroom presentation to a large rally involving thousands of participants. Members learned different aspects of event planning including logistics (time, date, location, food if relevant, and venue; outreach to their target audiences; minute by minute programming; speaker and performer recruitment; supply lists; division of labor among leaders and volunteers; safety; and media outreach). This required coordinated teamwork, as Nancy explained:

> There are certain roles and tasks that need to be assigned. And we would learn about those little things that you wouldn't think about: timekeeper, note taker, who's bringing the supplies, who's passing out the snacks. How are you delegating these different tasks? We get to learn about those moving pieces during that coordinating committee time. You don't realize it, but you kind of put things together at the end of it. You're like, "Wow, I'm a great organizer. I can do these things."

To further refine their organizational skills, members evaluated the event after its completion, a reflexive practice common in youth and adult community organizing groups.[18] Debriefing sessions identified what went well and what could be improved in the future. Dayanara, a member from Garfield High School, appreciated debriefing with her peers, as she believed discussions ultimately increased her competence and confidence: "At the end [of an event], we'd stay afterwards and talk about what's a rose, a thorn, and what's the soil." As she explained, a rose was something that went well, a thorn was something that did not go quite right, and the soil indicated resources or strategies for growth or improvement. "I really like this technique because it made me feel comfortable. Everyone was giving feedback, getting feedback, and it was nice to improve our skills," Dayanara said.

Experienced United Students members like Dayanara and Brandon significantly improved their ability to speak in public, communicate with a range of constituents, run meetings, and host events. Veteran ICS members acquired and fine-tuned basic civic skills that they could apply to a range of activities, political or not. One member even told me that being in United Students helped her plan her sister's quinceañera (a traditional, Latinx coming-of-age fifteenth-birthday celebration). However, within the context of United Students, members used these basic civic skills in the service of political causes.

Training in Collective Action

When I asked Brandon about what it took to win a grassroots campaign, he responded: "When you are pushing for a campaign, usually you have to ask: Who holds the power here? How can we uplift the voices of the people that are being affected in a strategic way? How can we get them to listen to our story?" Youth organizing groups trained adolescent members in garnering mass support for their demands or goals. Adopting lessons learned from prior movements, groups exposed their adolescent members to the mechanics behind what sociologist Charles Tilly calls "repertoires of collective action," or "the ways that people act together in pursuit of shared interests."[19] To compensate for their lack of financial capital and formal political power, these community-based organizations pursue broad-based support through direct outreach to peers, constituents, and other potential allies (for example, the audience at the March for Our Lives rally), as well as coalitional efforts and media outreach. With encouragement and guidance from staff and experienced peers, members gained practice in applying the basic civic skills they acquired to collective policy change and voter mobilization efforts. Those repertoires of collective action are the focus of this next section.

Mapping Power

As United Students advanced campaigns, 1.5- and second-generation members used a strategy known as power mapping, a practice that became more widespread in grassroots organizing circles after the 1992 LA Civil Unrest.[20] In power mapping, participants identify the key players in their campaign, distinguishing between the decision-makers responsible for the policy change and other stakeholders (like peers, parents, educators, residents, or voters) who might influence these decision-makers.[21] In my observations over the years, youth organizations implemented power mapping in various ways. In most cases, participants represented the key players on a grid that illustrated their level of opposition or support for the campaign goal on one axis and their degree of influence over the decision on another axis. Participants then discussed strategies for gaining sufficient support from the decision-makers themselves or relevant stakeholders.

The power mapping exercise helped youth understand the importance of public presentations, communicating with adults and decision-makers, and organizing events—the basic skills discussed earlier in this chapter. Specifically, they came to understand that a winning strategy for any campaign required building a coalition of stakeholders (peers, residents, school personnel, and sometimes the general public), then promoting a cause through multiple media. At ICS, members learned to visualize a power map for both policy change and electoral campaigns. The entire process, from power mapping to carrying out a strategy, allowed adolescents to use their relatively limited formal political power as minors to collectively effect change. "When you don't have any knowledge of [this process], you think it's hard, you think [change is] impossible" said Rafael, a member from Roosevelt High School. Rafael appreciated how power mapping helped him and his peers identify and win over influential allies who could pressure school board members to approve increased funding for schools serving high-poverty communities. Reflecting on the process, he added: "It really, really opens your eyes! You get a sense of how things are done. It's not that impossible when you get so much support."

Engaging Community Stakeholders

ICS trained their members in base building, which entailed educating, gathering data from, and securing the support of their peers at school, then replicating this process with other young and adult community members. J-Mo, Brandon's mentor and site organizer at Wilson High School's United Students, explained: "I try to instill in them that the bigger the base, the more likelihood the decision maker [will] listen and . . . act."

To achieve broad support, United Students conducted classroom and community presentations; they also canvassed their neighborhoods, knocking on doors to gather information (such as survey data), collect signatures on petitions, and garner support for campaign efforts. This guided experience enhanced the civic capacities of second-generation Latinx immigrant members and arguably advanced the political incorporation of peers and other community members whom they engaged.

ICS and many other groups utilized youth participatory action research to solicit the insights of peers and initiate conversations about new campaigns. Specifically, youth codesigned and implemented studies that collected data from constituencies about local concerns in order to advance their campaigns.[22] Like other core leaders of United Students, Brandon conducted surveys for multiple campaigns, including the campaign for health services at Wilson High School, for which Brandon asked students about their opinions on a possible wellness center. Brandon and his peers administered several hundred surveys during classroom presentations and at lunchtime, and the outcome was clear to him: "We identified a need. Students wanted a wellness center. We did all this work to have the research, because they [the administrators] don't care if you don't have any evidence or have any proof." After manually entering the data and analyzing it on Microsoft Excel— a process that Brandon described as "tedious"—the students shared the results with the student body and principal. Like the surveys in many ICS youth-led campaigns, the wellness survey prompted dialogue and provided data that fueled multiyear campaigns.

In another approach to base building, ICS prepared members to gather signatures for various campaigns, including those involving education reforms, lunchtime menu options, lowering the voting age, increasing school-based mental health counseling services, and rent controls. Iris, a member of United Students at Lincoln High School, recalled working on the 2015 Equity in A-G campaign, which sought to strengthen the A-G for All resolution that had passed a decade earlier. The 2015 campaign sought to increase access to and support for college prep courses required for admission into the University of California UC and California State University CSU systems. That spring, Iris and her peers conducted multiple class presentations and individually spoke to students to help them understand what was at stake and convince them to sign the petition. As Ben Kirshner notes, members of youth organizing groups often receive training in persuasive speech.[23] In this regard, Iris explained what she learned about effectively approaching other students:

> We definitely wanted to highlight how this was going to impact them and how they may benefit from either getting involved or signing a form and how they could make a difference in their community. So it always came back to why was this important to the person that I was talking to.

Iris also learned to think through different approaches depending on her audience. For example, in talking to parents during this campaign, she emphasized how the Equity in A-G campaign would increase their children's chances of getting into college. Most United Students members recalled having to speak to many people about their various campaigns. In 2019, ICS joined a coalition of groups seeking to secure the right to vote in school board elections for sixteen-year-olds. For Jackie, such an effort required buy-in from Garfield High School students and East Los Angeles residents. She was prepared to engage in multiple outreach methods: "We did door knocking, phone banking, classroom presentations. That's a way we connected with other people." Meanwhile, Mariana, who joined the same campaign at Mendez High School, spoke at large community gatherings and school presentations to reach students who did not attend ICS-affiliated schools and other residents.

In preparing novice members for neighborhood door knocking (also known as canvassing), ICS imparted strategies for maintaining personal safety and making the process enjoyable. For example, youth learned how to avoid aggressive dogs, and they paired up with parent chaperones. One youth member, Mariana, appreciated how the group prioritized safety: "You know, I don't want to be fearing for my life."

Canvassing is hard work—and not without an element of risk—but it is also a social activity that above all is fun, according to Mariana. Indeed, students often socialized and engaged in friendly competitions (like racing to knock on the greatest number of doors) during outreach efforts.

Working in Coalition

Youth organizing groups provide structured opportunities for adolescent members to work alongside adult allies in order to wield political influence and advance policy change.[24] In a localized political context receptive to immigrant rights, ICS tapped into a dense network of potential coalition partners. As Brandon explained, "I've met a lot of wonderful people through the work that I've done with different organizations. My network has grown a lot."

ICS campaigns focused on policy change at the municipal (and occasionally the state) level. Specifically, adolescent efforts targeted the school site, school district, the city, and the county; members also visited Sacramento government offices to weigh in on state-level policies. ICS rarely took on issues alone, as it represented only one cluster of neighborhoods within the nation's second-largest school district, second-largest city, largest county, and largest state. Thus, in the course of campaigns, adolescent members came to recognize the importance of accessing coalitions that exercise power at the appropriate jurisdictional level.

As minors who often lacked private transportation, United Students members were most active in the Eastside, where they could easily practice coalition building at the school site. For example, in the 2010s, they worked with other student clubs on campaigns advancing local school concerns, among them: wellness centers, school disciplinary practices, bathroom access, and course offerings. Lincoln High School's Iris emphasized the importance of this coalitional work:

> Getting these other clubs, these other student organizations, on board was important, whether it was to make sure that we could use the bathrooms, or that the district gave more funding for restorative justice. It was important to show that unity. It wasn't just United Students who cared about these things; other clubs did as well.

Iris added that these groups "would come to the rally, they would help us with the events to show their support." Given overlapping memberships and shared interests in social change, Movimiento Estudiantil Chicano de Aztlán (MEChA), a student organization with roots in the civil rights movement, and the gender and sexualities alliance (formerly known as the gay–straight alliance) were frequent allies. At Wilson High School, the Key Club (a community service group) and AVID (a college prep program) tended to support United Students campaigns—at least while Brandon was a member. At other schools, United Students members sometimes collaborated closely with student government or the school's leadership class, although in some cases student leadership distanced itself from the politicized work of United Students. As research suggests, overlapping memberships (or lack thereof) can determine whether coalition building occurs among groups.[25]

Beyond forming peer coalitions at the school site, United Students also aligned with parent groups and other local agencies. ICS's coalition partners often included the Community Coalition (featured in chapter 1), as well as other neighborhood and youth organizing groups. For example, in 2020, ICS joined with youth organizing groups like Students Deserve, Youth Justice Coalition, and the Labor Community Strategy Center in a successful campaign to redirect school police funding toward student services.[26]

During his junior and senior years in high school, Brandon served as a Brothers, Sons, and Selves coalition liaison involving ICS and other Los Angeles County–based groups featured in this book. Through these coalitional efforts focused on improving life outcomes for young men, he also met and learned from African American and Southeast Asian youth, who were not well represented demographically in the Los Angeles Eastside. This experience taught him that other groups faced challenges that were both similar to and different from his own: "It helped me realize what goes on in other communities," Brandon said, adding that the coalition "wouldn't mean anything if there wasn't actually any trust or foundation. It requires a lot of meetings, a lot of understanding." Developing a shared agenda, therefore, was time well spent in Brandon's opinion, and the work paid off. The LAUSD school board conceded to the coalition's demand that it maintain funding commitments to restorative justice programs as a way of reducing school suspensions and expulsions.[27]

Another notable coalitional effort occurred in the latter part of the 2010s, when ICS began working on gentrification and affordable housing issues affecting the Eastside, including neighborhoods within the city boundary lines and unincorporated areas in the surrounding county. ICS's Familias Unidas parents took the lead in these efforts since their schedules were more conducive to attending important city and county hearings during the school day. But outside of school hours, youth contributed to peer-to-peer outreach, canvassing in the community, and mobilizing for rallies. These efforts were part of a broader coalition called Eastside Leads, connecting young members to stakeholders whom

United Students had not worked with as closely in prior campaigns. During this campaign, Dayanara, who was from unincorporated East Los Angeles, learned about the challenges of fighting for affordable housing, as well as the benefits of working in coalition: "There's a lot of opposition to affordable housing, a lot of misunderstanding of what affordable housing means." Dayanara explained that corporate developers and landlords presented well-funded opposition to the groups' demands. Yet, in attending strategy sessions and public hearings, she also witnessed how a coalition could make a powerful case for new developments that limited displacing current residents and incorporated affordable housing: "Having other organizations join together, and different types of people on your side, it really gives you power."

Beyond grassroots campaigns, members also worked in coalitions to educate and mobilize young voters, sometimes with impressive success.[28] Adolescents' engagement in these efforts are further detailed in the following chapter.

Media Engagement

Beyond working with allies, ICS trained members on strategies for using public media to reach broad audiences. Core leaders typically participated in a weeklong Media Justice Academy that equipped them with tools for publicizing their cause, telling their own story, and engaging with news outlets and social media. This initial exposure laid the groundwork for additional workshops throughout the year, as well as direct engagement with media during campaigns.

The training appeared effective. For example, over the course of the 2010s, the *Los Angeles Times*, *LA School Report*, *The Wall Street Journal*, *La Opinión*, and *Hoy* quoted United Students members, and English and Spanish network news channels and local radio also featured them.[29] Youth voiced their views on campaigns focused on school funding, college access, school discipline reform, school-based health services, affordable housing, voter registration, gun violence, and other topics.

Mariana, a United Students member from Mendez High School, recalled "figuring out how we can use the media to uplift our story to make sure that . . . our narrative is not told in a bad way." With guidance and coaching, adolescents challenged negative public perceptions of Eastside Latinx youth and immigrants. As minors, adolescents acquired strategies for convincing adults to take them seriously through role-playing and one-on-one coaching. Mariana was among the group's media spokespeople for a rally demanding the right to vote in school board elections at age sixteen. "They prepared me to speak to media or just be ready," she said. "I had some talking points to stay on message."

She noted that she developed a sense of confidence and conviction that her voice mattered during these exercises: "I'm not just some foolish teenager. I have this viewpoint. I know it's important."

When they felt ready, youth volunteered to join the United Students media team, responsible for talking to reporters at government meetings, rallies, or press conferences. Brandon was on the media team at a school board meeting in which his peers testified about the importance of changing school discipline policy. Taught to stay on message, he said: "We are always taught to prep. We have media strategy meetings because we don't want [reporters] to randomly approach a student [who says] something dumb." The organizers, he continued, "let you know that [reporters] try to steer you off topic, and [staff] tell you to always bring it back to the message, to make sure that you're always getting across what you want to say."

Additionally, staff and youth members disseminated best practices on how to advance campaign efforts using social media. Ixchel, who attended Roosevelt High School, shared, "I learned to navigate social media." She enjoyed sharing pictures and videos related to the work of the United Students with her personal network. Other members reported acquiring valuable marketing techniques. As Carolina from Roosevelt High School explained, "I learned how [to] better catch the eye of the viewer, [and] how important it's to just keep things neat." Members encouraged each other to use humor, pop culture references, local references, and colorful images in creating posts or memes. Moreover, members who felt comfortable with the media spotlight tagged their friends, asked them to share the posts, or included links to additional information. Overall, United Students offered a learning environment in which adolescents became better equipped to utilize public media in service of their campaigns.

Applying Basic Skills and Collective Action Repertoires: The November 14, 2016, Walkout

Perhaps the clearest evidence that adolescents experienced a transformative political socialization comes from the civic actions youth themselves organized. Next, I describe one such action that reflects the capacity for collective action acquired by youth organizing group members.

Like many young people across the country, United Students members were shocked by the election of Donald Trump on November 8, 2016.[30] Equipped with strong civic skills and trained in collective action, they were poised to play a leadership role and respond in a way that reflected the views of many people in their community. Taking a page from the local Chicano movement, they turned to a historical political action: the walkout. "The walkouts weren't new to me. Well, organizing a walkout was completely new to me, but we had read about them. We had presented on them. It's a part of our history here," said Nancy, who was a senior at Garfield High School in 2016. Brandon and core leaders at the six ICS-affiliated schools shared her views. Acting under their own direction, students led a walkout on Monday, November 14.

Planning began on November 9, the day following the presidential election. United Student leaders across all six campuses decided to refocus their regular Wednesday after-school coordinating committee meeting agenda to plan the protest. As Brandon explained, "We'd map out everything that we want to do and how we're going to approach it and everything. There is always so much preparation that goes on behind the scenes. It just doesn't happen like, 'Hey, there is going to be a walkout, let's, like, do it.' Like, no!" Nancy also recalled the November 9 planning discussion. "I think a really important piece we thought about in the beginning was timing. Okay, it's basic, but what time are we walking out? How does it affect our students?" she said. Members then recalled their training in organizing public events to iron out the logistics of the walkout; Nancy listed some of the elements they had to think through:

> What's our messaging? That should have been the first thing, because we're all angry, but what's the messaging? Are we all in agreement about this message? We took into consideration [questions] around messaging and then figuring out, okay, with messaging comes . . . what media will say about us? And who is going to be assigned to talk to the media? How are we going to use social media platforms? What hashtags are we going to use? How are we going to share this information with our peers?

Nancy explained that students took some time to decide on their message. In the end, they agreed that instead of the election victory, or even Trump himself, they would protest his agenda, which attacked immigrants and other vulnerable people and threatened to eliminate vital social services. Their message was intersectional, recognizing that immigrants were not the only ones under attack. They wanted their local government institutions to protect them, their rights, and the services that help those most vulnerable, including immigrants, people of color, women, and queer and trans individuals. Once in agreement, students then assigned roles around media and outreach, as they had for prior political actions and events.

United Students also assigned committees to come up with chants, make posters, and gather supplies (like megaphones and noisemakers). They devised a route that would bring students from the six Eastside high schools to city hall, and youth leaders settled on meetup places like Mariachi Plaza in Boyle Heights where contingents would gather and march together. "We wanted this route to make sense because it was a long walk," said Nancy, who led the Garfield High School contingent, which was farthest (more than five miles away) from city hall. Nancy recognized that her own experience with United Students enabled her to play a leadership role at Garfield High School:

> All the meetings that we do helped. We're not just on the sidelines. Like in any meeting, they're always pushing us to be involved. You get used to it. . . . But there's always that continuous growth for all the youth, which is cool to see. Definitely those rallies, our lunchtime meetings, being able to go with Maria [the ICS executive director] to . . . conferences and speaking on behalf of the organization, being a media representative— all that was also helpful. I was ready!

As they had in prior actions, United Students members adopted a coalitional approach to ensure the participation of thousands of students, reflecting the historic 1968 walkouts. Representatives from each school site tapped established networks involving other student clubs at their own schools and beyond. Students called a general meeting with all the clubs at Plaza de la Raza in Lincoln Park on Saturday, November 12, to finalize shared plans and messaging. Given the communications efforts over the two previous days, most students arrived at this coalition meeting having already bought into the plans laid out by United Students members and other key student organizations they had enlisted. "Once we had that meeting with the coalition, it was left to us to make sure that it actually went through on our end," said Brandon.

Remembering lessons learned from the 1968 blowouts and subsequent LA walkouts they had studied, students knew that organizing a walkout was risky: "I thought I was going to get reprimanded," Brandon recalled. The school administrators had indicated that students should stay in school, but to Brandon's relief, students did not face consequences for their protest. Benefiting from a localized political context supportive of immigrant and civil rights and prior networking, youth secured widespread support, including from the teacher's union, United Teachers Los Angeles.[31]

Overall, the November 14 walkout was a success, given that thousands of students peacefully and safely marched and their demonstration garnered national media attention. For example, CNN reported: "Hundreds of high school students from at least six schools in East Los Angeles, home to a large Latino population, took to the streets chanting 'No papers, no fear' and 'Say it loud, say it clear, immigrants are welcome here.'"[32] Meanwhile, the *Chicago Tribune* published part of a student statement: "Eastside students know that this is the time to show our targeted community members that we stand in unity with them and exercise our right to protest to ensure that Los Angeles County leaders commit to doing everything in their power to support all vulnerable communities."[33] The article went on to highlight the intersectional politics of these second-generation youth, noting that "students identified themselves proudly on handmade signs and flags as Latinos, transgender and supporters of women's rights." The *Los Angeles Times* also included this intersectional messaging, quoting one fifteen-year-old student as saying, "A lot of people are worried about being deported and violence against them because of their sexual and ethnic identity."[34]

The November 2016 march serves as one example of how ICS members leveraged their transformative political socialization, and specifically their training in taking civic action, to exercise their voice. Given the formative experience gained in adolescence, many alumni members of ICS and other youth organizing groups have remained politically active as adults, bringing others along as they respond to local, state, or national political developments.

Youth Power in Practice

Brandon's path represents an emerging trajectory common to young people who experience a transformative political socialization. After graduating from high school, he enrolled at the University of California, San Diego, where he was eventually elected to the board of MEChA. He also spearheaded a multiracial student coalition addressing racial justice issues on campus. Additionally, he occasionally returned home to East Los Angeles to assist United Students with local campaigns. "I want to help my community and give back," he said.

As an influential agent of adolescents' political socialization, ICS's United Students offered Brandon and his peers numerous opportunities to develop basic civic skills. Through structured activities, members expanded their abilities to speak in public, run effective meetings, and coordinate events. With guidance from staff and experienced peers, members also gained experience in developing repertoires for collective action: building a base of supporters, participating in coalitions both within and outside of their schools, and spreading the message via digital media. This guidance in taking civic action constitutes a key element of the transformative socialization process, in which youth gain hands-on experience in policy change and voter outreach campaigns. As such, ICS presents a clear case of how youth gain invaluable practice in collectively exercising political power.

While United Students offered members similar training as other groups, the organization pursued, and often won, large-scale campaigns that may not have been viable in other parts of the state. These victories included successful efforts to open new schools; alter school curricular, disciplinary, and funding policies; secure millions in funding for school-based wellness centers and other health services; and lock in a multi-million-dollar community benefits agreement. Adapted to the localized political context, ICS leveraged a deep and broad network of supporters in the public school system, local Eastside associations, and broader Los Angeles civil society. Moreover, this local context supportive of immigrant and civil rights has made it easier for young people to work in coalition on ambitious campaigns and protest activities, including those countering federal efforts to undermine immigrant and other rights. Such bold collective actions tend to face greater constraints in less-welcoming regions, especially those lacking an extensive civil and immigrant rights civic infrastructure.

The next chapter elaborates on how youth organizing group members in the Central Valley engaged in broad-based electoral outreach. Groups in this region lacked access to a broad-based civic infrastructure supportive of immigrant and civil rights. Nonetheless, members learned to take civic action in an environment that was sometimes unwelcoming of young voices.

═ Chapter 8 ═

Growing Young Leaders in the Conservative Central Valley

I think it's really important for Latinx and Hmong folks and other groups to work together because here in the Central Valley, our struggles are tied. We're organizing because many of our elders, even many of our friends, our peers, are not showing up. And honestly, our people devote so much time and energy in working to survive, so they really are not able to show up and speak up for what they want all the time. And so to bring change, we need to educate each other, educate our white peers, and we have to register voters and mobilize our community because we know damn well that no one else is going to do it but us.
—Eugene Vang, 99Rootz member, Merced, California

In 2018, seventeen-year-old high school senior Eugene Vang was pre-registered to vote and determined to get his classmates and friends to preregister or register themselves. "My role was to connect with teachers and do classroom presentations. I also recruited a lot of my friends, classmates, and siblings to help out," Eugene recalled. As members of 99Rootz, a youth organizing group in California's agricultural Central Valley region, Eugene and his mostly Latinx and Hmong American peers were taking advantage of Senate Bill 113, which had been approved in September 2014, enabling sixteen- and seventeen-year-olds to preregister to vote. The bill allowed youth organizers to go into high school classrooms and talk about preregistration and to register students who had already turned eighteen. Making a nonpartisan argument for voting to fellow high schoolers, Eugene and his peers shared statistics about how young people in their communities were severely underrepresented among the electorate. Referencing data from the California Center for Civic Engagement Project, they highlighted that 51 percent of Merced County residents who were older than sixty-five voted in the 2014 midterm election, compared with only 7 percent of eligible eighteen-to-twenty-four-year-olds.[1] In other words, senior citizens

https://doi.org/10.7758/gert1126.8554

were about seven times more likely than the youngest age group of voters to exercise their right to vote.

In a typical presentation, Eugene and his peers would remind their mostly second-generation immigrant audiences that this age gap in voting also represented a racial disparity, asking, "What are the racial demographics of the senior citizens in our county?" Most youth would respond correctly: "They're white." They also asked: "What are the demographics of young people?" The typical responses were "Latinos," "people of color," or "not white." Occasionally someone would say, "Mexican." Leaders would then engage students in a discussion about how the profound age gap in voting could impact government officials' responsiveness to the needs of younger people in their communities.

At 99Rootz, Eugene and his peers experienced a transformative political socialization that prepared them to conduct extensive and effective nonpartisan voter outreach. They accessed developmental supports, including exposure to healing and self-care practices and college preparation. And through a critical civics education, Eugene learned about his own Hmong and other identities, as well as the identities and histories of his mostly Latinx peers. Moreover, he took part in workshops that helped him understand how immigrant rights, environmental justice, education funding, and housing issues affected local communities.

99Rootz also offered Eugene and his peers guidance in civic action. Members took part in grassroots policy change campaigns, such as those demanding access to clean water, increased mental health services for youth, and reduced funding for the police. When making these bold demands associated with progressive social movements, young people typically faced an uphill battle in the conservative Central Valley. Eugene understood that 99Rootz did not, at the time, possess the political power or allies to effectively influence major decisions: "I feel like we don't get taken seriously when we show up and try to get the elected officials to listen to us." Lacking access to a strong civic infrastructure and a deep network of influential allies who could champion their causes, 99Rootz and other Central Valley youth organizing groups were more likely than groups across the state to devote significant resources to voter outreach during the first Trump administration. Young people understood that increasing voter turnout was one strategic way to amplify diverse younger perspectives, at least at the local level.

This chapter details how and to what effect second-generation youth in organizing groups learn to conduct voter registration, education, and mobilization. I feature 99Rootz and other Central Valley youth organizing groups operating in the fairly hostile and localized political context of the Central Valley, which I describe in the pages that follow. In an environment in which ambitious, youth-led grassroots policy change campaigns faced a significant uphill battle, organizations adapted by prioritizing voter outreach. The youth who were part of these campaigns still expressed support for broader social movement efforts, but their involvement in nonpartisan voter education efforts represented a strategic avenue for wielding measurable political influence. As such, I demonstrate that young people can and do experience a transformative political socialization even when growing up in a hostile political context. By guiding youth in civic actions focused on widespread mobilization, organizations prepare their second-generation immigrant members to act as agents of horizontal (or peer-to-peer) political socialization, including in contexts in which immigrants encounter hostility.[2]

This chapter relies on multiple sources of data collected in 2018 and 2019 (further detailed in the appendix). These include survey data describing how 20 groups in the region engaged members around elections and in-depth interviews with 59 members of these groups. My student research team and I also conducted more than 1,600 hours of participant observations as part of the 2018 Central Valley Freedom Summer Participatory Action Research Project.[3] In addition, the findings presented here draw on 2018 surveys collected from 50 Central Valley second-generation youth leaders, as well as on results from an experiment designed to reveal how these efforts influenced turnout among young voters. My analysis is informed by mixed-methods research on statewide young voter engagement efforts that I began observing and tracking in 2016.

The Central Valley Context

Extending from the Sacramento–San Joaquin River Delta south to the Tehachapi Mountains, the Central Valley includes the larger urban areas of Fresno, Stockton, and Bakersfield and the small-to-midsize cities of Visalia, Modesto, and Merced. Agricultural farmland surrounds the Central Valley's urbanized areas. The region is the ancestral homeland of the Maidu, Miwok, and Yokuts tribes, whom successive waves of colonizers and settlers subjected to genocide and displacement. In the late nineteenth and twentieth centuries, these newcomers came to work in agricultural and other industries. White Americans from the South began arriving in large numbers after the Civil War, bringing with them hostile (and lingering) racial attitudes toward non-whites; they were followed by other American Midwestern settlers and Portuguese, Swedish, Yugoslavian, Dutch, German, Basque, Italian, and Armenian immigrants.[4] These groups found relative success in the region, and some of their descendants currently occupy influential positions in the economy and government.

Non-whites also made the region their home. African Americans began settling in the northern part of the Valley as early as the 1860s, arriving in larger numbers in the 1910s and 1920s and continuing in successive waves through the 1960s.[5] Meanwhile, Chinese laborers settled in the region after the completion of the transcontinental railroad in the late 1800s.[6] Japanese, Sikh, and Filipinx immigrants followed in the early twentieth century.[7]

Mexicans had resided in the region well before the United States' 1848 annexation of California, but they only began arriving in larger numbers in the early twentieth century.[8] In the 1930s, the United States forcibly repatriated some Mexicans, curbing the growth of this population. During and after World War II, however, the Mexican-origin population grew tremendously as part of the exponential expansion of the agricultural industry and related demands for low-wage labor. In this period, the Bracero Program (1942–1965) actively recruited Mexican men to work in the fields.[9] Some of these workers eventually settled in the Central Valley's growing cities and rural towns, where their families joined them or they formed new ones. Decades of sustained labor migration have made the Mexican-origin population the largest ethnic group in the region, including sizable Indigenous populations from Oaxaca and other regions of Mexico.[10]

Refugees who were forced from their homelands in the final decades of the twentieth century also reside in the region. These include Eugene's Hmong refugee community, as well as Vietnamese refugees, who are concentrated in Fresno and Stockton. Refugees also include a small number of Central Americans who escaped war and violence, fled natural disasters, or migrated for economic reasons.

Given these rich histories of migration and settlement, the Central Valley in 2020 was ethnically diverse. It was also relatively young. Nearly half—46 percent—of the region's residents were under the age of thirty, compared with 39 percent statewide. Among residents younger than thirty, the racial composition was 62 percent Latinx, 22 percent white, 8 percent AAPI, 4 percent black, and the remainder Native American or mixed race.[11]

White Supremacy and Local Resistance

The second generation of these communities has been coming of age within a context historically hostile to non-whites and immigrants. Throughout the 1920s and 1930s, Ku Klux Klan chapters in Tulare, Fresno, Kings, and Kern Counties actively terrorized communities of color and maintained a significant presence in local police departments and other government agencies.[12] The drought-driven influx of poor white Americans from the Midwest in the 1930s further reinforced the legacy of conservative politics, racism, and white supremacy.[13] White political domination continued throughout the twentieth century via the segregation and redlining of non-white communities after World War II, as well as the exclusion of people of color from lucrative jobs in the growing oil industry.[14]

In the 2010s, older white residents dominated the active electorate, which leaned right and overwhelmingly supported Donald Trump in the 2016 and 2020 elections.[15] Nationally prominent Trump allies Devin Nunes and Kevin McCarthy were two of the region's six all-white, all-male Congressional representatives during the forty-fifth president's term. Participant observations also confirmed the occasional display of Confederate flags, signaling an undercurrent of support for white supremacist values among some residents of the region.

Against this backdrop, anti-immigrant sentiments and opposition to the Black Lives Matter movement echoed not only through talk radio but in the statements of some locally elected government officials in the latter half of the decade. It is not surprising, then, that second-generation immigrant youth often confronted hostile opposition when seeking to advance the rights of immigrants, people of color, women, and LGBTQ+ groups.

Nonetheless, youth activists drew inspiration from, and occasionally connected with, veteran social movement leaders who had fought against labor exploitation, racism, and other forms of exclusion. After all, Filipinx and Mexican American members of the UFW from the Central Valley had garnered national attention for their labor organizing and boycotts in the 1960s and 1970s.[16] Although political opposition and infighting eventually weakened the union, the UFW continued to organize and advocate for worker health and safety throughout the 2010s and during the COVID-19 pandemic. There were other bright spots. For example, Dolores Huerta, a former UFW leader, started her own organization, which includes a youth organizing group. During my research, I observed Huerta and other movement veterans such as Cecilia Mendoza (in Merced) and Guadalupe Martinez (in Delano) meeting with, encouraging, and guiding young leaders. The presence of distinguished elders who supported youths' leadership on their own terms, however, remained limited.

Still, a patchwork of early twenty-first-century Central Valley organizations formed to address the needs of immigrants and other people of color. These included organizations focused on environmental concerns caused by local agribusiness, oil, and trash-processing industries,[17] as well as those drawing attention to the proliferation of prisons in the region.[18] ESPINO (which stood for ¡Escuelas Si! ¡Pintas No!),[19] a coalition that raised awareness about the school-to-prison pipeline and organized around education and juvenile justice, was an important forerunner of some of the youth groups of the 2010s I feature here.[20]

The Prioritization of Young Voter Outreach in the Central Valley

Despite the Central Valley's organizing tradition described previously, the civic infrastructure supporting second-generation immigrant youth organizing efforts remained fairly limited and diffuse in the 2010s—especially when compared with the concentrated immigrant rights and social movement networks in Los Angeles, the Bay Area, and even Santa Ana. Yet, through my field work and interviews with informants, I was able to identify twenty 501(c)3 Central Valley youth organizing groups with adolescent members, all of which I surveyed in 2019. Out of the twenty groups in the region, only one, Californians for Justice, had systematically engaged youth for more than a decade, enlisting them as the principal protagonists of grassroots campaigns. Other established organizations, such as the Youth Leadership Institute and Barrios Unidos, limited their focus on youth development until 2012 and did not systematically involve young people in campaigns. In general, when I observed these groups, they had not yet developed the political power and ties that would allow them to exercise significant political influence.

Youth organizing groups in the Central Valley did, however, involve their members in activities that could yield a transformative political socialization. Overlapping staff and statewide intermediaries diffused effective shared practices, although organizations unequally executed staff- and youth-led training sessions. Notably, Central Valley groups tended to be smaller and newer than many of those on the California coast, and hence not all groups in the region had developed a stable program with experienced staff and members. Overall, then, Central Valley groups incorporated the key elements of the transformative political socialization process—developmental supports and critical civics education—but the scope of this programming varied.

Both survey and interview data collected in 2018 and 2019 confirm that youth organizing group members accessed training in civic action, gaining at least some experience in meeting with government officials and urging school district, city, or county officials to change social policies. However, at that time, certain Central Valley groups had more rigorous and disciplined training programs than others, and even the best-resourced groups lacked the political power and influence to advance viable, large-scale policy change campaigns like those in friendlier contexts and more robust civic infrastructures of Los Angeles and the

Figure 8.1   Youth Organizing Groups' Focus on Voter Outreach Campaigns by Region, 2019 (*N* = 124)

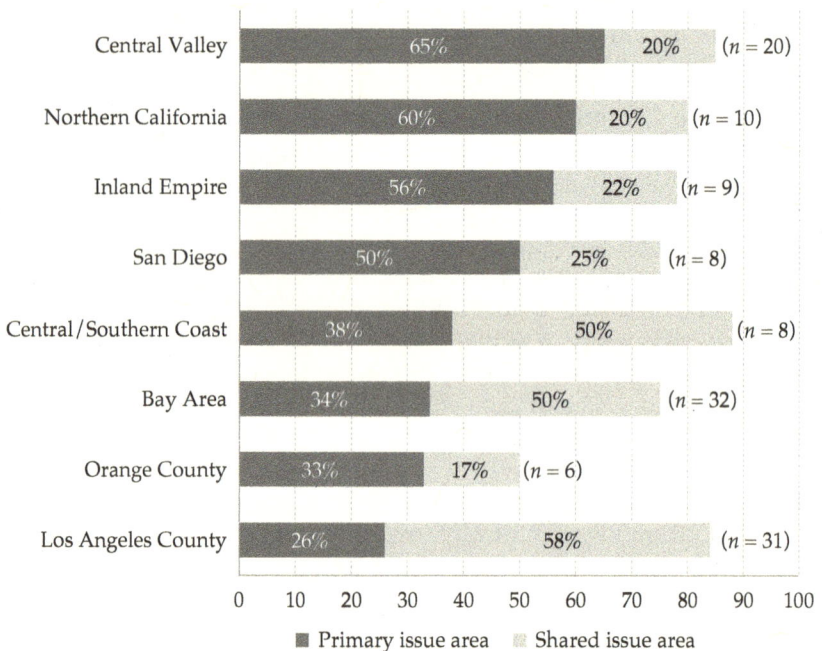

Central Valley	65% · 20% (*n* = 20)
Northern California	60% · 20% (*n* = 10)
Inland Empire	56% · 22% (*n* = 9)
San Diego	50% · 25% (*n* = 8)
Central/Southern Coast	38% · 50% (*n* = 8)
Bay Area	34% · 50% (*n* = 32)
Orange County	33% · 17% (*n* = 6)
Los Angeles County	26% · 58% (*n* = 31)

0 10 20 30 40 50 60 70 80 90 100

■ Primary issue area   ▨ Shared issue area

Source: Author's calculations based on the FCYO Youth Organizing Field Scan 2019.
Note: Central/Southern Coast includes Monterey, San Luis Obispo, Santa Barbara, and Ventura Counties.

Bay Area. Central Valley groups have had some policy change victories, but the local policy campaigns they waged and sometimes won prior to the COVID-19 pandemic tended to be modest in nature, as described at the end of this chapter.

Within a hostile localized political context, most youth organizing groups in the region adapted by training members through a political strategy that did not necessarily require support from political elites, allowing young people to make a measurable short-term electoral impact in terms of numbers of young people registered, voters contacted over the phone, text responses, or other metrics measuring social media communications. In the longer term, such peer-to-peer political outreach, if maintained, could grow an electorate that seeks to protect immigrant communities and align with youth-led campaigns.

Figure 8.1 evidences a regional focus on voter outreach. The chart illustrates responses to the 2019 survey of California youth organizing groups, which asked staff to list both leading and supportive roles for youth members on various campaign issues. Survey results indicate that 65 percent of Central Valley groups said that voting was a primary campaign issue, more than in any other region. Interestingly, more than 50 percent of groups in Northern California (here including Sacramento and northern rural counties) and the Inland Empire (Riverside and San Bernardino Counties) also prioritized voter outreach; these were two other regions where youth organizing groups also encountered significant political opposition.

Across the state, some groups viewed voter outreach as a shared issue area, meaning that they engaged their members in election-related efforts even when they were not taking the lead in these campaigns; 20 percent of groups in the Central Valley saw voter outreach in this light, compared with 17 percent in Orange County and 58 percent in Los Angeles County. Fresno Barrios Unidos was one such group viewing outreach as a shared issue. Best known for advocating for health equity, the group encouraged youth members to join older adult members and other organizations in going door to door to speak with voters. These partnerships allowed groups like Fresno Barrios Unidos to focus on their policy change efforts while exposing their members to elections and engaging people in the voting process.

Civic Action Reaching Broad Audiences

Staff surveys from the twenty Central Valley groups, along with semi-structured interviews with youth and participant observations, evidence how youth gained hands-on experience in voter education and mobilization even though they were not always old enough or eligible to vote themselves. Their training in such broad-based political outreach could be considered similar to an apprenticeship, wherein members learn by doing and receive coaching from more experienced members or young staff.[21] Participation in a range of voting-related activities contributes to the second generation's transformative political socialization, enhancing youths' abilities to engage peer and older audiences.

Figure 8.2, compiled from 2019 staff surveys, shows the various ways in which Central Valley groups guided their members to educate and mobilize young voters. Social media outreach was the most common form of outreach, which is not surprising given that millennials and Gen Z youth grew up with access to multiple sources of digital media.[22] Interviews with youth leaders and participant observations support these survey findings, as during the 2018 midterms (before TikTok became a preferred platform), youth members most frequently used

Figure 8.2   Central Valley Youth Organizing Groups' Voter Outreach Activities, 2019 (N = 20)

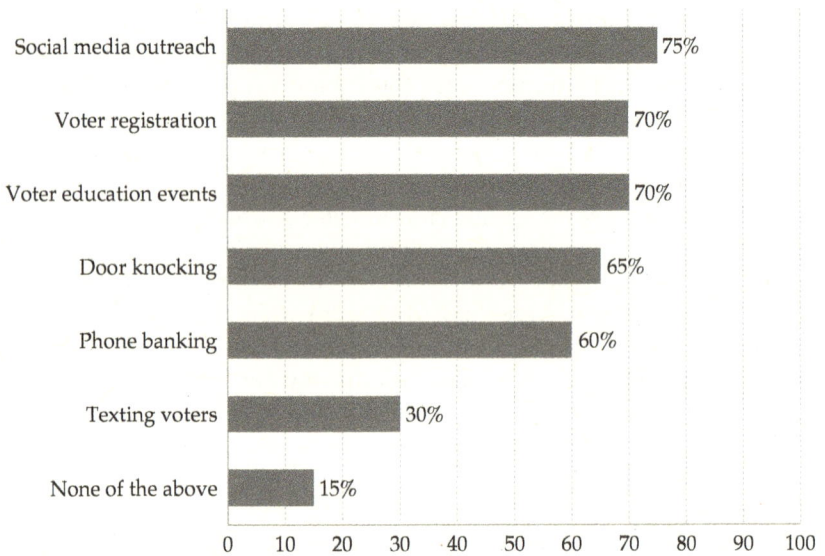

Source: Author's calculations based on the FCYO Youth Organizing Field Scan 2019.

their Instagram accounts to encourage their networks to vote, though some also used their Facebook or Twitter accounts.

Some studies have celebrated how young people utilize social media platforms to share news, opinions, and opportunities for political action.[23] However, my research also suggests that second-generation youth benefit from guidance on how to strategically engage in such online political discourse. Organizing groups provided their members with training, assistance, or encouragement to use their platforms to promote voter education or other campaigns. Such guidance, I argue, can contribute to second generation youths' efficacy in the public arena.

Eugene's experience with social media in his organizing group was illustrative. "I've been on social media for so long, I knew how to use it, obviously," he said. "But I think at 99Rootz, I started to learn how to use it strategically or intentionally to outreach, to get attention from other young people." Eugene said he received multiple training lessons on social media, during which he learned how to personalize political messages and tell his own story in a way that might inspire others to take action. He and his peers also gave each other feedback as they created their own memes and flyers to encourage voting.

In this supportive environment, young members grew accustomed to sharing their perspectives with broad audiences by utilizing their organization's or their own social media accounts. For example, Alang, a member of Hmong Innovating Politics, learned to share videos on voting, AAPI issues, Southeast Asian community issues, and other topics on his personal accounts. At the time, he mostly posted on Instagram — "It's where I have my biggest following" — but he also sometimes used Facebook. Additionally, Delano-based Loud for Tomorrow, a group of predominantly Latinx and Filipinx adolescents who had developed a reputation for their visibility on Instagram, hosted social media training sessions to develop multiplatform strategies for promoting voter registration and turnout among eligible local high school students, their families, and other constituents.

However, not every group devoted significant resources to digital media training. In some cases, staff merely created or disseminated voter materials, sharing them through their organization's social media accounts. They subsequently encouraged members to share these posts with their own networks. On various occasions, my research team and I witnessed staff or experienced members remind young leaders that they could make a difference in turnout by sharing social media content with nonmembers who were not as well informed as they were. This reposting of existing digital content, without additional context or personalization, required minimal training.

In terms of the focus of the political outreach, 70 percent of groups trained members to conduct voter preregistration and registration, sometimes using a shared curriculum circulated by Power California (an intermediary focused on increasing young voter turnout). This curriculum typically reiterated the importance of voting, laid out voting eligibility requirements, and guided youth leaders on how to fill out the preregistration or registration forms. This training emphasized current age and citizenship voting requirements, with organizers and experienced leaders reminding young people that DACA recipients and other noncitizens were ineligible to vote, sometimes speaking from personal experience. As one nineteen-year-old trainer from Merced recalled telling youth members:

> I can't vote because I don't have papers. However, I play a role by registering others and also getting people to vote on my behalf. So I need those of you who are citizens to register and vote for me. If you are not a citizen, you can't register to vote, but you can take that registration card and give it to someone else who can — a family member, a friend, anybody who is going to have your back and vote in favor of immigrant rights.

In other cases, when the people conducting the training were citizens, they told stories about undocumented youth "showing their power" by registering hundreds of people to vote on their behalf. As such, these organizations were socializing all youth, including noncitizens, toward engaging in government elections in some capacity.

In an attempt to broaden the electorate, these groups ensured that the registration training also informed members about the eligibility of citizens with criminal records. "Most people don't know that if you've got a misdemeanor, or if you were convicted of a felony and finished your sentence, you can vote," Ofelia, a twenty-year-old youth member of Mi Familia Vota in Modesto told a group of adolescents. She proceeded to explain how she registered her uncle, who had served a prison sentence and was excited to vote for the first time. "A lot of people in our communities got a criminal record. We got to make sure they know they have the right to vote," said Ofelia.

She and others reminded young leaders that they must remain nonpartisan. As one organizer explained, "You are there to tell people they should vote, but you are not there to tell them *how* to vote." Furthermore, members anticipated questions about which political party affiliation people should check on the registration forms. One organizer told youth members, "The answer you should give is: 'That's up to you. If you don't know what party you like the most, you can leave that part blank or register as no party preference.'" The organizer provided further instruction to members: "Tell them you don't need to identify with a party in order to be registered. That question is optional. They can go home and do some research, and then update their party affiliation at a later date." The training also included an overview of typical mistakes made during the registration process, one of the most common being failing to sign the registration form.

As also demonstrated in figure 8.2, survey results indicate that 70 percent of groups engaged their members in events and activities that encouraged people to vote. Prepared to discuss the importance of the youth vote, members gave classroom presentations like those Eugene organized at his high school, in which youth preregistered and registered their peers. With staff guidance and support, they also organized conferences, rallies, or other events that connected youths' interests to voting. For example, 99Rootz members in Sanger (Fresno County) developed a workshop that linked gun reform to voting, then shared the curriculum widely among peers. In Visalia, ACT for Women and Girls became fluent in explaining to peers how local elections could shape environmental policies.

Furthermore, 65 percent of youth organizing groups provided members with experience in door-to-door canvassing leading up to elections. Through role-playing, members practiced engaging adult voters directly in face-to-face conversations about why voting mattered to their communities. In some groups, like the Dolores Huerta Foundation, adolescents joined older adult members during canvassing efforts; youth learned to read paper voter lists, deliver a friendly message about the importance of voting, and track the outcomes of attempts to reach individual voters. Through these activities, many young people received their first exposure to a grassroots voter mobilization.

In addition, 60 percent of groups involved their members in phone banking, or calling voters to remind them to mail in their ballots or show up at the polls. My team and I observed four groups (of the twenty in our study) training their members in phone banking: 99Rootz, ACT for Women and Girls, Californians for Justice, and Mi Familia Vota, all of which were participating in a nonpartisan campaign coordinated by Power California at the time. Hence, these observations do not apply to all groups, but they do illustrate one set of approaches to preparing members (including some noncitizens) to get out the vote.

The training was systematized across the four Power California groups. Staff trained members and occasional volunteers on Political Data Inc., an online platform used to contact voters and track their progress. In reading a script that had been codeveloped by select staff and youth leaders, young volunteers first emphasized the importance of closing the age and racial gaps in voting before asking voters between the ages of eighteen and thirty-four if they were planning to vote. Through role-playing activities facilitated by either staff or an experienced youth leader, members learned to anticipate and respond to positive, negative, and even disrespectful responses from voters. Because many of the contacted people were first-time or occasional voters, leaders (many of whom had not yet voted themselves because they did not meet age or citizenship requirements) learned to give clear instructions on the voting process, including polling center dates and hours, whether it was permissible to skip items on the ballot, and identification requirements, as well as answer other frequently asked questions.

As someone who had participated in numerous phone banking efforts over the years, I saw similarities in the training processes of adult campaigns and those of these youth-led campaigns. However, the phone banking sessions for youth incorporated fun activities to break up the tedium, including teen-friendly icebreakers, breaks that included music and games, and friendly competition. Importantly, to maintain morale—the process could be demoralizing since most people do not pick up their phones—youth organizations acknowledged every commitment to vote from the people they called as a small victory. Around halfway through the typical three- or four-hour session, a staff or youth leader would facilitate a debriefing session with young volunteers on their experience. In the discussion, members routinely shared what went well, discussed challenging questions raised by voters, vented about difficult conversations, or diagnosed technical issues with the Political Data Inc. platform. These peer discussions likely helped members refine their messaging and scripts as they worked to convince people that voting was worth their time.

Importantly, to maintain energy and focus, members engaged in friendly competitions to recognize those who obtained the most affirmative responses from voters who agreed to cast a ballot. For example, at ACT for Women and Girls, members shared a round of applause for the volunteer who had received the most voting commitments during a ninety-minute session and awarded them a unicorn headband to wear during their next shift. At the end of a session, youth leaders typically tallied affirmative responses to measure their collective progress. These activities facilitated peer accountability for campaign goals. In cases where we did not observe such group norms, young members tended to be more distracted, spending more time on their cell phones or in side conversations with each other.

Finally, 30 percent of groups involved their members in texting voters, a voter outreach strategy that became common in the mid-2010s. This required youth to learn how to use an app that incorporated prepopulated messages and responses reminding young voters of the election and polling location.

Survey, interview, and participant observation data reveal how Central Valley youth organizing groups provided their members with a range of guided opportunities to contribute to voter outreach. As I detail in the next section, the extent to which individual members took part in and learned from their groups' activities varied.

Self-Reported Impact on Second-Generation Youth Members

Hands-on experience and guidance in civic action contributed to the transformative political socialization of second-generation members. Surveys collected from fifty second-generation members of youth organizing groups affiliated with the Power California network offer tentative evidence that members' capacity to take action in the civic arena increased, although results varied. The participants in the survey ranged in age from fifteen to thirty; 52 percent were current high school students, and 18 percent were noncitizens. Most young members (62 percent) were ineligible to vote because they did not meet age or citizenship requirements; yet they nonetheless exercised agency in government elections through education and outreach.

Figure 8.3   Members' Self-Reported Gains in Skills Relevant to Voter Outreach (N = 50)

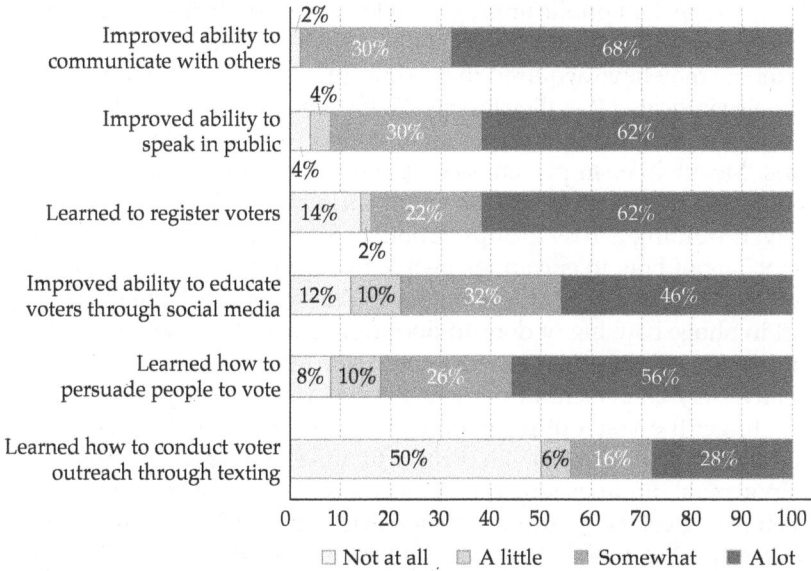

Source: Author's calculations based on the Survey of Central Valley Power California Fall Campaign Participants 2018.

Survey data (further detailed in an online appendix) provides self-reported information regarding the extent to which youth members acquired the confidence to conduct broad-based outreach around elections and other issues. Did group involvement in their organizations, including voter engagement efforts, affect their personal behavior or growth? Members had four answer options: their involvement had "no impact," "very little impact," "some impact," or "a lot of impact." As discussed in earlier chapters, such self-reports might suffer from a social desirability bias. However, the range of responses received indicates that participants were not reluctant to express honest opinions, and our observations of participants generally supported the varying results across groups. For example, our observations found that some groups offered their members more guidance on social media outreach than others, whereas some had a particularly strong focus on voter registration.

Figure 8.3 indicates that youth organizing groups paved the way for transformative political socialization. Findings suggest that 1.5- and second-generation youth felt they had enhanced their capacity to politicize broader audiences, but to varying degrees. For example, 68 percent of survey participants reported that their ability to communicate with others increased "a lot," while 62 percent said that their ability to speak in public improved "a lot." Most participants attributed their improved communication skills to their organizations, but some members may have acquired these skills prior to joining. About 62 percent also indicated that they learned "a lot" about how to register voters, and this finding was confirmed in interviews and participant observations. Meanwhile, 46 percent of respondents reported learning "a lot" about how to educate voters through social media, which reflects the uneven training across groups. Another 56 percent said they learned "a lot" about how to encourage people to vote, but 18 percent said they learned nothing or very little about how to do so, as not all members took part in phone banking or door-to-door canvassing. Thus, some members felt more confident than others about their ability to get out the vote. Finally, only 28 percent of participants reported learning "a lot" about how to get the vote out through texting, reflecting the fact that only a subset participated in training on how to utilize the texting platform.

In general, findings suggest that members enhanced their abilities to reach young voters as a result of their participation in their youth organizing groups. Yet, members unequally benefited from their involvement, either because they were novices who were still learning, because they had previously gained civic experience elsewhere, or because of uneven and inconsistent programming across organizations, among other possible explanations. Regardless, in a region with limited infrastructure, these youth organizing groups functioned as one of few training grounds for low-income, young second-generation immigrants to exercise their political muscle.

Impact on Young Voters

The transformative political socialization young people experienced in their Central Valley youth organizing groups facilitated their abilities to successfully engage their peers in the political process. These second-generation youth members represented a political force through their voter registration and mobilization efforts leading up to the 2018 November election. My research team and I observed more than sixty-five youth-led voter registration drives. While groups claimed to have preregistered and registered tens of thousands of voters, we unfortunately did not have noninvasive methods of gathering verifiable data on the unduplicated number of young residents who filled out voter registration cards. However, 2018 voting records offer more conclusive evidence that youth leaders influenced voter turnout. Here, I focus on the

Figure 8.4   The Impact of Youth Organizing Groups' Phone Banking
                Efforts on Turnout Among Central Valley Voters
                Aged Eighteen to Thirty-Four ($N = 105,512$)

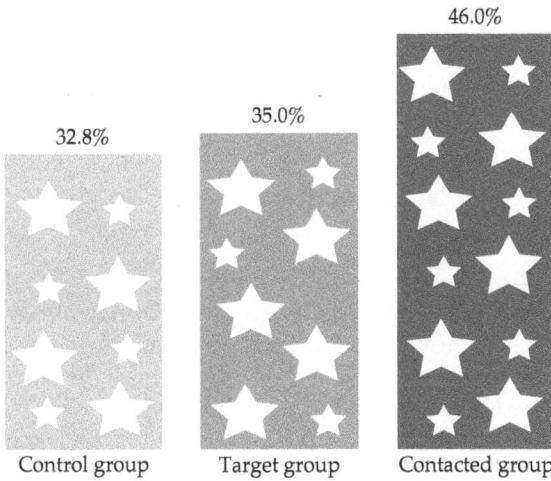

Source: Author's calculations based on Political Data Inc. and Power California.

more than 105,000 registered voters aged eighteen to thirty-four whom the Power California youth organizing groups targeted for mobilization. I compare voter turnout among a randomly selected control group of voters whom groups removed from call lists before phone banking began with voters of the same age whom groups targeted for outreach. Like other voting outreach experiments, I hope to account for why some individuals are more likely to answer the phone than others. I analyzed voting records using two-stage least square regression to estimate the extent to which phone calls by group members affected turnout.[24] My analysis controls for voting history, gender, Democratic Party registration, age, number of registered voters per household, voting method (mail or poll site), and zip code–level fixed effects. (The full analysis is available in an online appendix.)

Results shown in figure 8.4 indicate that youths' phone calls significantly increased turnout among young voters. Compared with the control group's nearly 33 percent estimated turnout, voters who were targeted for outreach (regardless of whether they answered the phone) averaged a turnout of 35 percent. In other words, youths' efforts increased overall turnout by roughly 2 percentage points among the target population (including those who voted by mail and those who voted in person combined). As demonstrated in other voter outreach experiments in immigrant communities, this is a noteworthy bump.[25] However, only 16 percent (or 24,127) of potential voters actually answered the phone. Among those who did, the estimated turnout was an impressive 46 percent; in other words, actual youth-initiated phone conversations resulted in an estimated 13 percentage-point increase in turnout. This research evidences youths' potential to effectively mobilize a large constituency of young voters.

Youth-Led Voter Mobilization and Social Change

In the fall of 2020, I reconnected with Eugene, who was taking online courses as a third-year college student at the University of California, San Diego. He had moved back home to Merced during the pandemic, where he had reconnected with 99Rootz and peers in his network. While deeply saddened by the suffering, loss, and grief he saw as many people in his community fell ill with COVID-19, Eugene was also hopeful and energized by all the voter outreach, mutual aid efforts, and anti-racist youth organizing he had been a part of that year:

> Since I started getting involved in the youth movement, Merced County has been on the rise. We are organizing actions that are youth led and youth centered. We are phone banking, canvassing, and registering our friends to vote. We are mailing our ballots and showing up to cast them at the polls to make sure our voices are heard and our priorities are reflected. With social media, there has been an increased presence and opportunity to connect with other youth leaders from different parts of the Central Valley. Youth are speaking up and sharing their stories that are very similar to ours, and until our elected officials finally choose us and bring us to the table, we won't stop.

Such confidence in the face of adversity was widespread. Through interviews with youth leaders and personal participation in online meetings, I concluded that second-generation youth like Eugene felt emboldened in 2020 in the Central Valley and across the country. I argue that a transformative political socialization facilitated their political activism in the wake of the racial reckoning around police violence and the political response to COVID-19. During this period, Eugene and others worked to get out the vote, in addition to mobilizing their peers to support Black Lives Matter protests, demanding that rent payments be canceled during the COVID-19 crisis, and participating in mutual aid efforts. Experience in youth organizing provided them with the tools and the motivation to engage others in a range of causes, even after they had aged out of adolescent youth organizing groups. In particular, the extensive guidance they received in multiple strategies for mobilizing young voters enabled these young people to serve as agents of horizontal (or peer-to-peer) political socialization, capable of educating others and inspiring them to take action.[26]

As of 2021, Central Valley youth organizing groups' grassroots policy victories remained modest, even though groups did find shared success in voter outreach. 99Rootz, for example, prompted a change in a school district policy previously banning high school students from wearing decorated caps that expressed cultural or political messaging during graduation ceremonies. 99Rootz also successfully advocated for a school district resolution that reinforced nonpartisan voter registration on high school campuses, and through coalitional efforts, youth members successfully convinced the city of Merced to dedicate a portion of the American Rescue Funds Act dollars to youth programs. Other more ambitious campaigns, such as those to defund school police and increase access to clean drinking water, stalled in 2020 and 2021. Meanwhile, other groups claimed a range of policy victories in the years prior to and during the pandemic; these included installing air quality monitors at local high schools, adding Wi-Fi access on buses, incorporating Punjabi language courses at select high schools, declaring sanctuary schools in a small district, and constructing hydration stations on school grounds.

Unfortunately, challenges during the COVID-19 pandemic undermined the stability of the nonprofit youth organizing sector the Central Valley. Nonetheless, the 2018 and 2020 elections demonstrated young people's potential to exercise their voice in a relatively hostile localized political context, inspiring groups like Delano-based Loud for Tomorrow to expand their geographic reach. As new organizational assemblages emerged in the early 2020s, young adult leaders continued to train younger cohorts, adapting their strategies to new technologies and evolving local and national political climates.

Youth-led voter mobilization efforts in the Central Valley demonstrate the possibilities for supporting young people's transformative political socialization, even within a more hostile localized political context. With appropriate guidance, adolescents can execute campaigns that achieve measurable impact. While continuing to innovate, such efforts must be properly calibrated to ensure participants' safety and be strategic to develop adolescents' skills and advance collective interests under conditions of constraint. Although requiring sustained commitment, long-term investments in comprehensive programming for adolescents can establish the foundation for immigrant and allied communities to cultivate durable forms of political power.

═ Chapter 9 ═

Leading for the Future

I N THE fall of 2020, Lilibeth Ramirez Gonzalez was struggling academically with online schooling during the COVID-19 pandemic. Living in the agricultural town of Santa Maria, California, she was also responsible for overseeing the online schooling of her younger sisters, aged eleven and thirteen, as well her two young cousins, aged five and six, who lived across the street. The educational responsibility disproportionately fell on Lilibeth because her parents, aunt, and uncle are migrants from Oaxaca with limited education. "At one point, I was basically failing all my classes, and all the homework was piling up. It was really hard for me," she said.

As Lilibeth's case demonstrates, the COVID-19 pandemic was particularly stressful for immigrant families and for economically and racially segregated communities of color. Lilibeth believed that Future Leaders of America (FLA) helped her get through this difficult time. With chapters in five cities throughout the adjacent coastal counties of Ventura and Santa Barbara, this youth organizing group met with members online weekly during the pandemic to check on their well-being. Lilibeth appreciated the ability to "reconnect with friends, since we weren't allowed to go out," and she felt these online gatherings helped her mental health. Like Lilibeth, many young people struggled with their mental health during the pandemic and the racial unrest occurring across the country,[1] and online meet-ups allowed members to process images of police violence, as well as their own experiences. Members shared tips and strategies for staying safe and managing online schooling. Staff adapted their regular college-preparatory support services to keep students motivated and invested in pursuing a postsecondary education. Through it all, FLA also managed to keep members involved in campaign-related work, though not always as consistently as it had before the pandemic. The various chapters continued to make progress—and in some cases, claim important victories—on campaigns focused on high school grading policies, local smoking bans, alcohol sales to minors, mental health resources in schools, an eviction moratorium, and local redistricting.[2]

176

https://doi.org/10.7758/gert1126.1368

Lilibeth stayed in school despite the pandemic-related mental health challenges and suboptimal learning conditions, but others in FLA were not as fortunate; some left school to work in the agricultural fields when their parents lost their jobs or became sick. As FLA's Santa Maria organizer Angel Lopez noted when I interviewed him in 2021, the pandemic was just the latest in a string of emotional hardships the students had experienced in recent years, along with, for example, the massive 2017 and 2018 Thomas Fire, which burned 281,893 acres in Ventura and Santa Barbara Counties and disproportionately threatened the health, lives, and livelihoods of immigrant farmworkers.[3]

FLA is located in California's Central Coast, a region characterized by moderate or mixed support for immigrant rights. Like the Santa Ana youth featured in chapter 5, FLA's members resided in a primarily Latinx city and could rely on an emerging network of allies. At the same time, FLA members were not insulated from the rhetoric of prominent Central Coast right-wing activists who vocally advocated against critical race theory, sexual health education, abortion access, and voting, immigrant, and LGBTQ rights.[4] Indeed, the dominant political discourse of the region likely added to the stresses youth were already experiencing during the pandemic.

In the midst of these trying circumstances, my research on young leaders and their organizations offers strategies for well-being, collective action, and resistance. I found that FLA and other youth organizing groups persisted during the darkest days of the COVID-19 pandemic; members participated in online healing circles, testified at virtual public hearings, shared public health guidance, and supported racial justice protests (virtually and in person). And, as I finalized this book in 2025 as the second Trump administration began mass deportations and defunding federal agencies, these organizations served as vehicles for disseminating "know your rights" information and mutual aid. Some also worked with local government institutions to safeguard residents' rights. Youth organizing groups and their alumni networks modeled responses to crises that centered the needs of racially diverse low-income residents and immigrant families.

Transformative Political Socialization and the Second Generation

Throughout this book, I have demonstrated how second-generation immigrant youth experience a transformative political socialization. Drawing on extensive data, I focused on young people's experiences across ethnically diverse communities and regions. While I spotlighted California, this research applies to other parts of the country with large or growing immigrant populations and varying receptivity toward immigrants. The young people featured came from poor and racially segregated communities and from immigrant and refugee families who disproportionately encountered barriers to political participation. Yet, many learned to exercise civic leadership through nonpartisan youth organizing groups, which provided targeted developmental supports, exposed them to a critical civics curriculum, and guided them in taking civic action. This youth-centered programming eclipsed that of other socializing agents (like parents, schools, and social media) that determine whether and how adolescents learn to take part in local political processes.

To varying degrees, organizing groups took an intersectional approach to their work. Programming prompted members to think about their own multiple identities and encouraged them to consider how—through collective efforts—they might address overlapping and unjust power dynamics. A transformative political socialization helped second-generation, low-income, and sometimes undocumented, queer, or trans youth to overcome the challenges of growing up in immigrant communities facing multiple injustices, eventually enabling them to exercise civic leadership.

Over the past few decades, grassroots youth organizing arguably developed into what DiMaggio and Powell call a distinct "organizational field."[5] As discussed in chapter 2, these 501(c)3 nonprofit groups have multiplied across the country since the 1990s, sharing and refining their practices along the way. In California, elders from late twentieth-century civil rights, labor, and sanctuary movements initially guided these groups with the goals of countering the injustices faced by young people of color, including immigrants. Statewide and local networks diffused early curricula, which embraced the historical memory and organizing repertoires of these iconic movements. In the 2010s, statewide intermediary organizations like YO Cali! and Power California helped disseminate best practices and furthered organizations' abilities to engage in nonpartisan election processes and policy reforms, sometimes in alignment with contemporaneous social movements. These nonprofit organizations introduced adolescents across the country to multiple approaches to advancing political change that fell outside partisan politics.

This book offers ample evidence of how robust programming can propel second-generation and other youth into civic leadership roles. Chapter 3 demonstrated that adolescents who had joined such organizations in high school tended to remain highly politically active in early adulthood. Many members self-reported that they had benefited from their involvement, offering evidence that they experienced a transformative political socialization, in spite of self-selection processes that inspired youth to join these organizations in the first place. In chapter 4, I shared the case of the undocumented youth leaders to demonstrate how civic competencies can be cultivated during adolescence in ways that can prepare young people to define national debates once they reach adulthood. I demonstrated that a significant proportion of young people at the helm of the immigrant youth movement in California benefited from their prior involvement in adolescent youth organizing groups. Formative experience in youth organizing groups that addressed health, education equity, environmental justice, or immigration issues facilitated young immigrants' abilities to lead the undocumented youth movement as it gained national attention in the early 2010s. At the time, many of those leaders were college students or recent graduates who had applied theories of intersectionality to make sense of their identity, manage their organizations, and define their campaigns. This intersectional approach contributed to the inclusivity of subsequent organizing efforts; some former leaders of the undocumented youth movement went on to work for or found youth organizing groups. For example, Eder Gaona-Macedo, an alumnus of FLA who was prominent in advocating for the Dream Act while an undergraduate at University of California, Los Angeles, returned to the organization as its executive director from 2014 to 2021, leveraging intersectional frameworks to guide a new focus on grassroots organizing. Meanwhile, other young immigrant leaders joined statewide and local intermediary organizations, further diffusing intersectional approaches to youth organizing.

In part II of this book, I outlined the elements of transformative political socialization in greater depth. Chapter 5 showed how ROC helped youth emotionally process everyday experiences and challenges. Their members resided in a largely undocumented immigrant community in Orange County, where the deportation and criminalization of their loved ones were legitimate concerns. ROC's attentiveness to the stress and trauma in this community provided members with the emotional bandwidth to take political action. While some groups across the state offered similar wellness programming that fostered young people's resilience and hopefulness, others placed a greater focus on ensuring members' academic success or connecting them with social services that could support their healthy transition to adulthood, as discussed in chapter 2. Regardless of their campaign priorities, most youth organizing groups devoted significant resources and time to helping low-income adolescents thrive during a stage of the life course characterized by tremendous growth and resilience. A focus on adolescent development set these groups apart from community organizing, social movement, and other political groups with adult memberships.

During adolescence, individuals deepen their exploration of who they are and their place in the world.[6] Capitalizing on this growing self-awareness, youth organizing groups incorporated a critical approach to civics education that focused on members' multiple and diverse identities. Similar to what Cohen and colleagues refer to as a "lived civics" approach, programs drew from ethnic, gender, and LGBTQ studies to prompt young people to reflect on their identities and their community's challenges.[7] In sharing the histories and struggles of their own and other marginalized groups through staff- and peer-led activities, members developed a critical consciousness that informed how they sought to change social conditions, for example by addressing multiple forms of inequality in their activities and campaigns. In this vein, chapter 6 featured AYPAL and YT, Oakland groups that used intersectional approaches to promote pride in their members' racial, ethnic, immigrant, refugee, gender, and queer identities while cultivating solidarity among diverse peers. They coupled this intersectional approach to power and inequality with training on how government systems can be pressured to be more inclusive. I argue that this critical approach to civics education laid the groundwork for members to participate in coalitional campaigns around youth concerns.

With guidance from staff and veteran peers, adolescents practiced leading civic actions, expanding on their abilities to collectively influence policies and get out the vote. For example, in chapter 7, I outlined the various ways in which ICS's United Students members developed their voice and planned activities; they also utilized these basic civic skills to educate and mobilize others. In a local political context like East Los Angeles, adolescents contributed to large intergenerational coalitions to carry out ambitious campaigns. Meanwhile, in a hostile political context like the Central Valley, where fewer allies could offer support, the goals of grassroots campaigns were often more modest. Nonetheless, youth effectively channeled their energy, for example through peer-to-peer outreach to get out the vote, as described in chapter 8.

Immigrant Incorporation

The concept of transformative political socialization draws from literatures on immigrant incorporation, adolescent political socialization and development, and intersectionality and politics. The sociological literature on immigration examines the unequal mobility trajectories of immigrant groups, or why some fare better socioeconomically than others.[8] Those who arrive in the United States with comparatively limited means, encounter a blocked pathway to citizenship, or face adverse racialization processes will likely encounter barriers to their upward mobility.[9] However, socioeconomic trajectories do not necessarily parallel patterns of political incorporation, as youth from marginalized back-grounds can exhibit higher levels of political activity when compared with peers from more advantaged backgrounds.[10]

My research emphasizes the importance of adolescents' political socialization in explaining why some second-generation youth from low-income and multiply marginalized backgrounds become influential civic leaders. Political socialization can be understood as the ongoing and interactive processes through which young people acquire knowledge about, attitudes toward, and a sense of agency in public affairs.[11] However, earlier research suggests that socializing agents can reproduce disparities in political participation.[12] Low-income, racialized, and immigrant adolescents often lack access to socializing agents directing them toward civic leadership or public actions in their own communities. After all, their parents may lack U.S. citizenship, English-language skills, formal schooling, and knowledge about government processes. Because they are focused on providing for their families' daily needs—and may possibly fear political entanglements—parents might be unable to model political participation within the household.[13] The children of immigrants face further disadvantages in that they often attend under-resourced schools that lack challenging civics curricula and extensive opportunities for extracurricular involvement.[14] This is not to say that parents or schools always fail to impart values, skills, or experiences that could lead to public engagement, only that doing so is often much more difficult in high-poverty communities.

Part of the problem is that mainstream political parties have often failed to meaningfully include immigrants in political discourse—and, at times, have enacted policies or adopted rhetoric that pushes them further into the margins. This can leave civic organizations to fill the void.[15] By demonstrating how young people become invested in and active contributors to the political life of their communities, my empirical findings align with a growing body of research that shows how social movement and other civic organizations facilitate immigrants' participation in political processes.[16] In this vein, I build on prior scholarship by emphasizing adolescence as a key period for shaping the political trajectories of second-generation youth from low-income communities.

Accordingly, I draw attention to the oft-overlooked political power of adolescents. Broader public discussions about politics often ignore adolescents in favor of eligible voters, including young adults who disproportionately participate in social movements and older adults who dominate elected and appointed positions of power. Yet, adolescents have successfully demanded policy changes and influenced voter turnout and will continue to do so in the future. By focusing on members of youth organizing groups, I show how socialization processes can prepare young people to exercise political influence. In the right group settings, adolescents can make sense of—and take action to address—public concerns in sophisticated ways.[17] I demonstrate that young people can aid in the political incorporation of their immigrant communities by engaging peers and other residents in policy change and electoral campaigns that ultimately pressure institutions to become more responsive to their shared concerns. As such, investments in adolescents' civic development can have both short-term and long-term consequences for altering power dynamics in immigrant communities.

Scholars have long puzzled over the relationship between social movements and electoral politics.[18] My research demonstrates how young people can develop an investment in both. In their political efforts, members of youth organizing groups drew inspiration from past social movements and reinforced the goals of contemporary ones. As they led campaigns around education reform, health equity, immigrant rights, environmental justice, and other social justice issues, they gained insights into how electoral measures could advance their causes and how responsive elected officials could boost their campaigns' momenta. And, while mobilizing around elections across different parts of California, young leaders also supported gun reforms in alliance with Parkland, Florida, youth; demanded the defunding of school police in solidarity with the Movement for Black Lives; and advocated for health insurance for undocumented immigrants in partnership with the broader immigrant rights movement. Through youth organizing, adolescent members gained formative exposure to multiple strategies for advancing political change.

Youth organizing thus exposes young people to different approaches to citizenship. In their influential study, Joel Westheimer and Joseph Kahne suggest that effective civic interventions in a healthy democracy may advance one of two approaches to citizenship: a participatory model focusing on informed engagement in government systems and community improvement efforts or a justice-oriented model facilitating critiques of social and political structures but offering young people limited direct experience in advancing change.[19] This research uniquely demonstrates that both participatory and justice-oriented conceptualizations of citizenship can be incorporated into age-appropriate programming so that adolescents can effectively exercise a voice in ways that concretely address injustices and promote equity and inclusion.

Intersectional Politics and Broader Social Change

Intersectional frameworks can help adolescents advance their understanding of social issues affecting their diverse communities and inform their civic actions. During adolescence, young people begin to reflect more deeply on how their race, gender, citizenship status, sexual orientation, and other identities have shaped their life; they also begin to understand how systems of oppression overlap to produce complex social inequalities.[20] This intersectional thinking can prompt adolescents to engage in more inclusionary organizational practices that attend to not only their own pressing needs but also those of their diverse peers. Moreover, intersectional thinking can prompt second-generation immigrant youth to work in solidarity with other groups that are primarily led by nonimmigrants (such as Black Lives Matter and March for Our Lives).

Such a collective, intersectional orientation challenges both U.S. individualism and right-wing authoritarianism by calling for systemic changes that ensure fairer treatment of historically marginalized immigrant and racial groups. In addition, this orientation spurs young people to fearlessly challenge gender norms and homophobia as they advance their own political agenda. In short, young people learn to fight for social and political changes that benefit not only their own ethnic groups or communities but also other constituencies suffering from social inequalities and injustices. In this regard, youth organizing begins to cultivate political imaginaries that resonate with what Daniel Martinez HoSang conceptualizes as "a wider type of freedom"—a vision of society that prioritizes collective liberation and interdependence, made possible through the dismantling of oppressive systems.[21]

Political Contexts and Local Programmatic Adaptations

Localized political contexts can define the strategies and characteristics of youth movements.[22] Nevertheless, I contend that adolescents may experience transformative political socialization across distinct geographies, making findings applicable outside of California. My research demonstrates that youth can develop the civic competencies to be at the forefront of campaigns, whether they live in welcoming localized political contexts (such as Los Angeles and Oakland) or moderate or mixed (Santa Ana and Santa Maria) or conservative (Central Valley) ones. Their organizations, however, make local adaptations to their curricula, strategies, campaign goals, or other aspects of their programming in ways that respond to the social terrain in which they operate.

Local demographics, histories of resistance, and the availability of supportive civic infrastructures define the contours of organizational programming. For example, in Santa Ana, Resilience OC adapted its program to respond to the criminalization of immigrants and young people; youth not only spearheaded campaigns to dismantle the school-to-prison-to-deportation pipeline but also offered its primarily Latinx membership the space to process how local policing and immigration enforcement impacted their emotional well-being. And as I demonstrated, groups in the comparatively welcoming contexts of the Bay Area and Los Angeles benefit from extensive civil and immigrant rights histories and networks. Specifically, I highlighted how Oakland-based AYPAL and Youth Together adapted their curricula to draw on the histories of local ethnic groups and social movements to advance a critical civics education attentive to wide-ranging ethnic diversity. Meanwhile, at InnerCity Struggle (ICS), located in the Eastside of Los Angeles, youth participated in ambitious intergenerational campaigns that leveraged a supportive civic infrastructure. In contrast, youth organizing groups in the Central Valley took a different approach, adapting to their hostile context and limited allied networks by prioritizing peer-to-peer outreach to mobilize voters. By highlighting local adaptations to youth programming, my research builds on prior work that demonstrates how subnational contexts alter the dynamics of immigrant civic organizations and social movements.[23] It also offers a framework for thinking about how civic organizations might make local adaptations when politically engaging immigrant communities outside of California.

Empirical Contributions and Limitations

This book offers an extensive empirical account of how second-generation immigrant youth learned to advance their own and their community's political incorporation. It demonstrates how youth organizing groups operating in segregated non-white communities fostered the transformative political socialization of small but highly active cadres of young people. Attentive to their community's diversity, adolescents exercised their political muscle across distinct localized political contexts.

While this study incorporates multiple sources of data gathered primarily throughout the 2010s, some key limitations (which I elaborate on in the appendix) offer opportunities for further research. Perhaps most obvious, I rely on cross-sectional survey and interview data that do not allow me to make causal claims that participation in youth organizing encourages the children of immigrants to become civic leaders. Moreover, I rely heavily on self-reported data, which are subject to the social desirability bias typical of survey and interview methods.[24] Although I triangulate self-reports with occasional participant observations and secondary sources to mitigate desirability bias, I cannot completely resolve the inherent limitations of self-reported data.[25] Experimental research could better measure the extent to which programming drives youths' political participation, while ethnographic methods would be better suited to capture the richness and nuance of organizational practices.

While this research offers strong evidence that developmental supports, a critical civics education, and guidance in civic action, in some combination, contribute to the transformative political socialization of second-generation immigrant youth, it does not offer a precise formula for success. Future studies might examine how organizations could achieve the right balance among the three components. Research might also account for the evolving national political climate, digital platforms, and AI in shaping youths' political development.

My findings also indicate that organizations tailor their programming to their localized political contexts. In the cases I feature in this book, I note how groups make local adaptations that respond to the demographics, histories of resistance, and civic infrastructures of the immigrant communities they serve. The local malleability of programming merits future study as communities respond to changing political dynamics. Still, my findings have important practical implications.

Applications

My research offers directions for those seeking to support adolescents in building their own political power. To begin with, youth organizing groups across the United States, and possibly elsewhere in the world, can disseminate best practices and continue to adapt to the evolving needs of adolescents and their communities. Additionally, schools, other youth-serving institutions, and informal collectives can adopt or expand on elements of the programming featured in this book. Amid a shifting national political climate and varied regional dynamics, localized adaptations to programming can help ensure that adolescents remain safe as they build their capacities to effectuate political change.

Implications for Youth Organizing Groups

My research suggests that youth organizing groups generally facilitate the transformative socialization of their members, but they do so to varying degrees. Adolescent members differ in the extent to which they benefit from developmental supports, access a critical civics education, and feel prepared to lead campaigns. Retention matters, as members who stay involved with their organizations for one year or longer tend to experience the most growth. Accordingly, findings offer insights into the elements of robust programming for nonprofit and other groups that seek to engage young people in building political power.

As a starting point, youth organizing and related groups should seek to offer comprehensive developmental supports, especially for young people who have the greatest needs. Attending to youths' emotional well-being is paramount, as they face numerous stressors related to poverty, anti-immigrant policies, racism, climate change, and political strife. Healing and self-care activities help adolescents cope with daily challenges as they collectively process their personal hardships and build a supportive community; these activities also empower them with a sense of hope and emotional resilience, enabling them to engage in contentious politics.

In addition to focusing on well-being, organizations should address adolescents' academic, professional, legal, and other needs. Connections to age-appropriate services distinguish these youth organizing groups from adult grassroots organizing groups that do not have to attend to the developmental needs of adolescents who experience multiple hardships and stressors. Youth organizations that encounter funding constraints may consider providing referrals to appropriate services available within their communities. Arguably, these developmental supports benefit individual youth members and contribute to their retention, thus strengthening the leadership capacity of the group as a whole.

In general, youth organizing groups offer a critical civics education that raises awareness of social diversity, power inequalities, and policy issues affecting their communities and beyond. The breadth, depth, and focus of the training curriculum can vary across organizations. Therefore, groups might consider sharing their curricula and best practices through intermediary organizations, regional gatherings, digital media, and allied networks. Moreover, curricula must adapt to evolving local demographics, power dynamics, and policy landscapes.

As demonstrated, youth organizing groups provide adolescents from immigrant and other low-income communities intensive guidance in participating in civic and political activities. However, in observing these groups for more than two decades, I have noticed that at times, staff themselves require training on how to best equip their adolescent members to find their own voice and take ownership of campaign efforts. Therefore, formal development training sessions, fellowship programs, or boot camps on grassroots organizing strategies and tactics could help adult allies more effectively empower adolescents to carry out grassroots policy change or voter mobilization campaigns on their own.[26] As demonstrated in chapters 7 and 8, with proper guidance and scaffolding, adolescents can grow in their abilities to drive political change.

Given the role of youth organizations in shaping the civic trajectory of their members and communities, government agencies arguably should provide monetary or in-kind support to expand their reach. Currently, these nonprofit groups disproportionately rely on private foundation support, which can be unstable and require continual investment in time to pursue.[27] Some groups, however, have managed to secure help from local city, county, or state governments to survive. Youth organizing groups in Oakland, Richmond, Long Beach, Sacramento, and Pomona, for example, are eligible to receive city funds, thanks to successful ballot initiatives promoted by youth organizing groups. This is a welcome development; as prominent immigration scholars have argued, municipal governments can and should play a stronger role in facilitating the political incorporation of immigrant groups.[28]

Implications for Schools and Other Youth-Serving Institutions

A very small proportion of low-income, second-generation immigrant adolescent youth across the United States can access nonprofit youth organizing groups. However, certain aspects of youth organizing programming can be brought to scale, with local adaptations, through more widespread and equitable adoption in schools or other youth-serving institutions.

Young people who experience multiple stressors often require a range of developmental supports to bolster their civic and political participation. In chapter 5, I highlighted youth organizing groups' healing and restorative practices that promote members' general well-being. Some of these collective healing activities overlap with those offered by school and community-based restorative justice programs that prepare young people and other community members to collectively address conflict, misbehavior, and crises. When properly implemented, such restorative justice programs also create safe spaces for young people to process their emotions and develop support networks.[29] With adequate funding, culturally competent staff, and buy-in from community leaders, restorative justice and other wellness programs can improve disciplinary issues and contribute to healthier behaviors among adolescents who are exposed to multiple stressors.[30] Healing can also inspire a form of radical hope, or a belief in a better future that persists in the face of hardship.[31] Hence, such programs may be a worthwhile investment for promoting well-being, expanding political imagination, and motivating political action among those most impacted by systemic inequalities.

Targeted programs that facilitate upward socioeconomic mobility for second-generation youth remain important.[32] For instance, many youth organizing groups provide members with academic and career guidance, even though engaging their members in campaigns is their primary focus. In this regard, my study echoes educational research emphasizing the need to invest in K–12 systems, career development, and mentoring programs in high-poverty communities.[33] However, academic and other developmental supports alone cannot provide second-generation youth with the analytic experience or concrete civic skills to take informed action.

Rather, these supports must be combined with the kind of critical civics education offered by youth organizing groups that inspires adolescents to participate in ways that attend to the diversity of their communities. Schools and other youth-serving institutions can offer similar and potentially more extensive critical civics curricula. For example, prior research shows that semester-long high school ethnic studies courses allow students to explore their identities and expand their understanding of social inequalities.[34] Moreover, courses that incorporate what is sometimes referred to as lived civics—or reading, assignments, lectures, discussions, and peer presentations covering local issues and identities—can further enhance students' civic development.[35] Such curricula should be made available to English-language learners.[36] And, whenever possible, it should take an intersectional approach and expose students to overlapping systems of oppression and the complex ways in which these systems manifest themselves locally. Educators, however, may encounter significant constraints to what they can teach in locales with strong political opposition to teaching about race, gender, and sexuality.[37]

Regardless of local political dynamics, educators may still be able to build on traditional and nonpartisan civics curricula to expose students to election procedures, local policy debates, and government decision processes. They can teach students how to find reliable information, host classroom debates, and clarify the roles of elected officials at different levels of government. Social studies teachers can appeal to young people's sense of fairness and justice by explaining the history of voting rights and the age gap in voting rates; they can raise questions about how voting can lead to more equitable representation within their local communities. Additionally, educators can incorporate service learning and youth participatory action into regular coursework, orienting diverse students toward policy debates and collective action.[38]

Outside of school, youth-serving organizations and institutions also offer a critical civics education. Youth arts programs focusing on the visual arts or poetry can spur students to reflect on their identity and local community concerns.[39] Programs connected to the juvenile justice system can also take a critical civics approach to educating adolescents.[40]

While curricular interventions help raise consciousness and increase political motivation, most adolescents from low-income and immigrant backgrounds will still need coaching on how to take civic action. As a starting point, teachers and other youth workers must strive to develop students' voices and enable them to collaborate with others around shared goals. This approach must involve classroom pedagogical practices that encourage active dialogue and public speaking.[41] Adolescents can further develop their basic civic skills through opportunities to run meetings, coordinate events, and communicate effectively through multiple forms of media.

Because certain students will be more eager to participate than others, effectively engaging the "average" (or more reticent) student may therefore require effort on the part of school leaders. To accomplish this, schools could follow the example of ICS, featured in chapter 7, and sponsor academies or training camps where students learn how to run meetings, plan activities, publicize events through various media, and conduct public outreach. In addition, schools—especially those serving students from less privileged backgrounds—can offer stipends or give course releases to teachers or other school personnel who train club members. For example, one Los Angeles high school employed a campus unification director to meet with the leaders of various social and cultural clubs to coordinate and plan school events, including those that raise student awareness about social justice concerns. Acting like a youth organizer, the unification director guided leaders on how to run their meetings effectively, engage their broader memberships, and organize school-wide activities.

As I have argued, youth organizing groups provide members with guidance in navigating political processes. Offering hands-on training in collective action can pose a challenge for schools and other youth-serving institutions due to time and staffing constraints, not to mention political opposition. Still, schools, perhaps in collaboration with the county registrar and recorder's office, can effectively promote peer-to-peer voter registration and preregistration in states where adolescents are eligible to preregister before their eighteenth birthday.[42] Staging mock elections is yet another way for schools to introduce students to voting processes.[43]

Students might gain further direct exposure to political processes through school governance.[44] Typically limited to a small number of students, such opportunities involve serving on school decision-making bodies, school district hearings, district-wide councils, or city and county youth commissions. These formalized decision-making bodies grant select adolescents a direct voice in policy debates but do not usually provide experience in taking collective action.[45] Adolescents will need additional training to engage in these processes; otherwise, their involvement risks being merely symbolic or disconnected from constituents' interests.[46] Furthermore, to guard against reproducing political inequalities, sponsoring agencies will need to extensively recruit and support adolescents from low-income, immigrant, and other underrepresented backgrounds.

Given their mission, youth organizing groups may be best equipped to train low-income and second-generation immigrant adolescents in collective political action focused on nonpartisan grassroots campaigns and voter outreach. As such, schools and other youth-serving institutions can actively seek to partner with local youth organizing groups (where possible) to expand the number of students participating in nonpartisan politics. In this regard, community schools—which provide staffing and communication infrastructure to connect school systems to local service providers, nonprofit agencies, and ethnic organizations—represent one promising reform initiative increasingly adopted nationally in the first half of the 2020s. Community schools (or similar initiatives) can serve as a mechanism for linking students to much-needed developmental supports as well as civic initiatives (including grassroots campaigns) aligned with community interests.[47] In strengthening linkages outside of the K-12 system, schools can potentially promote the transformative political socialization of greater numbers of diverse adolescents in ways that are responsive to local dynamics.

Leading for the Future

When I spoke to Lilibeth toward the end of her senior year, she was planning to go away to college. She intended to pursue a business-related degree, which she thought would enable her to contribute to her growing community as it experienced new economic development. "I am going to come back to Santa Maria just because my whole family's here, and I still feel like there's a lot of need for change here in Santa Maria," she asserted. Looking ahead, Lilibeth wanted to continue supporting FLA's campaign to pressure the school district to increase access to college-preparatory courses; she also wanted to help ensure that college graduates can return home to pursue careers that benefit their local community. "The new jobs should go to people who grew up here, who understand the community, and who will be considerate of what we need," she said. In addition, she sought to advocate for "more affordable and better family housing for the people who already reside in Santa Maria, so people don't need to cram their entire family into one room." Lilibeth was aware of the persistent patterns of racial and economic inequality, recognizing that outsiders, mainly more affluent whites, could easily take good jobs and spaces in new housing developments. "That's not right, and we need to stop that from happening," she said.

Thanks to FLA, Lilibeth was already well networked with former members who had maintained ties to their communities throughout and after college. This network included one of her mentors, Gloria Soto, an FLA alumnus who, at age twenty-eight, was elected to the Santa Maria City Council in 2018. Through her involvement, Lilibeth met other alumni who remained connected to the organization, including individuals who worked in government, schools, academia, nonprofits, philanthropy, and health care.

As this robust network demonstrates, youth organizing groups instill in their members a deep and lasting commitment to advancing social change in their communities and beyond. Indeed, the FLA alumni I met at events and gatherings were, like Lilibeth, intent on "giving back."[48] These young people represent a small but well-organized contingent of individuals who had invaluable formative experience in shifting social policies and educating voters. As the children of immigrants who are emboldened to take political action, they are not naive about the challenges to achieving their goals. As Lilibeth explained, "It's hard work, and it takes time, but at FLA, you learn that you can't give up, even when people are against you. Maybe you don't get exactly what you want, or when you want it, but together you can make a positive difference."

Lilibeth maintained a sense of hope in the summer of 2025, as she and others in her networks guided community members on how to prepare for ICE raids ordered by the second Trump administration. "Eventually, things will get better for everyone, but it's going to require a lot of people getting involved," she asserted. In addition to sharing valuable information and safety strategies, she underscored a critical step forward—educating voters. While taking a collective and pragmatic approach to politics, Lilibeth exemplified the commitment and perseverance of many youth organizing group members whom I met. Their young voices present alternative visions of democratic governance that stand in direct contrast to right-wing authoritarianism. Having undergone a transformative political socialization, Lilibeth and others like her have become better equipped to fight for a better future for their communities and the nation.

═ Appendix ═

Data Sources ·

*L*EARNING TO LEAD relies on extensive and layered data. The research behind this book includes multiple waves of surveys and semi-structured interviews collected over ten years, alongside secondary data sources and participant observations. As someone who is deeply invested in community-engaged research and has been connected to youth organizations for twenty-five years, I designed much of the data collection to address not only my own academic research questions but also topics raised by community partners. As such, I am deeply grateful to the young people, staff, and other community stakeholders who participated in and contributed to this research. I am also indebted to the graduate, undergraduate, and high school students who helped collect and analyze the data and added their own valuable insights to the project.

The manuscript synthesizes multiple overlapping and complementary studies I've carried out, including the CYAS from 2011 to 2013, the Youth Leadership and Health Study (YLHS) from 2013 to 2021, the Central Valley Freedom Summer Participatory Action Research Project in 2018, and the FCYO Field Scan in 2019. I triangulated results from these studies with secondary data—news stories, social media posts, and organizational websites. Taken together, these data—listed in table A.1—allow me to examine broad patterns in the field as well as different aspects of youth experiences in greater depth. The following summarizes key data sources, while a longer online methodological appendix provides more detailed information on my positionality, data, and approaches to data analysis.

Studies Included in *Learning to Lead*

The CYAS is a mixed-methods investigation of youth transitions to adulthood. Conducted between 2011 and 2013, it includes surveys of a representative sample of young adults (the general population), alumni members of eight youth organizing groups, and members of Dreamer organizations. My research team and I conducted follow-up interviews

https://doi.org/10.7758/gert1126.9130

Table A.1   Data Sources

Study	Total Sample Size	Relevant Chapters
California Young Adult Study (2011–2012)		
Surveys		
General population	2,200	3
Youth organizing	410	3
Undocumented youth activists	503	4
Semi-structured interviews		
General population	175	3, 4
Youth organizing	84	3, 4, 6, 7
Undocumented youth activists	66	4
Youth organizing staff	8	1, 2, 4, 6, 7
Youth Leadership and Health Study (2013–2021)		
Surveys		
Youth members (2014)	1,149	7
Youth members (2016)	1,396	3, 7
Semi-structured interviews		
Youth organizing members	180	1, 2, 3, 5, 6, 7, 8
Youth organizing staff	98	All
Central Valley Freedom Summer Participatory Action Research Project (2018)		
Participant observations	1,600 hours	8
Youth member surveys	71	8
Voting records	105,512	8
Funders Collaborative on Youth Organizing (2019)		
Survey		
Groups serving adolescents	283	2, 8
Other data		
Reviews of websites, social media, and news stories	NA	All
Informal participant observations	NA	All

Source: Author's compilation.

with a subsample of survey participants in each of the three target populations. The data also include in-depth interviews with a staff member in each of the eight youth organizing groups.

Building on findings from the CYAS, the book also draws on the YLHS, a more targeted examination of the civic learning processes within nonprofit youth civic groups (including youth organizing groups and apolitical public-oriented groups). As the field grew across the state,

I expanded the pool of youth organizing groups I observed. I commenced the study with an initial 2013 to 2014 survey of sixty-eight youth organizing staff in thirteen low-income communities across California, then carried out a membership census of most of these groups. Based on what I learned from staff and youth—and after identifying additional groups across the state to include—I administered a revised statewide 2015 staff survey, followed by a refined 2016 survey to members in ninety-six organizations (including forty-three youth organizing groups). Next, between 2018 and 2020, my research team and I conducted 180 in-depth interviews of youth organizing group members to gather more data on their experiences with everyday group activities and campaigns. To complement these semi-structured interview data, we also conducted eight focus groups and 98 interviews with youth organizing staff. AYPAL and Youth Together also generously shared their curriculum outlines to inform my understanding of their work. Given the breadth and scope of the YLHS, I only use a portion of the collected data in the book.

Through the 2018 Central Valley Freedom Summer Participatory Action Research Project, I deepened my analysis of how youth learn to take civic action to amplify their voice in government elections. In partnership with Power California and other youth organizing groups, my research team and I gathered extensive data in the Central Valley, where groups were investing significant time on voter education and where grassroots policy change campaigns tended to be relatively modest. As part of this study, I trained student researchers through coursework at the University of California at Santa Cruz (then my home institution) and Merced. I then placed twenty students (all Central Valley natives) as interns in youth organizing groups, where they gathered more than 1,600 hours of observational data on voter education efforts. Students also collected surveys from members of select youth organizing groups, and their responses provided additional information about how these groups enhanced their members' abilities to aid nonpartisan voter education efforts. Finally, in partnership with Power California, I also analyzed voting records to test the impact of youth organizations' voter outreach on turnout in the 2018 midterm election.

To contextualize my analyses of California groups, the book also incorporates a 2019 national survey of youth organizing groups. Collected in partnership with the Research Hub for Youth Organizing at the University of Colorado Boulder, the surveys were part of a national field scan of youth organizing groups commissioned by the Funders Collaborative on Youth Organizing (FCYO), a philanthropic intermediary organization. The universe for this survey came from FCYO's national registry of youth organizing groups, as well as my own comprehensive list of California youth organizing groups. I refer to this survey as the FCYO

Field Scan and restrict my analysis to groups that include adolescents, thus excluding organizations solely comprising young adults.

To further ensure that I had a comprehensive understanding of youth organizing groups, my team and I reviewed California groups' websites, public social media postings, and select news articles. These data were especially helpful in contextualizing the campaigns that youth members and staff referenced in interviews. Finally, I attended a variety of youth organizing events over the past twenty-five years, including a handful of statewide convenings in the 2010s. While my participant observations were in no way systematic, my occasional in-person presence over this extended period allowed me to watch the field grow, develop relationships with organizational staff and members, and contextualize my analysis in this book.

In sum, *Learning to Lead* is grounded in comprehensive data and shaped by my years of involvement in the field. Readers may consult the online appendix to further evaluate the empirical analyses that drive the arguments in this book. Readers may also review the disaggregated data featured in more than forty-five reports that students and I published through the University of Southern California Equity Research Institute; the University of California, Santa Cruz, Institute for Social Transformation; and the University of California, Los Angeles, Chicano Studies Research Center.

═ Notes ═

Chapter 1: Ain't No Power Like the Power of the Youth

1. Frey 2014. The board's action was supported by a new state law, the Local Control Funding Formula, which earmarked additional resources for school districts for which at least 55 percent of students were identified as being low-income, English language learners, or foster youth.

2. I use the term "Latinx" because it was the dominant term adopted by study participants when I finished data collection. I recognize that self-identification among young people whose ancestors hail from Mexico, Central America, South America, and the Spanish-speaking Caribbean varies and evolves.

3. Hondagneu-Sotelo and Pastor 2021.

4. The Equity Research Institute (2024) estimates that approximately 41 percent of all families in South Central and Southeast Los Angeles in 2021 were of mixed status.

5. H. Kwon 2024.

6. Niemi and Hepburn 1995.

7. Flood et al. 2021.

8. Akee et al. 2019; Chetty et al. 2014.

9. Dreby 2015; Valdivia 2021; Asad 2020.

10. Hagerman 2024; Phoenix and Arora 2018; Rodriguez 2022.

11. Rios 2011; Warren 2021; Lo 2018.

12. Flood et al. 2021.

13. Gates 2017.

14. Robert Smith 2024.

15. Feliciano and Lanuza 2017.

16. Bean et al. 2015; R. Gonzales 2015.

17. Monk 2021; Telles and Ortiz 2008.

18. García-Castañon et al. 2019; Waters et al. 2010; Kasinitz et al. 2008.

19. Terriquez 2015a; Street et al. 2017; Nicholls 2013.

20. Collins and Bilge 2020; Crenshaw 1989, 1991.

21. Milkman 2017; Ransby 2018; Escudero 2020; Garcia et al. 2024; Terriquez 2015a.

22. Terriquez and Lin 2019.

23. Kasinitz et al. 2008.

24. On mirroring the politics of nonimmigrant peers, see Callahan and Muller (2013); on Latinos who do not sympathize with immigrants, see Ramos (2024).

25. Examples include adolescent involvement in South Africa's anti-apartheid movement, the Hong Kong prodemocracy movement, the Arab Spring, child labor rights activism in India, and contemporary climate activism (especially outside the United States). Featuring children's activism in Peru, Jessica Taft's (2019) work demonstrates how children and adolescents can assert their rights and actively participate in organizing.

26. On young adults in social movements, see McAdam (1988); on older individuals in power, see Roberts and Wolak (2023).

27. National Academies of Sciences, Engineering, and Medicine 2019.

28. Additionally, during adolescence, individuals become increasingly attuned to the behaviors of adult authorities, and they can begin to question the legitimacy and fairness of institutions around them. Relative to those of younger children, adolescents' peers also play a more central role in determining their interests, behaviors, and priorities (Wasburn and Adkins-Covert 2017).

29. Flanagan 2013.

30. Ojeda and Hatemi 2015.

31. Wasburn and Adkins-Covert 2017.

32. Wasburn and Adkins-Covert 2017.

33. Niemi and Hepburn 1995; Wasburn and Adkins-Covert 2017.

34. Terriquez and Kwon 2014.

35. At times, the political engagement of second-generation adolescents can spark family conflict as parents may have different priorities, fear for their safety of their children, or express different political ideologies from those of their children (Terriquez and Kwon 2014).

36. Levinson 2012.

37. Kahne and Rogers 2024.

38. Cammarota 2016; De los Rios 2019; Mirra and Rogers 2016.

39. T. Maher and Earl 2019; Jenkins et al. 2016; Kahne et al. 2013.

40. Kahne and Bowyer 2018; T. Maher and Earl 2019; P. Howard et al. 2021.

41. Terriquez 2015b.

42. McFarland and Thomas 2006.

43. Eliasoph 2011.

44. Arguably, these groups promote what Joel Westheimer and Joseph Kahne (2004) call "participatory citizenship," which enables young people to intervene in government decision-making processes, as well as "justice-oriented citizenship," which seeks to address societal inequalities.

45. DiMaggio and Powell 1983, 147, 149.

46. Valladares et al. 2021.

47. Fuhrmann et al. 2015; Eaton et al. 2022; Bradshaw et al. 2012; Lamblin et al. 2017.

48. Rogers et al. 2013.

49. For a robust description of earlier grassroots groups targeting adults, see Han (2014).

50. Robert Smith (2014) also shows how black culture can be beneficial to immigrants, demonstrating how Mexican immigrant youth adopt a black culture of mobility to enhance their economic prospects.

51. For a comparative perspective of panethnic identity formation in the civil rights era, see G. Mora and Okamoto (2020).

52. Kirschner 2006.

53. Wong 2006.

54. Bloemraad et al. 2022.

55. Portes and Rumbaut 2014. On political engagement, see Bloemraad (2006); Mollenkopf and Pastor (2016).

56. Burciaga and Martinez 2017. A long (and oft-debated) list of contextual influences includes local demographics, histories of movement activism, and the availability of immigrant-serving civic infrastructures (Mollenkopf and Pastor 2016; Tran et al. 2013; Bloemraad et al. 2022).

57. The online appendix is available at https://www.russellsage.org/publications /book/learning-lead.

Chapter 2: Rooted in Resistance: The Origins and State of the Nonprofit Youth Organizing Field

1. Meyer and Whittier 1994.

2. McAdam 1988; Shaw 2010.

3. Clay 2012; Pastor et al. 2020.

4. Clay 2012.

5. Shaw 2010.

6. Menjivar 2000; Hamilton and Chinchilla 2001.

7. Portes and Rumbaut 2014.

8. Menjívar 2006.

9. Bloemraad et al. 2011; Ramirez 2015.

10. Milkman 2020.

11. Pastor 2018; Terriquez, Sanchez, et al. 2020.

12. Braxton 2016.

13. HoSang 2006.

14. State Task Force on Gang Violence 1986; Rios 2011.

15. HoSang 2010.

16. HoSang 2006; Braxton 2016.

17. Settlement houses were first established in the 1880s to provide a range of services to immigrants who were experiencing poverty. In the 1970s, settlement houses became deeply involved in community organizing and advocating for systemic change (Fabricant and Fisher 2001).

18. Hosang 2006.

19. Valladares et al. 2021.

20. Terriquez and Dominguez 2014.

21. DiMaggio and Powell 1983.

22. More assimilated third-plus generation Latinx and AAPI youth often reside outside the poorest neighborhoods where nonprofit youth organizing groups are situated.

23. The term *significantly* can be interpreted in a variety of ways, but these reports nonetheless provide important insights into young members' demographic characteristics.

24. Youth organizing groups rarely possess the capacity to engage young immigrants who arrive in the United States during their adolescent years, as these young people tend to be focused on learning the language and adjusting to life in their adopted country.

25. On school segregation, see Ochoa (2013); Fuller et al. (2019); Stewart et al. (2021).

26. Rogers et al. 2022; Terriquez and Milkman 2021.

27. Sherwood and Terriquez 2020.

28. Lopez 2003.

29. Fan and Parreñas 2018.

30. García Bedolla 2005; Jones-Correa 1998; Robnett 1996; Aguirre and Lio 2008; Shah 1997.

31. Milkman and Terriquez 2012; Terriquez and Milkman 2021.

32. Warren 2021; Rios 2011; Lo 2018; Peguero and Bondy 2015; Cammarota 2004; Lopez 2002.

33. The first set of bars indicates that groups may include transgender youth, within the broader category of LGBTQ.

34. Fisher 2012.

35. For further illustration, see May Lin's (2022) ethnographic study, which demonstrates how KGA members articulated their campaigns using terms that aligned with broader racial and health justice movements.

36. Warren 2021; Domina et al. 2017.

37. Pastor et al. 2018.

38. Groups in California received financial support from The California Endowment, the California Wellness Foundation, and the Sierra Health Foundation. These support streams may have encouraged some California groups to adopt this focus.

39. Terriquez and Xu 2020.

40. Ramirez 2015; García Bedolla and Michelson 2012; Wong 2006.

41. Munguia 2018a, 2018b.

42. Washburn 2018.

43. Sherwood and Terriquez 2020.

44. Terriquez and Milkman 2021.

45. Serrano 2020.

46. Chaudhary and Moss 2019.

Chapter 3: Finding Power: The Developmental Roots of Civic Leadership

1. Levinson 2012; Terriquez and Kwon 2014.

2. Terriquez and Lin 2019.

3. McFarland and Thomas 2006.

4. These young people responded "yes" to two questions: the first asked respondents if they were involved in a group that tried to make a difference in the community or broader society; the second asked if the group was political. While the 2011 measure included members of youth organizing groups as well as other political groups such Human Rights Watch and MeCHA (Movimiento Estudiantil Chicano de Aztlán, a political student group), additional survey data corroborate the results from this representative sample of California young adult residents.

5. Control variables include socioeconomic status, parents' political participation, and access to rigorous high school curricula, among other factors.

6. Kasinitz et al. 2008.

7. Vogelsang 2021.

8. McFarland and Thomas 2006.

9. Terriquez 2015b; Terriquez, Xu, et al. 2021.

10. Most participants came from groups dominated by adolescents, but some groups also included young adult members.

11. van Goethem et al. 2014.

12. Terriquez 2015b.

13. Bradshaw et al. 2012; Fuhrmann et al. 2015; Guyer et al. 2016; Eaton et al. 2022; Lamblin et al. 2017.

14. Terriquez, Santos, et al. 2020.

15. Terriquez and Rogers 2017; Terriquez, Xu, et al. 2021.

16. Noguera et al. 2006; S. Kwon 2013; Kirshner 2015; Rogers et al. 2012; Watts and Hipolito-Delgado 2015.

17. Snell 2010; Kasinitz et al. 2008.

18. Turner 2021; Serrano 2020; Turner et al. 2022.

19. Turner 2021.

20. Cammarota and Fine 2008; Ozer 2017; Rogers and Morrell 2011; Scorza et al. 2013; Mirra et al. 2016; Turner 2021; Dolan et al. 2015.

21. My interest at the time of this survey was health-related grassroots organizing (broadly defined); survey questions therefore focused on knowledge young people acquired about health in particular.

22. Rivas-Drake et al. 2014; Cross et al. 2017; Umaña-Taylor et al. 2014; Freer and Lopez 2011; Ginwright 2009.

23. Kirshner 2006.

24. Feliciano and Lanuza 2017; Bean et al. 2015; R. Gonzales 2015.

25. Bloemraad et al. 2011; Kasinitz et al. 2008; Wong et al. 2011.

Chapter 4: Youth Organizing, Intersectionality, and the Making of the Immigrant Youth Movement

1. Benford and Snow 2000.

2. Greenman and Hall 2013.

3. R. Gonzales 2015.

4. On learning theory, see Rogoff (1990).

5. McCarthy and Zald 1977; Morris 1984.

6. Nicholls 2013.

7. Ramirez 2015; Pastor 2018.

8. Milkman 2020.

9. In the early-to-mid 2010s, when I was collecting data from the CDN, the network regularly hosted two statewide retreats offering leadership development training. In addition, it coordinated a statewide steering committee that included two representatives from each region in California. This steering committee held weekly conference calls and monthly in-person meetings to coordinate outreach, political campaigns, and local educational events.

10. Abrams 2022.

11. Abrego and Negrón-Gonzales 2020.

12. At the time, some groups also called themselves AB 540 organizations, after the 2001 California state legislation that allowed immigrants and students born in other U.S. states to pay in-state tuition for state colleges if they attended high school in California.

13. Additional sample descriptions can be found in the online appendix.

14. The questionnaire did not explicitly ask study participants if they were part of a "youth organizing group." Two proxy questions were used to identify members of youth organizing and similar groups: "While in high school, did you participate in an organization that tried to make a difference at your school, the community, or broader society?"; if they responded "yes," then they were asked a series of follow-up questions, including "Was this group political in any way?" A "yes" response to the second question indicated that the study participant belonged to a political group in high school. Follow-up interviews indicated that many of these youth were indeed part of youth organizing groups. However, some were also part of groups such as Amnesty International, Human Rights Watch, and MEChA that provided them with similar, although not generally as intensive, political experience.

15. While experience in adolescent public-oriented groups was positively correlated with participation in other political activities illustrated in figure 4.2, differences between these youth and their nonmember peers were not statistically significant.

16. Robert Smith 2024.

17. Abrego 2006.

18. Abrego 2008.

19. Seif 2004.

20. Nicholls 2013.

21. McAdam 1988.

22. Nicholls 2013; Terriquez 2015a.

23. Nash 2019.

24. Seif 2014.

25. Terriquez 2015a; Zimmerman 2012; Nicholls 2013.

26. Benford and Snow 2000.

27. Terriquez et al. 2018.

28. Milkman 2017; Ransby 2018.

29. Benford and Snow 2000.

30. Lachica Buenavista 2018.

31. Escudero 2020.

32. Zimmerman et al. 2013. A couple of interviewees mentioned challenges working with religious organizations. Some religious groups that might otherwise support immigrant rights efforts likely did not align with the pro-LGBTQ stance of the Dream movement.

33. DACA also allowed other young adults to pursue legal employment in the field of study outside of social movements, and hence they became less involved in politics as they had been prior to obtaining work permits.

Part II: Localized Political Contexts and the Transformative Political Socialization Process

1. Burciaga and Martinez 2017.

2. Mollenkopf and Pastor 2016; Tran et al. 2013; de Graauw et al. 2013.

Chapter 5: Healing, Self-Care, and Fighting the School-to-Prison-to-Deportation Pipeline in Orange County

1. Dreby 2015; Valdivia 2021; Asad 2020.

2. Verma et al. 2017.

3. García 2019.

4. Warren 2021, 21.

5. HoSang 2010.

6. Warren 2021.

7. California Education Code 48900(k).

8. Rios 2011; Lopez 2002; Lo 2018.

9. Terriquez et al. 2014.

10. Verma et al. 2017; Warren 2021.

11. Whipple 2019.

12. Armenta 2017; Geron and Levinson 2018.

13. Verma et al. 2017.

14. Shedd 2015; Sojoyner 2016.

15. Burciaga and Malone 2021; Moreno et al. 2021.

16. Lacayo 2017; García 2019.

17. McCarty 2007.

18. Sarmiento 2020.

19. Carcamo 2018.

20. García 2019.

21. K. Maher 2004.

22. Walton 2017.

23. Lacayo 2017.

24. R. Mora and Christianakis 2013.

25. Lacayo 2017.

26. Barajas 2007; Muniz 2014.

27. Dreby 2015; Valdivia 2021.

28. A. Gonzales 2009, 44.

29. A. Gonzales 2009.

30. Seemiller and Grace 2018.

31. Hampel and Petermann 2005; Reisner et al. 2015; Eisenberg et al. 2017.

32. Zavella 2020; Gorski 2019.

33. Ginwright 2009; Ortega-Williams et al. 2018; Sánchez Carmen et al. 2015; Lin 2022.

34. Caldwell and Witt 2011; London 2019.

35. Rosenbaum and Talmor 2022.

36. Kieffer 2020.

37. Lorde 1988, 130.

38. Eaton et al. 2022; Rivas-Drake et al. 2014; Santos and Toomey 2018; Bradshaw et al. 2012.

39. French et al. 2019; Mosley et al. 2020; Ortega-Williams et al. 2018; Ginwright 2009; Lin 2022.

40. Nicholls 2013.

41. Hampel and Petermann 2005; Amin et al. 2018.

42. Gray and Lauderdale 2007.

43. Michaels 2002.

44. National Compadres Network n.d.

45. Rendon 2019.

46. Busch et al. 2012; Monk-Turner 2003; Tan 2016; Perciavalle et al. 2017.

47. Goodwin et al. 2020; Mosley et al. 2020.

48. French et al. 2019, 26.

49. Gould 2009.

50. Zavella 2020; Gorski 2019.

51. K. Smith and Christakis 2008.

52. Harding 2009; Haynie 2001; Shek et al. 2019; Christens and Peterson 2012; Ballard et al. 2019.

53. Sanchez Carmen et al. 2015.

54. Cruwys et al. 2013.

55. Stanton-Salazar and Spina 2005; Oliver and Cheff 2014; French et al. 2019; Curran and Wexler 2017.

56. Arbeit et al. 2019; Rhodes 2004.

57. Beck 2012.

58. Bazemore 2001.

59. Bazemore 2001; Beck 2012; Roger Smith 2009; Winn 2018.

60. Haskins 2021.

61. Eaton et al. 2022; Bradshaw et al. 2012; National Academies of Sciences, Engineering, and Medicine 2019.

62. French et al. 2019; Mosley et al. 2020; Ortega-Williams et al. 2018; Ginwright 2009; Lin 2022.

Chapter 6: "Know Yo' History, Know Yo' Self": Youth Organizing and Critical Civics Education in Multiracial Oakland

1. Rogers et al. 2022.

2. de Graauw et al. 2013.

3. Menendian and Gambhir 2019.

4. Author calculations of 2020 American Community Survey data.

5. Schafran 2018.

6. Lung-Amam 2017.

7. Schafran 2018.

8. Johnson and Oliver 2013; McCall and Parker 2005.

9. Clay 2012; Alvarez and Widener 2008.

10. Hobson 2019; Armstrong 2002.

11. Araiza 2013; Bae 2017.

12. Chung and Chang 1998; X. Bañales and Lee-Oliver 2019.

13. Bae 2017.

14. Bae 2017; G. Mora and Okamoto 2020.

15. Maria Garcia 2006.

16. Clay 2012, 7.

17. Terriquez and Milkman 2021; Clay 2012; Lin 2020; S. Kwon 2006; Hope 2019; Lee et al. 2020; Freer and Lopez 2011.

18. Molina et al. 2019, 7.

19. Luna 2016.

20. Freer and Lopez 2011.

21. California Department of Education 2025a, 2025b. For example, the percent of students who identified as white was 1.1 percent at Castlemont High, 2.5 percent at Fremont High 2.5 percent at McClymonds High, 2.3 percent at Oakland High. In contrast Skyline High, located in an affluent neighborhood, included 10.8 percent white students.

22. Umaña-Taylor et al. 2014; Santos and Toomey 2018.

23. Vasquez 2011; Telles and Ortiz 2008.

24. Cross et al. 2017.

25. Ginwright 2009; Desai 2021.

26. Cammarota 2016; Sleeter and Zavala 2020.

27. Molina et al. 2019.

28. Mora and Okamoto 2020.

29. Okamoto and Mora 2014.

30. Tatum 2017.

31. Freer and Lopez 2011; Nicholson et al. 2018.

32. Rumbaut 2005; Kelly 1986.

33. Poon et al. 2016; Suzuki 1977.

34. Terriquez and Milkman 2021; Lee et al. 2020; Hope 2019.

35. Flanagan 2013.

36. Collins and Bilge 2020; Terriquez 2015a; Zavella 2020; Lorde 1984; Greenwood 2008; Sandoval 1991.

37. Robinson and Schmitz 2021; McGlashan and Fitzpatrick 2018.

38. Whipple 2019; Cerezo and Bergfeld 2013.

39. Ward 2008.

40. Umaña-Taylor et al. 2014.

41. Mathews et al. 2020; J. Bañales et al. 2020.

Chapter 7: Building on the Legacies of the Chicano Movement: Guiding Youth to Lead Campaigns in the Los Angeles Eastside

1. Holland et al. 2018.

2. Rogers et al. 2012; Watts and Flanagan 2007; Conner et al. 2013; Kirshner 2015; Ginwright et al. 2006.

3. Garcia and Castro 2011; Chávez 2002; Sánchez 2021.

4. García Bedolla 2005.

5. Rogers and Morrell 2011.

6. Oakes and Rogers 2006; Rogers and Morrell 2011; Perez and Madera 2015; Kruzman 2019.

7. de Tocqueville 2003; Putnam 2000; Verba et al. 1995.

8. Flanagan 2013.

9. Rogoff 1990.

10. Lave and Wenger 1991.

11. Kirshner 2006.

12. Han 2014.

13. Terriquez 2017; Han 2014.

14. Flanagan 2013; Levinson 2012; Wasburn and Adkins-Covert 2017.

15. Kirshner 2006, 2015.

16. Terriquez 2011; Valdés 1996; Quin and Han 2014.

17. McFarland and Thomas 2006; Flanagan 2013; Hart et al. 2007.

18. Han 2014; Dolan et al. 2015.

19. Tilly 1993, 253.

20. Pastor and Prichard 2012.

21. Noy 2008.

22. Cammarota and Fine 2008; Ozer 2017; Rogers and Morrell 2011; Mirra et al. 2016; Turner 2021; Dolan et al. 2015.

23. Kirschner 2006.

24. Tivaringe and Kirshner 2022.

25. Van Dyke and McCammon 2010; Baldassarri and Diani 2007.

26. Serrano 2020.

27. Turner 2021.

28. Terriquez and Carmona Mora 2018.

29. Alpizar 2012; Gaglianone 2019; Mesa and Chavolla 2019; Blume and Kohli 2018; Fabian 2012; Greanias 2018; Blume 2015; Kohli 2018; Kohli et al. 2017; Phillips 2013.

30. Gajanan 2016.

31. Bloom et al. 2016.

32. Grinberg and Shoichet 2016.

33. Resmovits, Kohli, et al. 2016.

34. Resmovits, Rocha, et al. 2016.

Chapter 8: Growing Young Leaders in the Conservative Central Valley

1. Romero 2014.

2. Terriquez, Villegas, et al. 2020.

3. Terriquez et al. 2019.

4. Parsons 1986.

5. Gregory 2005; Kirby 1983.

6. Chan 1986.

7. Gonzalez 1986; Mabalon 2013; Matsumoto 1993.

8. Weber 1994.

9. Walker 2004.

10. Fox 2004; Rivera-Salgado 2015.

11. Author calculations of 2020 American Community Survey data.

12. Humes 1999.

13. Lytle-Hernández 2010; Walker 2004.

14. Schwaller 2018.

15. Vestal et al. 2021; Rancaño 2016.

16. Ganz 2009; Matthew Garcia 2014; Cruz 2016.

17. Cole and Foster 2001; Del Real 2019; Borrell 2018.

18. Gilmore 2007, 129.

19. Spanish translation of "Schools not jails," a phrase that activists used in the 2000s to represent their efforts to dismantle the school-to-prison pipeline.

20. Wright 2007.

21. Kirshner 2006; Rogers et al. 2012.

22. Milkman 2017; Katz et al. 2022.

23. Jenkins et al. 2016; Kahne et al. 2013; Kahne et al. 2016.

24. Green et al. 2003.

25. García Bedolla and Michelson 2012; Wong 2005.

26. Terriquez, Villegas, et al. 2020.

Chapter 9: Leading for the Future

1. Lund 2020; Fegert et al. 2020; U.S. Department of Health and Human Services 2021.

2. Terriquez et al. 2022.

3. Mendez 2020.

4. Rosenberg and Fenkner 2022; Rogers et al. 2021; Lanham 2021.

5. DiMaggio and Powell 1983.

6. Flanagan 2013.

7. Cohen et al. 2020.

8. See, for examples: Feliciano and Lanuza 2017; Portes and Rumbaut 2014; Alba and Nee 2003.

9. R. Gonzales 2016; Massey 2009; Telles and Ortiz 2008; Vasquez 2011.

10. Kasinitz et al. 2008.

11. Niemi and Hepburn 1995; Wong and Tseng 2008.

12. Wasburn and Adkins-Covert 2017.

13. Terriquez and Kwon 2014.

14. Levinson 2012.

15. Wong 2006.

16. García Bedolla and Michelson 2012; Mollenkopf and Pastor 2016; Ramakrishnan and Bloemraad 2008; Bloemraad et al. 2022.

17. Flanagan 2013; Kirshner 2015.

18. Fisher 2012.

19. Westheimer and Kahne 2004.

20. Umaña-Taylor et al. 2014.

21. HoSang 2021.

22. Burciaga and Martinez 2017.

23. Mollenkopf and Pastor 2016; Tran et al. 2013; Burciaga and Martinez 2017; de Graauw et al. 2013.

24. Gaia 2020; Small and Cook 2021.

25. Small and Cook 2021.

26. Terriquez and Soto 2019; Terriquez, Soto, et al. 2021.

27. Shah 2020.

28. Bloemraad 2006; Gulasekaram and Ramakrishnan 2015; Mollenkopf and Pastor 2016; Pastor 2018.

29. Bazemore 2001; Nissen 2011.

30. Winn 2018; Katic et al. 2020; Song et al. 2020.

31. Mosley et al. 2020; French et al. 2019; Ginwright 2009.

32. Robert Smith 2024.

33. Weiss and Reville 2019; Milner 2015; T. Howard 2019; Mendoza 2019; Suárez-Orozco et al. 2010.

34. Cammarota 2015; Sleeter and Zavala 2020.

35. Cohen et al. 2020.

36. De los Rios 2019.

37. Rogers et al. 2021.

38. Cammarota and Fine 2008; Ozer and Wright 2012; Schensul and Marlene 2004; Westheimer and Kahne 2004.

39. Goessling et al. 2021; Ibrahim et al. 2022.

40. Desai 2021.

41. Campbell 2008.

42. Terriquez and Carmona Mora 2018.

43. McDevitt and Chaffee 2000.

44. Koller and Schugurensky 2010.

45. Flutter 2006.

46. Lundy 2018.

47. Murillo et al. 2021; Daniel et al. 2019.

48. Vallejo 2012.

References

Abrams, Kathryn. 2022. *Open Hand, Closed Fist: Practices of Undocumented Organizing in a Hostile State*. University of California Press.

Abrego, Leisy J. 2006. "'I Can't Go to College Because I Don't Have Papers': Incorporation Patterns of Latino Undocumented Youth." *Latino Studies* 4(3): 212–31.

Abrego, Leisy. 2008. "Legitimacy, Social Identity, and the Mobilization of Law: The Effects of Assembly Bill 540 on Undocumented Students in California." *Law & Social Inquiry* 33(3): 709–34.

Abrego, Leisy, and Genevieve Negrón-Gonzales, eds. 2020. *We Are Not Dreamers: Undocumented Scholars Theorize Undocumented Life in the United States*. Duke University Press.

Aguirre, Adalberto, Jr., and Shoon Lio. 2008. "Spaces of Mobilization: The Asian American/Pacific Islander Struggle for Social Justice." *Social Justice* 35(2): 1–17.

Akee, Randall, Maggie R. Jones, and Sonya R. Porter. 2019. "Race Matters: Income Shares, Income Inequality, and Income Mobility for All U.S. Races." *Demography* 56(3): 999–1021.

Alba, Richard, and Victor Nee. 2003. *Remaking the American Mainstream: Assimilation and Contemporary Immigration*. Harvard University Press.

Alpizar, Marvelia. 2012. "Promueven el voto latino en Los Ángeles." *La Opinion*, November 12. https://laopinion.com/2012/11/04/promueven-el-voto-latino-en-los-angeles-2.

Alvarez, Luis, and Daniel Widener. 2008. "A History of Black and Brown: Chicana/o-African American Cultural and Political Relations." *Aztlán: A Journal of Chicano Studies* 33(1): 143–54.

Amin, Avni, Anna Kågesten, Emmanuel Adebayo, and Venkatraman Chandra-Mouli. 2018. "Addressing Gender Socialization and Masculinity Norms Among Adolescent Boys: Policy and Programmatic Implications." *Journal of Adolescent Health* 62(3): S3–S5.

Araiza, Lauren. 2013. *To March for Others: The Black Freedom Struggle and the United Farm Workers*. University of Pennsylvania Press.

Arbeit, Miriam R., Haley E. Johnson, Anita A. Grabowska, Victoria A. Mauer, and Nancy L. Deutsch. 2021. "Leveraging Relational Metaphors: An Analysis of Non-Parental Adult Roles in Response to Youth Needs." *Youth & Society* 53(1): 104–30.

Armenta, Amada. 2017. *Protect, Serve, and Deport: The Rise of Policing as Immigration Enforcement*. University of California Press.

Armstrong, Elizabeth. 2002. *Forging Gay Identities: Organizing Sexuality in San Francisco, 1950–1994*. University of Chicago Press.

Asad, Asad L. 2020. "Latinos' Deportation Fears by Citizenship and Legal Status, 2007 to 2018." *Proceedings of the National Academy of Sciences* 117(16): 8836–44.

Bae, Aaron B. 2017. "The Struggle for Freedom, Justice, and Equality Transcends Racial and National Boundaries: Anti-Imperialism, Multiracial Alliances, and the Free Huey Movement in the San Francisco Bay Area." *Pacific Historical Review* 86(4): 691–722.

Baldassarri, Delia, and Mario Diani. 2007. "The Integrative Power of Civic Networks." *American Journal of Sociology* 113(3): 735–80.

Ballard, Parissa J., Lindsay T. Hoyt, and Mark C. Pachucki. 2019. "Impacts of Adolescent and Young Adult Civic Engagement on Health and Socioeconomic Status in Adulthood." *Child Development* 90(4): 1138–54.

Barajas, Frank P. 2007. "An Invading Army: A Civil Gang Injunction in a Southern California Chicana/o Community." *Latino Studies* 5: 393–417.

Bañales, Josefina, Channing Mathews, Noorya Hayat, Nkemka Anyiwo, and Matthew A. Diemer. 2020. "Latinx and Black Young Adults' Pathways to Civic/Political Engagement." *Cultural Diversity and Ethnic Minority Psychology* 26(2): 176–88.

Bañales, Xamuel, and Leece Lee-Oliver. 2019. "Fifty Years of Ethnic Studies: Foundations, Challenges, and Opportunities." *Ethnic Studies Review* 42(2): 7–14.

Bazemore, Gordon. 2001. "Young People, Trouble, and Crime: Restorative Justice as a Normative Theory of Informal Social Control and Social Support." *Youth & Society* 33(2): 199–226.

Bean, Frank D., Susan K. Brown, and James D. Bachmeier. 2015. *Parents Without Papers: The Progress and Pitfalls of Mexican American Integration*. Russell Sage Foundation.

Beck, Elizabeth. 2012. "Transforming Communities: Restorative Justice as a Community Building Strategy." *Journal of Community Practice* 20(4): 380–401.

Benford, Robert D., and David A. Snow. 2000. "Framing Processes and Social Movements: An Overview and Assessment." *Annual Review of Sociology* 26: 611–39.

Bloemraad, Irene. 2006. *Becoming a Citizen: Incorporating Immigrants and Refugees in the United States and Canada*. University of California Press.

Bloemraad, Irene, Ali R. Chaudhary, and Shannon Gleeson. 2022. "Immigrant Organizations." *Annual Review of Sociology* 48: 319–41.

Bloemraad, Irene, Kim Voss, and Taeku Lee. 2011. "The Protests of 2006: What Were They, How Do We Understand Them, Where Do We Go?" In *Rallying for Immigrant Rights*, edited by Kim Voss and Irene Bloemraad. University of California Press.

Bloom, Tracy, Christina Pascucci, and Kareen Wynter. 2016. "LAUSD Students Walk Out of Classes as Anti-Trump Protests Continue." KTLA 5, November 14. https://ktla.com/news/local-news/l-a-students-planning-anti-trump-walkouts-monday.

Blume, Howard. 2015. "L.A. Unified Retreats in Higher Graduation Standards." *Los Angeles Times*, June 9. https://www.latimes.com/local/education/la-me-lausd-20150610-story.html.

Blume, Howard, and Sonali Kohli. 2018. "Ready, Set, Walk Out: Schools Prepare for Expected Student Protests on Wednesday." *Los Angeles Times*, March 13. https://www.latimes.com/local/lanow/la-me-edu-school-walkouts-20180312-story.html.

Borrell, Brendan. 2018. "California's Fertile Valley Is Awash in Air Pollution." *Mother Jones*, December 10. https://www.motherjones.com/environment/2018/12/californias-fertile-valley-is-awash-in-air-pollution.

Bradshaw, Catherine, Asha Goldweber, Diana Fishbein, and Mark T. Greenberg. 2012. "Infusing Developmental Neuroscience into School-Based Preventive Interventions: Implications and Future Directions." *Journal of Adolescent Health* 51(2): 41–47.

Braxton, Eric. 2016. "Youth Leadership for Social Justice: Past and Present." In *Contemporary Youth Activism: Advancing Social Justice in the United States*, edited by Jerusha Conner and Sonia M. Rosen. Praeger.

Buckley, James Michael, and William Littmann. 2010. "Viewpoint: A Contemporary Vernacular: Latino Landscapes in California's Central Valley." *Buildings & Landscapes: Journal of the Vernacular Architecture Forum* 17(2): 1–12.

Burciaga, Edelina M., and Aaron Malone. 2021. "Intensified Liminal Legality: The Impact of the DACA Rescission for Undocumented Young Adults in Colorado." *Law & Social Inquiry* 46(4): 1092–114.

Burciaga, Edelina M., and Lisa M. Martinez. 2017. "How Do Political Contexts Shape Undocumented Youth Movements? Evidence from Three Immigrant Destinations." *Mobilization: An International Quarterly* 22(4): 451–71.

Busch, Volker, Walter Magerl, Uwe Kern, Joachim Haas, Göran Hajak, and Peter Eichhammer. 2012. "The Effect of Deep and Slow Breathing on Pain Perception, Autonomic Activity, and Mood Processing—An Experimental Study." *Pain Medicine* 13(2): 215–28.

Caldwell, Linda L., and Peter A. Witt. 2011. "Leisure, Recreation, and Play from a Developmental Context." *New Directions for Youth Development* 2011(130): 13–27.

California Department of Education. 2025a. "2019–20 Enrollment by Ethnicity: Oakland Unified Report." *DataQuest*. Accessed August 20, 2025. https://dq.cde.ca.gov/dataquest/dqcensus/EnrEthLevels.aspx?cds=0161259&agglevel=district&year=2019-20.

California Department of Education. 2025b. "2019–20 Enrollment by Ethnicity and Grade: Oakland Unified Report," *DataQuest*. Accessed August 20, 2025. https://dq.cde.ca.gov/dataquest/dqcensus/EnrEthGrd.aspx?cds=0161259&agglevel=district&year=2019-20.

Callahan, Rebecca M., and Chandra Muller. 2013. *Coming of Political Age: American Schools and the Civic Development of Immigrant Youth*. Russell Sage Foundation.

Cammarota, Julio. 2004. "The Gendered and Racialized Pathways of Latina and Latino Youth: Different Struggles, Different Resistances in the Urban Context." *Anthropology and Education Quarterly* 35(1): 53–74.

Cammarota, Julio. 2016. "The Praxis of Ethnic Studies: Transforming Second Sight into Critical Consciousness." *Race Ethnicity and Education* 19(2): 233–51.

Cammarota, Julio, and Michelle Fine, eds. 2008. *Revolutionizing Education: Youth Participatory Action Research in Motion*. Routledge.

Campbell, D. E. 2008. "Voice in the Classroom: How an Open Classroom Climate Fosters Political Engagement Among Adolescents." *Political Behavior* 30(4): 437–54.

Carcamo, Cindy. 2018. "Orange County Quits Program That Exemplified Its Tough Stance on Illegal Immigration." *Los Angeles Times*, January 6, 2018. https://www.latimes.com/local/california/la-me-orangecounty-halts-immigration-program-20180103-story.html.

Cerezo, Alison, and Jeannette Bergfeld. 2013. "Meaningful LGBTQ Inclusion in Schools: The Importance of Diversity Representation and Counterspaces." *Journal of LGBT Issues in Counseling* 7(4): 355–71.

Chan, Sucheng. 1986. *This Bittersweet Soil: The Chinese in California Agriculture, 1860–1910*. University of California Press.

Chaudhary, Ali R., and Dana M. Moss. 2019. "Suppressing Transnationalism: Bringing Constraints into the Study of Transnational Political Action." *Comparative Migration Studies* 7(9). https://doi.org/10.1186/s40878-019-0112-z.

Chavez, Ernesto. 2002. *Mi Raza Primero, My People First: Nationalism, Identity, and Insurgency in the Chicano Movement in Los Angeles, 1966–1978*. University of California Press.

Chetty, Raj, Nathaniel Hendren, Patrick Kline, and Emmanuel Saez. 2014. "Where Is the Land of Opportunity? The Geography of Intergenerational Mobility in the United States." *Quarterly Journal of Economics* 129(4): 1553–623.

Christens, Brian D., and N. Andrew Peterson. 2012. "The Role of Empowerment in Youth Development: A Study of Sociopolitical Control as Mediator of Ecological Systems' Influence on Developmental Outcomes." *Journal of Youth and Adolescence* 41(5): 623–35.

Chung, Angie Y., and Edward Taehan Chang. 1998. "From Third-World Liberation to Multiple Oppression Politics: A Contemporary Approach to Inter-ethnic Coalitions." *Social Justice* 25(3): 80–100.

Clay, Andreana. 2012. *The Hip Hop Generation Fights Back: Youth, Activism and Post-Civil Rights Politics*. New York University Press.

Cohen, Cathy, Joseph Kahne, and Jessica Marshall. 2020. *Let's Go There: Race, Ethnicity and Lived Civics Approach to Civics Education*. GenForward at the University of Chicago. https://static1.squarespace.com/static/5e20c70a7802d9509b9aeff2/t/5e66cd4feddd0f57bb759f21/1583795568756/LetsGoThere_Paper_V17.pdf.

Cole, Luke W., and Sheila R. Foster. 2001. *From the Ground Up: Environmental Racism and the Rise of the Environmental Justice Movement*. New York University Press.

Collins, Patricia Hill, and Sirma Bilge. 2020. *Intersectionality*. 2nd ed. Polity.

Conner, Jerusha, Karen Zaino, and Emily Scarola. 2013. "Very Powerful Voices: The Influence of Youth Organizing on Educational Policy in Philadelphia." *Educational Policy* 27(3): 560–88.

Crenshaw, Kimberle. 1989. "Demarginalizing the Intersection of Race and Sex: A Black Feminist Critique of Antidiscrimination Doctrine, Feminist Theory and Antiracist Politics." *University of Chicago Legal Forum* 1989(1): 139–67.

Crenshaw, Kimberle. 1991. "Mapping the Margins: Intersectionality, Identity Politics, and Violence Against Women of Color." *Stanford Law Review* 43(6): 1241–99.

Cross, William E., Jr., Eleanor K. Seaton, Tiffany Yip, Richard M. Lee, Deborah Rivas, Gilbert C. Gee, Wendy D. Roth, and Bic Ngo. 2017. "Identity Work: Enactment of Racial-Ethnic Identity in Everyday Life." *Identity* 17(1): 1–12.

Cruwys, Tegan, Genevieve A. Dingle, Catherine Haslam, S. Alexander Haslam, Jolanda Jetten, and Thomas A. Morton. 2013. "Social Group Memberships Protect Against Future Depression, Alleviate Depression Symptoms and Prevent Depression Relapse." *Social Science and Medicine* 98: 179–86.

Cruz, Adrian. 2016. "The Union Within the Union: Filipinos, Mexicans, and the Racial Integration of the Farm Worker Movement." *Social Movement Studies* 15(4): 361–73.

Curran, Tess, and Lisa Wexler. 2017. "School-Based Positive Youth Development: A Systematic Review of the Literature." *Journal of School Health* 87(1): 71–80.

Daniel, Julia, Karen Hunter Quartz, and Jeannie Oakes. 2019. "Teaching in Community Schools: Creating Conditions for Deeper Learning." *Review of Research in Education* 43(1): 453–80.

de Graauw, Els, Irene Bloemraad, and Shannon Gleeson. 2013. "Funding Immigrant Organizations: Suburban Free Riding and Local Civic Presence." *American Journal of Sociology* 119(1): 75–130.

De los Rios, Cati V. 2019. "Revisiting Notions of Social Action in Ethnic Studies Pedagogy: One Teacher's Critical Lessons from the Classroom." In *Rethinking Ethnic Studies*, edited by R. Tolteka Cuauhtin, Miguel Zavala, Christine Sleeter and Wayne Au. Rethinking Schools.

de Tocqueville, Alexis. 2003. *Democracy in America*. Penguin Books.

Del Real, Jose A. 2019. "They Grow the Nation's Food, but They Can't Drink the Water." *New York Times*, May 21. https://www.nytimes.com/2019/05/21/us/california-central-valley-tainted-water.html.

Desai, Shiv R. 2021. "From Being System-Involved to Changing the System: Infiltrating the System." *Education and Urban Society* 54(1): 77–98.

DiMaggio, Paul J., and Walter W. Powell. 1983. "The Iron Cage Revisited: Institutional Isomorphism and Collective Rationality in Organizational Fields." *American Sociological Review* 48(2): 147–60.

Dolan, Tom, Brian D. Christens, and Cynthia Lin. 2015. "Combining Youth Organizing and Youth Participatory Action Research to Strengthen Student Voice in Education Reform." *Teachers College Record: The Voice of Scholarship in Education* 117(13): 153–70.

Domina, Thurston, Andrew Penner, and Emily Penner. 2017. "Categorical Inequality: Schools as Sorting Machines." *Annual Review of Sociology* 43(1): 311–30.

Dreby, Joanna. 2015. *Everyday Illegal: When Policies Undermine Immigrant Families*. University of California Press.

Eaton, Steve, Harriet Cornwell, Catherine Hamilton-Giachritsis, and Graeme Fairchild. 2022. "Resilience and Young People's Brain Structure, Function and Connectivity: A Systematic Review." *Neuroscience and Biobehavioral Reviews* 132: 936–56.

Eisenberg, Marla E., Amy L. Gower, Barbara J. McMorris, G. Nicole Rider, Glynis Shea, and Eli Coleman. 2017. "Risk and Protective Factors in the Lives of Transgender/Gender Nonconforming Adolescents." *Journal of Adolescent Health* 61(4): 521–26.

Eliasoph, Nina. 2011. *Making Volunteers: Civic Life After Welfare's End*. Princeton University Press.

Equity Research Institute. 2024. "California Immigrant Data Portal." https:// immigrantdataca.org/.

Escudero, Kevin. 2020. *Organizing While Undocumented: Immigrant Youth's Political Activism Under the Law*. New York University Press.

Fabian, Esmeralda. 2012. "Preparatoria elimina la 'tolerancia cero.'" *La Opinion*, June 7. https://laopinion.com/2012/06/07/preparatoria-elimina-la-tolerancia -cero/.

Fabricant, Michael B., and Robert Fisher. 2001. *Settlement Houses Under Siege: The Struggle to Sustain Community Organizations in New York City*. Columbia University Press.

Fan, Yu-Kang, and Rhacel Salazar Parreñas. 2018. "Who Cares for the Children and the Elderly? Gender and Transnational Families." In *Childhood and Parenting in Transnational Settings*, edited by Viorela Ducu, Mihaela Nedelcu and Aron Telegdi-Csetri. Springer.

Fegert, Jörg, Benedetto Vitiello, Paul L. Plener, and Vera Clemens. 2020. "Challenges and Burden of the Coronavirus 2019 (COVID-19) Pandemic for Child and Adolescent Mental Health: A Narrative Review to Highlight Clinical and Research Needs in the Acute Phase and the Long Return to Normality." *Child and Adolescent Psychiatry and Mental Health* 14(20). https:// doi.org/10.1186/s13034-020-00329-3.

Feliciano, Cynthia, and Yader R. Lanuza. 2017. "An Immigrant Paradox? Contextual Attainment and Intergenerational Educational Mobility." *American Sociological Review* 82(1): 211–41.

Fisher, Dana R. 2012. "Youth Political Participation: Bridging Activism and Electoral Politics." *Annual Review of Sociology* 38: 119–37.

Flanagan, Constance A. 2013. *Teenage Citizens: The Political Theories of the Young*. Harvard University Press.

Flood, Sarah, Miriam King, Renae Rodgers, Steven Ruggles, J. Robert Warren, and Michael Westberry. 2021. "Integrated Public Use Microdata Series, Current Population Survey: Version 9.0 [dataset]." Minneapolis, MN: IPUMS.

Flutter, Julia. 2006. "This Place Could Help You Learn': Student Participation in Creating Better School Environments." *Educational Review* 58(2): 183–93.

Fox, Jonathan 2006. "Reframing Mexican Migration as a Multi-Ethnic Process." *Latino Studies* 4: 39–61.

Freer, Regina M., and Claudia S. Lopez. 2011. "Black, Brown, Young, and Together." In *Just Neighbors? Research on African American and Latino Relations in the United States*, edited by Edward Telles, Mark Q. Sawyer and Gaspar R. Salgado. Russell Sage Foundation.

French, Bryana H., Jioni A. Lewis, Della V. Mosley, Hector Y. Adames, Nayeli Y. Chavez-Dueñas, Grace A. Chen, and Helen A. Neville. 2019. "Toward a Psychological Framework of Radical Healing in Communities of Color." *Counseling Psychologist* 48(1): 14–46.

Frey, Susan. 2014. "LAUSD Allots Funds to Schools with Highest Student Need." EdSource, June 23. https://edsource.org/2014/l-a-unified-allocates-funds-to-schools-with-highest-student-need/64305.

Fuhrmann, Delia, Lisa J. Knoll, and Sarah-Jayne Blakemore. 2015. "Adolescence as a Sensitive Period of Brain Development." *Trends in Cognitive Sciences* 19(10): 558–66.

Fuller, Bruce, Yoonjeon Kim, Claudia Galindo, Shruti Bathia, Margaret Bridges, Greg J. Duncan, and Isabel García Valdivia. 2019. "Worsening School Segregation for Latino Children?" *Educational Researcher* 48(7): 407–20.

Gaglianone, Virginia. 2019. "Medida EE busca fondos para educación." *La Opinion*, May 23. https://www.innercitystruggle.org/medida_ee_busca_fondos_para_educaci_n_la_opini_n.

Gaia, Alessandra. 2020. "Social Desirability Bias and Sensitive Questions in Surveys." In *Sage Research Methods Foundations*, edited by Paul Atkinson, Sara Delamont, Alexandru Cernat, Joseph W. Sakshaug, and Richard A. Williams. SAGE Publications.

Gajanan, Mahita. 2016. "Students Across the U.S. Stage Walkouts to Protest Donald Trump." *Time*, September 14. https://time.com/4570871/students-protest-donald-trump/.

Ganz, Marshall. 2009. *Why David Sometimes Wins: Leadership, Organization, and Strategy in the California Farm Worker Movement*. Oxford University Press.

Garcia, Ana, Dora Rebelo, Juliana Diógenes-Lima, Maria Fernandes-Jesus, and Carla Malafaia. 2024. "Intersectionality in Youth Climate Activism as Educational Practice: Political, Pragmatic, and Pedagogical Dimensions." *Frontiers in Education* 9. https://doi.org/10.3389/feduc.2024.1491387.

García, Angela S. 2019. *Legal Passing: Navigating Undocumented Life and Local Immigration Law*. University of California Press.

Garcia, Maria Cristina. 2006. *Seeking Refuge: Central American Migration to Mexico, the United States, and Canada*. University of California Press.

Garcia, Mario, and Sal Castro. 2011. *Chicano Blowouts*. University of North Carolina Press.

Garcia, Matthew. 2014. *From the Jaws of Victory: The Triumph and Tragedy of Cesar Chavez and the Farm Worker Movement*. University of California Press.

García Bedolla, Lisa. 2005. *Fluid Borders: Latino Power, Identity, and Politics in Los Angeles*. University of California Press.

García Bedolla, Lisa, and Melissa R. Michelson. 2012. *Mobilizing Inclusion: Transforming the Electorate through Get-Out-the-Vote Campaigns*. Yale University Press.

García-Castañon, Marcela, Kiku Huckle, Hannah L. Walker, and Chinbo Chong. 2019. "Democracy's Deficit: The Role of Institutional Contact in Shaping Non-White Political Behavior." *Journal of Race, Ethnicity, and Politics* 4(1): 1–31.

Gates, Gary J. 2017. "LGBT Data Collection Amid Social and Demographic Shifts of the US LGBT Community." *American Journal of Public Health* 107(8): 1220–22.

Geron, Tatiana, and Meira Levinson. 2018. "Intentional Collaboration, Predictable Complicity, and Proactive Prevention: U.S. Schools' Ethical Responsibilities in Slowing the School-to-Deportation Pipeline." *Journal of Global Ethics* 14(1): 23–33.

Gilmore, Ruth Wilson. 2007. *Golden Gulag: Prisons, Surplus, Crisis, and Opposition in Globalizing California*. University of California Press.

Ginwright, Shawn. 2009. *Black Youth Rising: Activism and Radical Healing in Urban America*. Teachers College Press.

Goessling, Kristen P., Dana E. Wright, Amanda C. Wager, and Marit Dewhurst. 2021. *Engaging Youth in Critical Arts Pedagogies and Creative Research for Social Justice: Opportunities and Challenges of Arts-based Work and Research with Young People*. Routledge.

Gonzales, Alfonso. 2009. "The 2006 Mega Marchas in Greater Los Angeles: Counter-Hegemonic Moment and the Future of El Migrante Struggle." *Latino Studies* 7(1): 30–59.

Gonzales, Juan L. 1986. "Asian Indian Immigration Patterns: The Origins of the Sikh Community in California." *International Migration Review* 20(1): 40–54.

Gonzales, Roberto G. 2015. *Lives in Limbo: Undocumented and Coming of Age in America*. University of California Press.

Goodwin, Renee D., Andrea H. Weinberger, June H. Kim, Melody Wu, and Sandro Galea. 2020. "Trends in Anxiety Among Adults in the United States, 2008–2018: Rapid Increases Among Young Adults." *Journal of Psychiatric Research* 130: 441–46.

Gorski, Paul C. 2019. "Fighting Racism, Battling Burnout: Causes of Activist Burnout in US Racial Justice Activists." *Ethnic and Racial Studies* 42(5): 667–87.

Gould, Deborah B. 2009. *Moving Politics: Emotion and ACT UP's Fight Against AIDS*. University of Chicago Press.

Gray, Barbara, and Pat Lauderdale. 2007. "The Great Circle of Justice: North American Indigenous Justice and Contemporary Restoration Programs." *Contemporary Justice Review* 10(2): 215–25.

Greanias, Laura. 2018. "It Gets Worse for LAUSD: This Week Both the County and the State Showed Up to Say, 'Get Your Fiscal House in Order or Else We're Taking Over.'" *LA School Report*, September 12. https://www.laschoolreport .com/it-gets-worse-for-lausd-this-week-both-the-county-and-the-state-showed -up-to-say-get-your-fiscal-house-in-order-or-else-were-taking-over/.

Green, Donald P., Alan S. Gerber, and David W. Nickerson. 2003. "Getting Out the Vote in Local Elections: Results from Six Door-to-Door Canvassing Experiments." *Journal of Politics* 65(4): 1083–96.

Greenman, Emily, and Matthew Hall. 2013. "Legal Status and Educational Transitions for Mexican and Central American Immigrant Youth." *Social Forces* 91(4): 1475–98.

Greenwood, Ronni Michelle. 2008. "Intersectional Political Consciousness: Appreciation for Intragroup Differences and Solidarity in Diverse Groups." *Psychology of Women Quarterly* 32(1): 36–47.

Gregory, James N. 2005. *The Southern Diaspora: How the Great Migrations of Black and White Southerners Transformed America.* University of North Carolina Press.

Grinberg, Emanuella, and Catherine E. Shoichet. 2016. "Students stage anti-Trump walkouts." *CNN,* November 14. https://www.cnn.com/2016/11/14/us /protests-elections-trump/index.html.

Gulasekaram, Pratheepan, and Subramanian Karthick Ramakrishnan. 2015. *The New Immigration Federalism.* Cambridge University Press.

Guyer, Amanda E., Jennifer S. Silk, and Eric E. Nelson. 2016. "The Neurobiology of the Emotional Adolescent: From the Inside Out." *Neuroscience Biobehavioral Review* 70: 74–85.

Hagerman, Margaret A. 2024. *Children of a Troubled Time: Growing Up with Racism in Trump's America.* New York University Press.

Hamilton, Nora, and Norma Stoltz Chinchilla. 2001. *Seeking Community in a Global City: Guatemalans and Salvadorans in Los Angeles.* Temple University Press.

Hampel, Petra, and Franz Petermann. 2005. "Age and Gender Effects on Coping in Children and Adolescents." *Journal of Youth and Adolescence* 34: 73–83.

Han, Hahrie. 2014. *How Organizations Develop Activists: Civic Associations & Leadership in the 21st Century.* Oxford University Press.

Harding, David. J. 2009. "Violence, Older Peers, and the Socialization of Adolescent Boys." *American Sociological Review* 74(3): 445–64.

Hart, Daniel, Thomas M. Donnelly, James Youniss, and Robert Atkins. 2007. "High School Community Service as a Predictor of Adult Voting and Volunteering." *American Educational Research Journal* 44(1): 197–219.

Haskins, Ron. 2021. "Child Welfare Financing: What Do We Fund, How, and What Could Be Improved?" *Annals of the American Academy of Political and Social Science* 692(1): 50–67.

Haynie, Dana L. 2001. "Delinquent Peers Revisited: Does Network Structure Matter?" *American Journal of Sociology* 106(4): 1013–57.

Hobson, Emily. 2019. *Lavender and Red: Liberation and Solidarity in the Gay and Lesbian Left.* University of California Press.

Holland, Gale, Andrea Castillo, and Laura J. Nelson. 2018. "Tens of Thousands Gather in Downtown Los Angeles for March for Our Lives Rally." March 24, 2018. https://www.latimes.com/local/lanow/la-me-ln-los-angeles-march -20180324-story.html.

Hondagneu-Sotelo, Pierrette, and Manuel Pastor. 2021. *South Central Dreams: Finding Home and Building Community in South L.A.* New York University Press.

Hope, Jeanelle K. 2019. "This Tree Needs Water!: A Case Study on the Radical Potential of Afro-Asian Solidarity in the Era of Black Lives Matter." *Amerasia Journal* 45(2): 222–37.

HoSang, Daniel. 2006. "Reframing Youth Resistance: Building Theories of Youth Activism." In *Beyond Resistance! Youth Activism And Community Change: New Democratic Possibilities For Practice And Policy For America's Youth,* edited by Pedro Noguera, Julio Cammarota, and Shawn Ginwright. Routledge.

HoSang, Daniel. 2010. *Racial Propositions: Ballot Initiatives and the Making of Postwar California*. University of California Press.

HoSang Martinez, Daniel. 2021. *A Wider Type of Freedom*. University of California Press.

Howard, Philip N., Lisa-Maria Neudert, and Nayana Prakash. 2021. *Digital Misinformation/Disinformation and Children*. UNICEF. https://www.ictworks.org/wp-content/uploads/2021/10/UNICEF-Global-Insight-Digital-Mis-Disinformation-and-Children-2021.pdf.

Howard, Tyrone C. 2019. *Why Race and Culture Matter in Schools: Closing the Achievement Gap in America's Classrooms*. 2nd ed. Teachers College Press.

Humes, Edward. 1999. *Mean Justice: A Town's Terror, A Prosecutor's Power, A Betrayal of Innocence*. Simon & Schuster.

Ibrahim, Deanna A., Erin B. Godfrey, Elise Cappella, and Esther Burson. 2022. "The Art of Social Justice: Examining Arts Programming as a Context for Critical Consciousness Development Among Youth." *Journal of Youth Adolescence* 51(3): 409–27.

Jelinek, Lawrence J. 1982. *Harvest Empire: A History of California Agriculture*. Heinle & Heinle Pub.

Jenkins, Henry, Sangita Shresthova, Liana Gamber-Thompson, Neta Kligler-Vilenchik, and Arely Zimmerman. 2016. *By Any Media Necessary: The New Youth Activism*. New York University Press.

Johnson, James H. Jr., and Melvin L. Oliver. 2013. "Interethnic Minority Conflict in Urban America: The Effects of Economic and Social Dislocations." *Urban Geography* 10(5): 449–63.

Jones-Correa, Michael. 1998. "Different Paths: Gender, Immigration, and Political Participation." *International Migration Review* 32(2): 326–49.

Kahne, Joseph, and Benjamin Bowyer. 2018. "The Political Significance of Social Media Activity and Social Networks." *Political Communication* 35(3): 470–93.

Kahne, Joseph, Erica Hodgin, and Elyse Eidman-Aadahl. 2016. "Redesigning Civic Education for the Digital Age: Participatory Politics and the Pursuit of Democratic Engagement." *Theory & Research in Social Education* 44(1): 1–35.

Kahne, Joseph, Nam-Jin Lee, and Jessica Feezell. 2013. "The Civic and Political Significance of Online Participatory Cultures Among Youth Transitioning to Adulthood." *Journal of Information Technology & Politics* 10(1): 1–20.

Kahne, Joseph, and John Rogers. 2024. "Facing Partisan Conflict: How Social Studies Educators Can Lead Towards a Diverse Democracy." *Social Education* 88(1): 13–19.

Kasinitz, Philip, John H. Mollenkopf, Mary C. Waters, and Jennifer Holdaway. 2008. *Inheriting the City: The Children of Immigrants Come of Age*. Russell Sage Foundation.

Katic, Barbara, Laura A. Alba, and Austin H. Johnson. 2020. "A Systematic Evaluation of Restorative Justice Practices: School Violence Prevention and Response." *Journal of School Violence* 19(4): 579–93.

Katz, Roberta, Sarah Ogilvie, Jane Shaw, and Linda Woodhead. 2022. *Gen Z Explained: The Art of Living in a Digital Age*. University of Chicago Press.

Kelly, Gail P. 1986. "Coping with America: Refugees from Vietnam, Cambodia, and Laos in the 1970s and 1980s." *Annals of the American Academy of Political and Social Science* 487: 138–49.

Kieffer, Kira G. 2020. "Manifesting Millions: How Women's Spiritual Entrepreneurship Genders Capitalism." *Nova Religio: The Journal of Alternative and Emergent Religion* 24(2): 80–104.

Kirshner, Ben. 2006. "Apprenticeship Learning in Youth Activism." In *Beyond Resistance! Youth Activism and Community Change: New Democratic Possibilities for Practice and Policy for America's Youth*, edited by Pedro Noguera, Julio Cammarota, and Shawn Ginwright. Routledge.

Kirshner, Ben. 2015. *Youth Activism in an Era of Education Inequality*. New York University Press.

Kohli, Sonali. 2018. "School Board Approves a New Formula for Funding High-Need Schools." *Los Angeles Times*, April 10. https://www.latimes.com/local/education/la-me-edu-lausd-meeting-20180410-story.html.

Kohli, Sonali, Cindy Carcamo, and Corina Knoll. 2017. "DACA sacó a los 'Dreamers' de las sombras; ahora, algunos planean subir el volumen a sus reclamos." *Hoy*, September 8. https://www.hoylosangeles.com/noticias/estadosunidos/hoyla-lat-daca-saco-a-los-dreamers-de-las-sombras-ahora-algunos-planean-subir-el-volumen-a-sus-reclamos-20170908-story.html.

Koller, Donna, and Daniel Schugurensky. 2010. "Examining the Developmental Impact of Youth Participation in Education Governance: The Case of Student Trustees." *Journal of Research on Adolescence* 21(2): 350–60.

Kruzman, Diana. 2019. "USC Pledges to Involve Residents in Boyle Heights Development Projects." *Boyle Heights Beat*, February 5. https://boyleheightsbeat.com/usc-pledges-to-involve-residents-in-boyle-heights-development-projects.

Kwon, Hyeyoung. 2024. *Language Brokers: Children of Immigrants Translating Inequality and Belonging for Their Families*. Stanford University Press.

Kwon, Soo Ah. 2006. "Youth of Color Organizing for Juvenile Justice." In *Beyond Resistance! Youth Activism and Community Change: New Democratic Possibilities for Practice and Policy for America's Youth*, edited by Pedro Noguera, Julio Cammarota and Shawn Ginwright. Routledge.

Kwon, Soo Ah. 2013. *Uncivil Youth: Race, Activism and Affirmative Governmentality*. Duke University Press.

Lacayo, Celia Olivia. 2017. "Perpetual Inferiority: Whites' Racial Ideology Toward Latinos." *Sociology of Race & Ethnicity* 3(4): 566–79.

Lachica Buenavista, Tracy. 2018. "Model (Undocumented) Minorities and 'Illegal' Immigrants: Centering Asian Americans and US Carcerality in Undocumented Student Discourse." *Race, Ethnicity and Education* 21(1): 78–91.

Lamblin, Michelle, Carsten Murawski, Sarah Whittle, and Alex Fornito. 2017. "Social Connectedness, Mental Health and the Adolescent Brain." *Neuroscience & Biobehavioral Reviews* 80: 57–68.

Lanham, Camillia. 2021. "Paso School District Passes Ban on Teaching Critical Race Theory." *New Times San Luis Obispo*, August 12. https://www.newtimesslo.com/sanluisobispo/paso-school-district-passes-ban-on-teaching-critical-race-theory/Content?oid=11405633.

Lave, Jean, and Etienne Wenger. 1991. *Situated Learning: Legitimate Peripheral Participation.* Cambridge University Press.

Lee, Stacey J., Choua P. Xiong, Linda M. Pheng, and Mai Neng Vang. 2020. "'Asians for Black Lives, Not Asians for Asians': Building Southeast Asian American and Black Solidarity." *Anthropology & Education Quarterly* 51(4): 405–21.

Levinson, Meira. 2012. *No Citizen Left Behind.* Harvard University Press.

Lin, May. 2020. "From Alienated to Activists: Expressions and Formation of Group Consciousness Among Asian American Young Adults." *Journal of Ethnic and Migration Studies* 46(7): 1405–24.

Lin, May. 2022. "Khmer Girls in Action and Healing Justice: Expanding Understandings of Anti-Asian Racism and Public Health Solutions." *Frontiers in Public Health* 10. https://doi.org/10.3389/fpubh.2022.956308.

Lo, Bao. 2018. "Criminalization and Second-Generation Hmong American Boys." *Amerasia Journal* 44(2): 113–26.

London, Rebecca A. 2019. *Rethinking Recess: Creating Safe and Inclusive Playtime for All Children in School.* Harvard Education Press.

Lopez, Nancy. 2003. *Hopeful Girls, Troubled Boys: Race and Gender Disparity in Urban Education.* Routledge.

Lorde, Audre. 1984. *Sister Outsider: Essays and Speeches.* Crossing Press.

Lorde, Audre. 1988. *A Burst of Light: Essays.* Firebrand Books.

Luna, Zakiya. 2016. "'Truly a Women of Color Organization': Negotiating Sameness and Difference in Pursuit of Intersectionality." *Gender & Society* 30(5): 769–90.

Lund, Emily. 2020. "Even More to Handle: Additional Sources of Stress and Trauma for Clients from Marginalized Racial and Ethnic Groups in the United States During the COVID-19 Pandemic." *Counseling Psychology Quarterly* 34(3–4): 321–30.

Lundy, Laura. 2018. "In Defence of Tokenism? Implementing Children's Right to Participate in Collective Decision-Making." *Childhood* 25(3): 340–54.

Lung-Amam, Willow. 2017. *Trespassers? Asian Americans and the Battle for Suburbia.* University of California Press.

Lytle-Hernández, Kelly. 2010. *Migra! A History of the U.S. Border Patrol.* University of California Press.

Mabalon, Dawn. 2013. *Little Manila Is in the Heart: The Making of the Filipina/o American Community in Stockton, California.* Duke University Press.

Maher, Kristen Hill. 2004. "Borders and Social Distinction in the Global Suburb." *American Quarterly* 56(3): 781–806.

Maher, Thomas V., and Jennifer Earl. 2019. "Barrier or Booster? Digital Media, Social Networks, and Youth Micromobilization." *Sociological Perspectives* 62(6): 865–83.

Massey, Douglas S. 2009. "Racial Formation in Theory and Practice: The Case of Mexicans in the United States." *Race and Social Problems* 1: 12–26.

Mathews, Channing J., Michael A. Medina, Josefina Bañales, et al. 2020. "Mapping the Intersections of Adolescents' Ethnic-Racial Identity and Critical Consciousness." *Adolescent Research Review* 5: 363–79.

Matsumoto, Valerie. 1993. *Farming the Home Place: A Japanese American Community in California, 1919–1982*. Cornell University Press.

McAdam, Douglas. 1988. *Freedom Summer*. Oxford University Press.

McCall, Patricia L., and Karen F. Parker. 2005. "A Dynamic Model of Racial Competition, Racial Inequality, and Interracial Violence." *Sociological Inquiry* 75(2): 273–93.

McCarthy, John D., and Mayer N. Zald. 1977. "Resource Mobilization and Social Movements: A Partial Theory." *American Journal of Sociology* 82(6): 1212–41.

McCarty, Justin A. 2007. "The Volunteer Border Patrol: The Inevitable Disaster of the Minuteman Project." *Iowa Law Review* 92(4): 1459–92.

McDevitt, Michael, and Steven H. Chaffee. 2000. "Closing Gaps in Political Communication and Knowledge: Effects of a School Intervention." *Communication Research* 27(3): 259–92.

McFarland, Daniel, and Reuben Thomas. 2006. "Bowling Young: How Youth Voluntary Association Influence Adult Political Participation." *American Sociological Review* 71(3): 401–25.

McGlashan, Hayley, and Katie Fitzpatrick. 2018. "'I Use Any Pronouns, and I'm Questioning Everything Else': Transgender Youth and the Issue of Gender Pronouns." *Sexual Education* 18(3): 239–52.

Mendez, Michael. 2020. *Climate Change from the Streets: How Conflict and Collaboration Strengthen the Environmental Justice Movement*. Yale University Press.

Mendoza, Cecilia. 2019. "Language Development Policies and Practices Impacting the College and Career Readiness of Long-Term English Learners (LTELs) in Secondary Schools." *Educational Leadership and Administration: Teaching and Program Development* 30: 14–34.

Menendian, Stephen, and Samir Gambhir. 2019. *Racial Segregation in the San Francisco Bay Area, Part 2*. Othering and Belonging Institute, University of California, Berkeley. https://belonging.berkeley.edu/racial-segregation-san -francisco-bay-area-part-2.

Menjivar, Cecilia. 2000. *Fragmented Ties: Salvadoran Immigrant Networks in America*. University of California Press.

Menjivar, Cecilia. 2006. "Liminal Legality: Salvadoran and Guatemalan Immigrants' Lives in the United States." *American Journal of Sociology* 111(4): 999–1037.

Mesa, Raymond, and Elizabeth Chavolla. 2019. "Inauguran nuevo centro para jóvenes en Boyle Heights." Telemundo 52, May 28. https://www.telemundo52 .com/noticias/local/inauguran-nuevo-centro-para-jovenes-en-boyle-heights /133554.

Meyer, David S., and Nancy Whittier. 1994. "Social Movement Spillover." *Social Problems* 41(2): 277–98.

Michaels, Cathleen L. 2002. "Circle Communication: An Old Form of Communication Useful for 21st Century Leadership." *Nursing Administration Quarterly* 26(5): 1–10.

Milkman, Ruth. 2017. "A New Political Generation: Millennials and the Post-2008 Wave of Protest." *American Sociological Review* 82(1): 1–31.

Milkman, Ruth. 2020. *Immigrant Labor and the New Precariat*. Polity.

Milkman, Ruth, and Veronica Terriquez. 2012. "'We Are the Ones Who Are Out in Front': Women's Leadership in the Immigrant Rights Movement." *Feminist Studies* 38(3): 723–52.

Milner, H. Richard. 2015. *Rac(e)ing to Class: Confronting Poverty and Race in Schools and Classrooms*. Harvard Education Press.

Mirra, Nicole, Antero Garcia, and Ernest Morrell. 2016. *Doing Youth Participatory Action Research: Transforming Inquiry with Researchers, Educators, and Students*. Routledge.

Mirra, Nicole, and John Rogers. 2016. "Institutional Participation and Social Transformation: Considering the Goals and Tensions of University-Initiated YPAR Projects with K–12 Youth." *International Journal of Qualitative Studies in Education* 29(10): 1255–68.

Molina, Natalia, Daniel Martinez HoSang, and Ramón A. Gutiérrez. 2019. "Introduction: Towards a Relational Consciousness of Race." In *Relational Formations of Race: Theory, Method, and Practice*, edited by Natalia Molina, Daniel Martinez HoSang, and Ramón A. Gutiérrez. University of California Press.

Mollenkopf, John H., and Manuel Pastor. 2016. *Unsettled Americans: Metropolitan Context and Civic Leadership for Immigrant Integration*. Cornell University Press.

Monk, Ellis P. 2021. "The Unceasing Significance of Colorism: Skin Tone Stratification in the United States." *Daedalus* 150(2): 76–90.

Monk-Turner, Elizabeth. 2003. "The Benefits of Meditation: Experimental Findings." *Social Science Journal* 40: 465–70.

Mora, G. Christina, and Dina Okamoto. 2020. "Boundary Articulation and Emergent Identities: Asian and Hispanic Panethnicity in Comparison 1970–1980." *Social Problems* 67(1): 56–76.

Mora, Richard, and Mary Christianakis. 2013. "Feeding the School-to-Prison Pipeline: The Convergence of Neoliberalism, Conservativism, and Penal Populism." *Journal of Educational Controversy* 7(1). https://cedar.wwu.edu/jec/vol7/iss1/5.

Moraga, Cherríe, and Gloria E. Anzaldúa, eds. 2015. *This Bridge Called My Back: Writings by Radical Women of Color*. State University of New York Press.

Moreno, Oswaldo, Lisa Fuentes, Isis Garcia-Rodriguez, Rosalie Corona, and Germàn A. Cadenas. 2021. "Psychological Impact, Strengths, and Handling the Uncertainty Among Latinx DACA Recipients." *Counseling Psychologist* 49(5): 728–53.

Morris, Aldon D. 1984. *The Origins of the Civil Rights Movement: Black Communities Organizing for Change*. Free Press.

Mosley, Della V., Helen A. Neville, Nayeli Y. Chavez-Dueñas, Hector Y. Adames, Jioni A. Lewis, and Bryana H. French. 2020. "Radical Hope in Revolting Times: Proposing a Culturally Relevant Psychological Framework." *Social and Personality Psychology Compass* 14(1). https://doi.org/10.1111/spc3.12512.

Munguia, Hayley. 2018a. "Long Beach Approves $3 Billion Budget for 2019, After Marathon Debate over 'People's Budget' Additions." *Long Beach Press Telegram*, September 5. https://www.presstelegram.com/2018/09/05/long-beach-approves-3-billion-budget-for-2019-after-marathon-debate-over-peoples-budget-additions.

Munguia, Hayley. 2018b. "Long Beach Kids Campaign for $500,000 Youth Fund in 2019 Budget." *Long Beach Press Telegram*, August 6. https://www.presstelegram .com/2018/08/06/long-beach-kids-campaign-for-500000-youth-fund-in-2019 -budget.

Muniz, Ana. 2014. "Maintaining Racial Boundaries: Criminalization, Neighborhood Context, and the Origins of Gang Injunctions." *Social Problems* 61(2): 216–36.

Murillo, Marco A., Christine Abagat Liboon, and Karen Hunter Quartz. 2021. "Immigrant Family Legal Clinic: A Case of Integrated Student Supports in a Community School Context." *Journal of Educational Change* 24(2): 365–92.

Nash, Jennifer C. 2019. *Black Feminism Reimagined: After Intersectionality*. Duke University Press.

National Academies of Sciences, Engineering, and Medicine. 2019. *The Promise of Adolescence: Realizing Opportunity for All Youth*. National Academies Press.

National Compadres Network. n.d. "Training Curricula." Accessed November 20, 2019. https://nationalcompadresnetwork.org/training-curricula/.

Nicholls, Walter J. 2013. *The DREAMers: How the Undocumented Youth Movement Transformed the Immigrant Rights Debate*. Stanford University Press.

Nicholson, Harvey L., Jr., J. Scott Carter, and Arjee Restar. 2018. "Strength in Numbers: Perceptions of Political Commonality with African Americans Among Asians and Asian Americans in the United States." *Sociology of Race and Ethnicity* 6(1): 107–22.

Niemi, Richard G., and Mary A. Hepburn. 1995. "The Rebirth of Political Socialization." *Perspectives on Political Science* 24(1): 7–16.

Nissen, Laura Burney. 2011. "Community-Directed Engagement and Positive Youth Development: Developing Positive and Progressive Pathways Between Youth and Their Communities in Reclaiming Futures." *Children and Youth Services Review* 33(S1): S23–S28.

Noguera, Pedro, Julio Cammarota, and Shawn Ginwright. 2006. *Beyond Resistance! Youth Activism and Community Change: New Democratic Possibilities for Practice and Policy for America's Youth*. Routledge.

Noy, Darren. 2008. "Power Mapping: Enhancing Sociological Knowledge by Developing Generalizable Analytical Public Tools" *American Sociologist* 39(1): 3–18.

Oakes, Jeannie, and John Rogers. 2006. *Learning Power: Organizing for Education and Justice*. Teachers College Press.

Ochoa, Gilda L. 2013. *Academic Profiling: Latinos, Asian Americans, and the Achievement Gap*. University of Minnesota.

Ojeda, Christopher, and Peter K. Hatemi. 2015. "Accounting for the Child in the Transmission of Party Identification." *American Sociological Review* 80(6): 1150–74.

Okamoto, Dina, and Cristina G. Mora. 2014. "Panethnicity." *Annual Review of Sociology* 40: 219–39.

Oliver, Vanessa, and Rebecca Cheff. 2014. "The Social Network: Homeless Young Women, Social Capital, and the Health Implications of Belonging Outside the Nuclear Family." *Youth & Society* 46(5): 642–62.

Ortega-Williams, Anna, Laura J. Wernick, Jenny DeBower, and Brittany Brathwaite. 2018. "Finding Relief in Action: The Intersection of Youth-Led Community Organizing and Mental Health in Brooklyn, New York City." *Youth & Society* 52(4): 618–38.

Ozer, Emily. 2017. "Youth-Led Participatory Action Research: Overview and Potential for Enhancing Adolescent Development." *Child Development Perspectives* 11(3): 173–77.

Ozer, Emily, and Dana Wright. 2012. "Beyond School Spirit: The Effects of Youth-Led Participatory Action Research in Two Urban High Schools." *Journal of Research on Adolescence* 22(2): 267–83.

Parsons, James J. 1986. "A Geographer Looks at the San Joaquin Valley." *Geographical Review* 76(4): 371–89.

Pastor, Manuel. 2018. *State of Resistance: What California's Dizzying Descent and Remarkable Resurgence Mean for America's Future.* New Press.

Pastor, Manuel, and Michele Prichard. 2012. *L.A. Rising: The 1992 Civil Unrest, the Arc of Social Justice Organizing, and the Lessons for Today's Movement Building.* University of Southern California Equity Research Institute. https:// dornsife.usc.edu/eri/wp-content/uploads/sites/41/2023/01/2012_LArising _full_report.pdf.

Pastor, Manuel, Veronica Terriquez, and May Lin. 2018. "How Community Organizing Promotes Health Equity and How Health Equity Impacts Organizing." *Health Affairs* 37(3): 358–63.

Pastor, Manuel, Ashley K. Thomas, Preston Mills, Rachel Rosner, and Vanessa Carter. 2020. *Bridges Puentes: Building Black-Brown Solidarities Across the U.S.* University of Southern California Equity Research Institute. https://dornsife .usc.edu/eri/publications/bridges-puentes/.

Peguero, Anthony A., and Jenifer M. Bondy. 2015. "Schools, Justice, and Immigrant Students: Assimilation, Race, Ethnicity, Gender, and Perceptions of Fairness and Order." *Teachers College Record* 117(7): 1–42.

Perciavalle, Valentina, Marta Blandini, Paola Fecarotta, et al. 2017. "The Role of Deep Breathing on Stress." *Neurological Sciences* 38(3): 451–58.

Perez, Henry M., and Perla Madera. 2015. "Mobilizing the Eastside of Los Angeles for Educational Justice." *Voice in Urban Education* 40: 18–26. https://files.eric .ed.gov/fulltext/EJ1056839.pdf.

Phillips, Erica E. 2013. "L.A. Schools Rethink Suspensions." *Wall Street Journal*, May 15. https://www.wsj.com/articles/SB10001424127887323398204578485353139641538.

Phoenix, Davin L., and Maneesh Arora. 2018. "From Emotion to Action Among Asian Americans: Assessing the Roles of Threat and Identity in the Age of Trump." *Politics, Groups, and Identities* 6(3): 357–72.

Poon, OiYan, Dian Squire, and Devita Bishundat. 2016. "A Critical Review of the Model Minority Myth in Selected Literature on Asian Americans and Pacific Islanders in Higher Education." *Review of Educational Research* 86(2): 469–502.

Portes, Alejandro, and Rubén G. Rumbaut. 2014. *Immigrant America: A Portrait.* Fourth ed. University of California Press.

Putnam, Robert. 2000. *Bowling Alone: The Collapse and Revival of American Community.* Simon & Schuster.

Quin, Desiree Baolian, and Eun-Jin Han. 2014. "Tiger Parents or Sheep Parents? Struggles of Parental Involvement in Working-Class Chinese Immigrant Families." *Teacher's College Record* 116(8). https://doi.org/10.1177/016146811411600807.

Ramakrishnan, S. Karthick, and Irene Bloemraad. 2008. "Introduction: Civic and Political Realities." In *Civic Hopes and Political Realities: Immigrants, Community Organizations, and Political Engagement*, edited by K. Karthick Ramakrishnan and Irene Bloemraad. Russell Sage Foundation.

Ramirez, Ricardo. 2015. *Mobilizing Opportunities: The Evolving Latino Electorate and the Future of American Politics*. University of Virginia Press.

Ramos, Paola. 2024. *Defectors: The Rise of the Latino Far Right and What It Means for America*. Pantheon.

Rancaño, Vanessa. 2016. "Why These Central Valley Republicans Stand by Donald Trump." KQED, October 22. https://www.kqed.org/news/11138262/why-these-central-valley-republicans-stand-by-donald-trump.

Ransby, Barbara. 2018. *Making All Black Lives Matter: Reimagining Freedom in the Twenty-First Century*. University of California Press.

Reisner, Sari L., Emily A. Greytak, Jeffrey T. Parsons, and Michele Ybarra. 2015. "Gender Minority Social Stress in Adolescence: Disparities in Adolescent Bullying and Substance Use by Gender Identity." *Journal of Sex Research* 52(3): 243–56.

Rendon, Maria G. 2019. *Stagnant Dreamers: How the Inner City Shapes the Integration of the Second Generation*. Russell Sage Foundation.

Resmovits, Joy, Sonali Kohli, and Veronica Rocha. 2016. "Los Angeles Students Stage Walkouts to Protest President-Elect Trump." *Los Angeles Times*, November 14. https://www.latimes.com/local/lanow/la-me-ln-student-protests-los-angeles-20161114-story.html

Resmovits, Joy, Veronica Rocha, Mark Boster, et al. 2016. "Anti-Trump Protest Updates: Los Angeles Students Stage Walkout." *Los Angeles Times*, November 14. https://www.latimes.com/local/california/la-live-major-anti-trump-protest-planned-los-angeles-20161112-htmlstory.html.

Rhodes, Jean E. 2004. "The Critical Ingredient: Caring Youth-Staff Relationships in After-School Settings." *New Directions for Youth Development* 101: 145–61.

Rios, Victor M. 2011. *Punished: Policing the Lives of Black and Latino Boys*. New York University Press.

Rivas-Drake, Deborah, Moin Syed, Adriana Umaña-Taylor, et al. 2014. "Feeling Good, Happy, and Proud: A Meta-Analysis of Positive Ethnic-Racial Affect and Adjustment." *Child Development* 85(1): 77–102.

Rivera-Salgado, Gaspar. 2015. "From Hometown Clubs to Transnational Social Movement: The Evolution of Oaxacan Migrant Associations in California." *Social Justice* 42: 118–36.

Roberts, Damon, and Jennifer Wolak. 2023. "Do Voters Care About the Age of their Elected Representatives?" *Political Behavior* 45: 1959–78.

Robinson, Brandon Andrew, and Rachel M. Schmitz. 2021. "Beyond Resilience: Resistance in the Lives of LGBTQ Youth." *Sociology Compass* 15(12): 1–15.

Robnett, Belinda. 1996. "African-American Women in the Civil Rights Movement, 1954–1965: Gender, Leadership, and Micromobilization." *American Journal of Sociology* 101(6): 1661–93.

Rodriguez, Sophia. 2022. "'Immigration Knocks on the Door . . . We Are Stuck . . .': A Multilevel Analysis of Undocumented Youth's Experiences of Racism, System Failure, and Resistance in Policy and School Contexts." *Teachers College Record* 124(6): 3–37.

Rogers, John, Joseph Kahne, Erica Hodgin, and Veronica Terriquez. 2022. *Educating Toward a Multiracial Democracy in California.* University of California, Los Angeles, Institute for Democracy, Education, and Access.

Rogers, John, Kavitha Mediratta, Seema Shah, and Joseph Kahne. 2012. "Building Power, Learning Democracy: Youth Organizing as a Site of Civic Development." *Review of Research in Education* 36: 43–66.

Rogers, John, and Ernest Morrell. 2011. "A Force to Be Reckoned With: The Campaign for College Access in Los Angeles." In *Public Engagement for Public Education: Joining Forces to Revitalize Democracy and Equalize Schools,* edited by Marion Orr and John Rogers. Stanford University Press.

Rogers, John, Mica Pollock, Alexander Kwako, et al. 2021. *The Conflict Campaign: Exploring Local Experiences of the Campaign to Ban "Critical Race Theory" in Public K–12 Education in the U.S., 2020–2021.* University of California, Los Angeles. https://idea.gseis.ucla.edu/publications/the-conflict-campaign.

Rogers, John, Veronica Terriquez, and Miguel Carvente. 2013. *Powerful Learning: Community Coalition SCYEA's Impact on the Educational and Civic Pathways of Youth Members.* University of California, Los Angeles, Institute for Democracy, Education, and Access.

Rogoff, Barbara. 1990. *Apprenticeship in Thinking: Cognitive Development in Social Context.* Oxford University Press.

Romero, Mindy. 2014. "Table 7–8: California Eligible Voter Turnout by Age: 2014 General Election." University of California, Davis, California Civic Engagement Project.

Rosenbaum, Susanna, and Ruti Talmor. 2022. "Self-Care." *Feminist Anthropology* 3(2): 362–72.

Rosenberg, Sheridan, and James Fenkner. 2022. "Critical Race Theory in Local Schools." *Santa Barbara News-Press,* January 16. https://newspaperarchive.com/santa-barbara-news-press-jan-16-2022-p-13/?utm_source=newspaperarchive&utm_medium=copy_link&utm_campaign=share_link&utm_content=newspaper_page/.

Rumbaut, Ruben. 2005. "Vietnamese, Laotian, and Cambodian Americans." In *Asian Americans: Contemporary Trends and Issues,* edited by Pyong G. Min. Sage Publications.

Sánchez Carmen, Sonia Abigail, Michael Domínguez, et al. 2015. "Revisiting the Collective in Critical Consciousness: Diverse Sociopolitical Wisdoms and Ontological Healing in Sociopolitical Development." *Urban Review* 47: 824–46.

Sanchez, George. 2021. *Boyle Heights: How a Los Angeles Neighborhood Became the Future of American Democracy.* University of California Press.

Sandoval, Chela. 1991. "US Third World Feminism: The Theory and Method of Oppositional Consciousness in the Postmodern World." *Genders* 10: 1–24.

Santos, Carlos E., and Russell B. Toomey. 2018. "Integrating an Intersectionality Lens in Theory and Research in Developmental Science." *New Directions for Child and Adolescent Development* 2018(161): 7–15.

Sarmiento, Carolina S. 2020. "From Jails to Sanctuary Planning: Spatial Justice in Santa Ana, California." *Journal of Planning Education and Research* 40(2): 196–209.

Schafran, Alex. 2018. *The Road to Resegregation: Northern California and the Failure of Politics.* University of California Press.

Schensul, Jean J., and Berg Marlene. 2004. "Youth Participatory Action Research: A Transformative Approach to Service-Learning." *Michigan Journal of Community Service Learning* 10(3): 76–88.

Schwaller, Shawn. 2018. "Greetings from Bakersfield! Law Enforcement Corruption, White Supremacy, and Latinx Lives in California's Deep Red South." *Boom California,* October. https://boomcalifornia.org/2018/10/16/greetings-from-bakersfield/.

Scorza, D'Artagnan, Nicole Mirra, and Ernest Morrell. 2013. "It Should Just Be Education: Critical Pedagogy Normalized as Academic Excellence." *International Journal of Critical Pedagogy* 4(2): 15–34.

Seemiller, Corey, and Meghan Grace. 2018. *Generation Z: A Century in the Making.* Routledge.

Seif, Hinda. 2004. "'Wise Up!' Undocumented Latino Youth, Mexican-American Legislators, and the Struggle for Higher Education Access." *Latino Studies* 2: 210–30.

Seif, Hinda. 2014. "'Coming Out of the Shadows' and 'Undocuqueer': Undocumented Immigrants Transforming Sexuality Discourse and Activism." *Journal of Language and Sexuality* 3: 87–120.

Serrano, Uriel. 2020. "Lessons Learned From the Los Angeles Youth Movement Against the Carceral State." Latinx Project, October 20. https://www.latinxproject.nyu.edu/intervenxions/lessons-learned-from-the-los-angeles-youth-movement-against-the-carceral-state.

Shah, Seema. 2020. *FCYO'S 2020 Funder Scan: Investing in the Power of Young People.* Funders Collaborative on Youth Organizing. https://fcyo.org/resources/fcyos-2020-funder-scan-investing-in-the-power-of-young-people.

Shah, Sonia, ed. 1997. *Dragon Ladies: Asian American Feminists Breathe Fire.* University of Chicago Press.

Shaw, Randy. 2010. *Beyond the Fields: Cesar Chavez, the UFW, and the Struggle for Justice in the 21st Century.* University of California Press.

Shedd, Carla. 2015. *Unequal City: Race, Schools, and Perceptions of Injustice.* Russell Sage Foundation.

Shek, Daniel T. L., Diya Dou, Xiaoqin Zhu, and Wenyu Chai. 2019. "Positive Youth Development: Current Perspectives." *Adolescent Health, Medicine and Therapeutics* 10: 131–41.

Sherwood, Yvonne, and Veronica Terriquez. 2020. *Indigenous Youth Leadership: Themes and Questions to Consider.* University of Southern California Equity Research Institute. https://dornsife.usc.edu/eri/indigenous-youth-leadership.

Sleeter, Christine E., and Miguel Zavala. 2020. *Transformative Ethnic Studies in Schools: Curriculum, Pedagogy, and Research.* Teachers College Press.

Small, Mario L., and Jenna M. Cook. 2021. "Using Interviews to Understand Why: Challenges and Strategies in the Study of Motivated Action." *Sociological Methods & Research* 52(4): 1591–631.

Smith, Kirsten P., and Nicholas A. Christakis. 2008. "Social Networks and Health." *Annual Review of Sociology* 34: 405–29.

Smith, Robert Courtney. 2014. "Black Mexicans, Conjunctural Ethnicity, and Operating Identities: Long-Term Ethnographic Analysis." *American Sociological Review* 79(3): 517–48.

Smith, Robert Courtney. 2024. *Dreams Achieved and Denied: Mexican Intergenerational Mobility*. Russell Sage Foundation.

Smith, Roger. 2009. "Childhood, Agency and Youth Justice." *Children & Society* 23(4): 252–64.

Snell, Patricia. 2010. "Emerging Adult Civic and Political Disengagement: A Longitudinal Analysis of Lack of Involvement With Politics." *Journal of Adolescent Research* 25(2): 258–87. https://doi.org/10.1177/0743558409357238.

Sojoyner, Damien M. 2016. *First Strike: Educational Enclosures in Black Los Angeles*. University of Minnesota Press

Song, Samuel Y., Jacqueline M. Eddy, Heather M. Thompson, Brian Adams, and Jennifer Beskow. 2020. "Restorative Consultation in Schools: A Systematic Review and Call for Restorative Justice Science to Promote Anti-Racism and Social Justice." *Journal of Educational and Psychological Consultation* 30(4): 462–76.

Stanton-Salazar, Ricardo D., and Stephanie U. Spina. 2005. "Adolescent Peer Networks as a Context for Social and Emotional Support." *Youth & Society* 36(4): 379–417.

State Task Force on Gang Violence. 1986. *Final Report*. California Council on Criminal Justice.

Stewart, Mahala Dyer, Ashley García, and Hannah Petersen. 2021. "Schools as Racialized Organizations in Policy and Practice." *Sociology Compass* 15(12): 1–13.

Street, Alex, Michael Jones-Correa, and Chris Zepeda-Millán. 2017. "Political Effects of Having Undocumented Parents." *Political Research Quarterly* 70(4): 818–32.

Suárez-Orozco, Carola, Marcelo M. Suárez-Orozco, and Irina Todorova. 2010. *Learning a New Land: Immigrant Students in American Society*. Harvard University Press.

Suzuki, Bob H. 1977. "Education and the Socialization of Asian Americans: A Revisionist Analysis of the 'Model Minority' Thesis." *Amerasia Journal* 4(2): 23–51.

Taft, Jessica K. 2019. *The Kids Are in Charge: Activism and Power in Peru's Movement of Working Children*. New York University Press.

Tan, Lucy B. G. 2016. "A Critical Review of Adolescent Mindfulness-Based Programmes." *Clinical Child Psychology and Psychiatry* 21(2): 193–207.

Tatum, Beverly D. 2017. *Why Are All the Black Kids Sitting Together in the Cafeteria? And Other Conversations About Race*. Revised ed. Basic Books.

Telles, Edward E., and Vilma Ortiz. 2008. *Generations of Exclusion: Mexican Americans, Assimilation, and Race*. Russell Sage Foundation.

Temple Kirby, Jack. 1983. "The Southern Exodus, 1910–1960: A Primer for Historians." *Journal of Southern History* 49(4): 585–600.

Terriquez, Veronica. 2011. "Schools for Democracy: Labor Union Participation and Latino Immigrant Parents' School-Based Civic Engagement." *American Sociological Review* 76: 581–601.

Terriquez, Veronica. 2015a. "Intersectional Mobilization, Social Movement Spillover, and Queer Youth Leadership in the Immigrant Rights Movement." *Social Problems* 62(3): 343–62.

Terriquez, Veronica. 2015b. "Training Young Activists: Grassroots Organizing and Youths' Civic and Political Trajectories." *Sociological Perspectives* 58(2): 223–42.

Terriquez, Veronica. 2017. "Legal Status, Civic Associations, and Political Participation among Latino Young Adults." *Sociological Quarterly* 58(2): 315–36.

Terriquez, Veronica, Tizoc Brenes, and Abdiel Lopez. 2018. "Intersectionality as a Multipurpose Collective Action Frame: The Case of The Undocumented Youth Movement." *Ethnicities* 18(2): 260–76.

Terriquez, Veronica, Alyssa Cazares, and Jose Negrete. 2022. *Future Leaders of America: The Critical Role of Youth Activism in Central Coast Communities.* University of California, Los Angeles, Chicano Studies Research Center. https://www.chicano.ucla.edu/about/news/csrc-report-future-leaders-america-critical-role-youth-activism-central-coast-communities.

Terriquez, Veronica, and Gabriela Dominguez. 2014. *Building Healthy Communities Through Youth Leadership: Summary of Key Findings from the 2013–2014 Youth Program Participant Survey.* University of Southern California Equity Research Institute. https://dornsife.usc.edu/eri/wp-content/uploads/sites/41/2023/01/2014BHCYouthSurveySummary.pdf.

Terriquez, Veronica, and Hyeyoung Kwon. 2014. "Intergenerational Family Relations, Civic Organisations, and the Political Socialisation of Second-Generation Immigrant Youth." *Journal of Ethnic and Migration Studies* 41(3): 425–47.

Terriquez, Veronica, and May Lin. 2019. "Yesterday They Marched, Today They Mobilized the Vote: A Developmental Model for Civic Leadership Among the Children of Immigrants." *Journal of Ethnic and Migration Studies* 46(4): 747–69. https://doi.org/10.1080/1369183X.2018.1556457.

Terriquez, Veronica, and Ruth Milkman. 2021. "Immigrant and Refugee Youth Organizing in Solidarity with the Movement for Black Lives." *Gender & Society* 35(4): 577–87.

Terriquez, Veronica, and Steven Carmona Mora. 2018. *The LA Youth Vote and the Activation of a Young and Diverse Electorate.* University of California, Santa Cruz, Institute for Social Transformation. https://transform.ucsc.edu/los-angeles-youth-vote.

Terriquez, Veronica, and John Rogers. 2017. "Time for Social Change: Youth Development and the Educational Outcomes of Youth Organizing." In *Learning Time: In Pursuit of Educational Equity,* edited by Jeannie Oakes, Marisa Saunders, and Jorge Ruiz. Harvard Education Press.

Terriquez, Veronica, Jeffrey Sacha, and Robert Chlala. 2014. *The Impact of Punitive High School Discipline Policies on the Postsecondary Trajectories of Young Men.*

University of California, Los Angeles, All Campus Consortion on Research for Diversity. https://pathways.gseis.ucla.edu/publications/Discipline_Report.pdf

Terriquez, Veronica, Luis Sanchez, and Marqueece Harris-Dawson. 2020. "On the Shoulders of Giants: The Lineage and Growth of California's Inter-generational, Multiracial Youth Movement." KCET, October 21. https://www.kcet.org/shows/city-rising/on-the-shoulders-of-giants-the-lineage-and-growth-of-californias-intergenerational-multiracial-youth-movement.

Terriquez, Veronica, Betania Santos, and May Lin. 2020. *Healing, Self-Care, and Youth Political Empowerment.* University of Southern California Equity Research Institute. https://dornsife.usc.edu/eri/wp-content/uploads/sites/41/2023/01/VT_TCE_Healing_Report_June_2021.pdf.

Terriquez, Veronica, and Jennifer Soto. 2019. *Organizational Capacity Building and the Mobilization of Young Voters: Results from the Power California Partner Survey.* University of Southern California Equity Research Institute. https://dornsife.usc.edu/assets/sites/242/docs/PowerCANetworkEval2019.FINAL.pdf.

Terriquez, Veronica, Jennifer Soto, and Nicole White. 2021. *YO! California's 2019 Emerging Organizers Fellowship Program Evaluation Findings.* University of Southern California Equity Research Institute. https://dornsife.usc.edu/eri/publications/building-a-statewide-youth-movement-yo-california-emerging-organizers-fellowship/.

Terriquez, Veronica, Randy Villegas, and Roxanna Villalobos. 2019. "Central Valley Freedom Summer." *Contexts* 18(3): 54–57.

Terriquez, Veronica, Randy Villegas, Roxanna Villalobos, and Jiayi Xu. 2020. "The Political Socialization of Latinx Youth in a Conservative Political Context." *Journal of Applied Developmental Psychology* 70. https://doi.org/10.1016/j.appdev.2020.101188.

Terriquez, Veronica, and Jiayi Xu. 2020. *Mobilizing Young Voters to the Polls: Lessons Learned from the Power California Network.* University of Southern California Equity Research Institute. https://dornsife.usc.edu/eri/publications/mobilizing-young-voters-to-the-polls/.

Terriquez, Veronica, Jiayi Xu, and Marlen Reyes. 2021. *Building Healthy Communities Youth Programming and Participants' Developmental Outcomes.* University of Southern California Equity Research Institute. https://dornsife.usc.edu/eri/wp-content/uploads/sites/41/2023/01/BHC_youth_outcomesTerriquezXuReyes2021.pdf.

Tilly, Charles. 1993. "Contentious Repertoires in Great Britain, 1758–1934." *Social Science History* 17(2): 253–80.

Tivaringe, Tafadzwa, and Ben Kirshner. 2022. "Learning to Claim Power in a Contentious Public Sphere: A Study of Youth Movement Formation in South Africa." *Journal of the Learning Sciences* 30(1): 125–50.

Tran, Van C., Corina Graif, Alison D. Jones, Mario L. Small, and Christopher Winship. 2013. "Participation in Context: Neighborhood Diversity and Organizational Involvement in Boston." *City & Community* 12(3): 187–210.

Turner, David C., III. 2021. "The (Good) Trouble with Black Boys: Organizing with Black Boys and Young Men in George Floyd's America." *Theory into Practice* 60(4): 422–33.

Turner, David C., III, Uriel Serrano, and Freeden Blume Ouer. 2022. "'Everyone Gets the Same 24 Hours a Day': An Intersectional Approach to Understanding the Time and Life Lost For Black Men and Boys." In *Getting Real About Inequality: Intersectionality in Real Life*, edited by Cherise A. Harris and Stephanie M. McClure. Sage Publishing.

Umaña-Taylor, Adriana J., Stephen M. Quintana, Richard M. Lee, et al. 2014. "Ethnic and Racial Identity During Adolescence and into Young Adulthood: An Integrated Conceptualization." *Child Development* 85(1): 21–39.

U.S. Department of Health and Human Services. 2021. *Protecting Youth Mental Health: The U.S. Surgeon General's Advisory*. Health and Human Services. https://www.hhs.gov/sites/default/files/surgeon-general-youth-mental-health-advisory.pdf.

Valdés, Guadalupe. 1996. *Con Respeto: Bridging the Distances Between Culturally Diverse Families and Schools*. Teachers College Press.

Valdivia, Carolina. 2021. "'I Became a Mom Overnight': How Parental Detentions and Deportations Affect Immigrant Young Adults' Roles and Educational Trajectories." *Harvard Educational Review* 91(1): 62–82.

Valladares, Michelle Renée, Siomara Valladares, Matt Garcia, et al. 2021. *20 Years of Youth Power: The 2020 National Youth Organizing Field Scan*. Funders Collaborative on Youth Organizing.

Vallejo, Jody. 2012. *Barrios to the Burbs: The Making of the Mexican American Middle-Class*. Stanford University Press.

Van Dyke, Nella, and Holly J. McCammon. 2010. "Introduction: Social Movement Coalition Formation." In *Strategic Alliances: Coalition Building and Social Movements*, edited by Nella Van Dyke and Holly J. McCammon. University of Minnesota Press.

van Goethem, Anne A. J., Anne van Hoof, Marcel A. G. van Aken, Bram Orobio de Castro, and Quinten A. W. Raaijmakers. 2014. "Socialising Adolescent Volunteering: How Important Are Parents and Friends? Age Dependent Effects of Parents and Friends on Adolescents' Volunteering Behaviours." *Journal of Applied Developmental Psychology* 35(2): 94–101.

Vasquez, Jessica M. 2011. *Mexicans Americans Across Generations: Immigrant Families, Racial Realities*. New York University Press.

Verba, Sidney, Kay L. Scholzman, and Henry E. Brady. 1995. *Voice and Equality: Civic Voluntarism in American Politics*. Harvard University Press.

Verma, Saunjuhi, Patricia Maloney, and Duke W. Austin. 2017. "The School to Deportation Pipeline: The Perspectives of Immigrant Students and Their Teachers on Profiling and Surveillance Within the School System." *Annals of the American Academy of Political and Social Science* 673(1): 209–29.

Vestal, Allan J., Andrew Briz, Annette Choi, Beatrice Jin, Andrew McGill, and Lily Mihalik. 2021. "Joe Biden Won in California." *Politico*, March 14. https://www.politico.com/2020-election/results/california/.

Vogelsang, Eric M. 2021. "Social Participation Across Mid- and Later-life: Evidence from a Longitudinal Cohort Study." *Sociological Perspectives* 64(6): 1187–205.

Walker, Richard. 2004. *The Conquest of Bread: 150 Years of Agribusiness in California*. New Press.

Walton, Emily. 2017. "Spatial Assimilation and Its Discontents: Asian Ethnic Neighborhood Change in California." *Urban Geography* 38(7): 993–1018.

Ward, Jane. 2008. "Diversity Discourse and Multi-Identity Work in Lesbian and Gay Organizations." In *Identity Work in Social Movements*, edited by Jo Reger, Daniel J. Myers and Rachel L. Einwohner. University of Minnesota Press.

Warren, Mark R. 2021. *Willful Defiance: The Movement to Dismantle the School-to-Prison Pipeline*. Oxford University Press.

Wasburn, Philo C., and Tawnya J. Adkins-Covert. 2017. *Making Citizens: Political Socialization Research and Beyond*. Springer.

Washburn, David. 2018. "Some California Districts Are Downplaying the National School Walkout as Others Embrace It." EdSource, March 6. https://edsource.org/2018/some-california-districts-are-downplaying-the-national-school-walkout-as-others-embrace-it/594339.

Waters, Mary C., Van C. Tran, Philip Kasinitz, and John H. Mollenkopf. 2010. "Segmented Assimilation Revisited: Types of Acculturation and Socioeconomic Mobility in Young Adulthood." *Ethnic and Racial Studies* 33(7): 1168–93.

Watts, Roderick J., and Constance Flanagan. 2007. "Pushing the Envelope on Youth Civic Engagement: A Developmental and Liberation Psychology Perspective." *Journal of Community Psychology* 35(6): 779–92.

Watts, Roderick J., and Carlos P. Hipolito-Delgado. 2015. "Thinking Ourselves to Liberation? Advancing Sociopolitical Action in Critical Consciousness." *Urban Review* 47(5): 847–67.

Weber, Devra. 1994. *Dark Sweat, White Gold: California Farm Workers, Cotton, and the New Deal*. University of California Press.

Weiss, Elaine, and Paul Reville. 2019. *Broader, Bolder, Better: How Schools and Communities Help Students Overcome the Disadvantages of Poverty*. Harvard Education Press.

Westheimer, Joel, and Joseph Kahne. 2004. "What Kind of Citizen? The Politics of Educating for Democracy." *American Educational Research Journal* 41(2): 237–69.

Whipple, Kyle S. 2019. "Supporting Transgender and Gender Non-Conforming Kids: A Review of Transgender Children and Youth." *Journal of LGBT Youth* 17(1): 123–25.

Winn, Maisha T. 2018. *Justice on Both Sides: Transforming Education Through Restorative Justice*. Harvard Education Press.

Wong, Janelle. 2005. "Mobilizing Asian American Voters: A Field Experiment." *Annals of the American Academy of Political Science* 601: 102–14.

Wong, Janelle. 2006. *Democracy's Promise: Immigrants and American Civic Institutions*. University of Michigan Press.

Wong, Janelle, S. Karthick Ramakrishnan, Taeku Lee, and Jane Junn. 2011. *Asian American Political Participation: Emerging Constituents and Their Political Identities*. Russell Sage Foundation.

Wong, Janelle, and Vivian Tseng. 2008. "Political Socialisation in Immigrant Families: Challenging Top-Down Parental Socialisation Models." *Journal of Ethnic and Migration Studies* 34(1): 151–68.

Wright, Dana. 2007. "Escuelas Si! ¡Pintas No! (Schools Yes! Prisons, No!): Connecting Youth Action Research and Youth Organizing in California." *Children, Youth and Environments* 17(2): 503–16.

Zavella, Patricia. 2020. *The Movement for Reproductive Justice: Empowering Women of Color Through Social Activism*. New York University Press.

Zimmerman, Arely. 2012. *Documenting Dreams: New Media, Undocumented Youth, and the Immigrant Rights Movement*. Case Study Working Paper for the Media, Activism, and Participatory Politics Project. https://clalliance.org/wp-content/uploads/files/documenting_dreams_-_working_paper-mapp_-_june_6_20121.pdf.

Zimmerman, Arely, Anthony Perez, Michelle Saucedo, Jennifer Ito, and Manuel Pastor. 2013. *Cultivating the Dream: Evaluating the Impact of Dream Summer on a New Generation of Leaders*. University of Southern California Equity Research Institute. https://dornsife.usc.edu/eri/publications/cultivating-the-dream/.

= Index =

Tables and figures are listed in **boldface**.